Patrick Kanouse

The NOOK Book

An Unofficial Guide Fourth Edition

  800 East 96th Street, Indianapolis, Indiana 46240

The NOOK® Book: An Unofficial Guide

Copyright © 2013 by Pearson Education

All rights reserved. No part of this book shall be reproduced, stored in a retrieval system, or transmitted by any means, electronic, mechanical, photocopying, recording, or otherwise, without written permission from the publisher. No patent liability is assumed with respect to the use of the information contained herein. Although every precaution has been taken in the preparation of this book, the publisher and author assume no responsibility for errors or omissions. Nor is any liability assumed for damages resulting from the use of the information contained herein.

ISBN-13: 978-0-7897-5060-0
ISBN-10: 0-7897-5060-0

The Library of Congress Cataloging-in-Publication Data is on file.

Printed in the United States of America

Second Printing: January 2013

Trademarks

All terms mentioned in this book that are known to be trademarks or service marks have been appropriately capitalized. Que Publishing cannot attest to the accuracy of this information. Use of a term in this book should not be regarded as affecting the validity of any trademark or service mark.

NOOK, NOOK HD+, NOOK HD, NOOK Color, NOOK Study, NOOK Tablet, NOOK Simple Touch, NOOK Simple Touch with GlowLight, NOOK for iPad, NOOK for iPhone, NOOK for Android, NOOK for PC, NOOK for Mac, NOOK Kids for iPad, NOOK Friends, LendMe, PubIt!, NOOK Kids, NOOK Book, NOOK Book enhanced, NOOK Bookstore, NOOK Store, NOOK Reading Apps, NOOK Profiles, NOOK Video, My NOOK, NOOK Magazine, NOOK Newspapers, and all other Barnes & Noble marks in the book are trademarks of Barnes & Noble, Inc. and its affiliates.

Use of terms in this book that are trademarks of Barnes & Noble, Inc. and its affiliates does not imply any association with or endorsement by Barnes & Noble, Inc. or its affiliates, and no association or endorsement is intended or should be inferred.

Warning and Disclaimer

Every effort has been made to make this book as complete and as accurate as possible, but no warranty or fitness is implied. The information provided is on an "as is" basis. The author and the publisher shall have neither liability nor responsibility to any person or entity with respect to any loss or damages arising from the information contained in this book or from the use of the programs accompanying it.

Bulk Sales

Que Publishing offers excellent discounts on this book when ordered in quantity for bulk purchases or special sales. For more information, please contact

    U.S. Corporate and Government Sales
    1-800-382-3419
    corpsales@pearsontechgroup.com

For sales outside of the U.S., please contact

    International Sales
    international@pearsoned.com

Editor-in-Chief
Greg Wiegand

Executive Editor
Loretta Yates

Development Editor
Todd Brakke

Managing Editor
Kristy Hart

Project Editor
Betsy Harris

Copy Editor
Apostrophe Editing Services

Senior Indexer
Cheryl Lenser

Proofreader
Sarah Kearns

Editorial Assistant
Cindy Teeters

Book Designer
Anne Jones

Compositor
Nonie Ratcliff

Table of Contents

About the Author

Patrick Kanouse works as the director of workflow services for Pearson Education. Always a bookworm, he has gladly adopted ebook reading technologies, while still appreciating and valuing the printed book.

Patrick also teaches business technical report writing at IUPUI. Outside of teaching about writing, reading on his NOOK®, and writing about his NOOK, he writes science fiction and poetry, having published a PubIt™ book at BN.com that you can read on your NOOK. His website is patrickkanouse.com. You can find him on Twitter at @patrickkanouse.

Patrick lives in Westfield, Indiana, with his wife and two Yorkies.

Dedication

This book is dedicated to my wife, Gina, who has always supported my every endeavor, even if it is immersed in some ancient history reading or volumes of poetry or dragging her to the latest science fiction movie. Without her support and encouragement, nothing that I attempt would be possible.

Acknowledgments

Thanks to Loretta Yates for asking me to revise and write this edition. Given the pace of writing this edition, I must give substantial thanks to the book team for taking my initial words and making them much better: Todd Brakke, Betsy Harris, San Dee Phillips, and everyone in production.

Thank you to Jeff at the Noblesville B&N store for his patience as I walked in one morning desperate to get my hands on a NOOK® HD+.

We Want to Hear from You!

As the reader of this book, *you* are our most important critic and commentator. We value your opinion and want to know what we're doing right, what we could do better, what areas you'd like to see us publish in, and any other words of wisdom you're willing to pass our way.

We welcome your comments. You can email or write to let us know what you did or didn't like about this book—as well as what we can do to make our books better.

Please note that we cannot help you with technical problems related to the topic of this book.

When you write, please be sure to include this book's title and author as well as your name and email address. We will carefully review your comments and share them with the author and editors who worked on the book.

Email: feedback@quepublishing.com

Mail: Que Publishing
           ATTN: Reader Feedback
           800 East 96th Street
           Indianapolis, IN 46240 USA

Reader Services

Visit our website and register this book at quepublishing.com/register for convenient access to any updates, downloads, or errata that might be available for this book.

Introduction

Congratulations on your purchase of the NOOK® HD, NOOK HD+, or NOOK Simple Touch™, Barnes & Noble's (simply B&N from here on) ebook readers. The NOOK HD+ and NOOK HD, released in November 2012, are a complete redesign of the NOOK Tablet™ and NOOK Color™, which debuted September 2011. Both the NOOK HDs feature high-definition color touch screens. The NOOK Simple Touch, which first went on sale in June 2011 and was updated in 2012 with GlowLight, features an E Ink reading display that bears a remarkable resemblance to paper. The NOOK HDs resemble a tablet like the iPad or Google Nexus, but B&N has intentionally focused it as an ereading device, so although it has apps and video and music, B&N has designed the NOOK HDs to be readers. This focuses attention on the reading experience of books, newspapers, and magazines while keeping the price down. The NOOK HDs are an attempt to balance the features of the tablet with the immersive experience of reading. With the high-definition display, you can read text so clearly that you may think it is better than paper. The NOOK HD+ and NOOK HD differ in size, but they pack in all the same software and features.

Beyond releasing the new devices, two other related items are worth mentioning. Since B&N has been releasing ereading devices, the company has never sold video content. With the release of the NOOK Tablet, it included apps for Netflix and Hulu Plus, but those services (although great) could not boast as wide a selection as some would prefer. In addition, you could not purchase and download movies and TV shows to watch when you have no Internet connection. In November 2012, B&N released NOOK Video™. This service, which debuts on the NOOK HDs and will have a separate app for laptops and other tablets eventually, will fill in a large gap in B&N's offerings compared to other tablets.

The other item is the introduction of profiles. Most tablets and ereading devices are set up for one person—all content is available to anyone with access to the tablet. But what if you are a family that shares a device? You may not want your 4 year old to watch R-rated movies at the touch of a button—or rack up credit card bills by buying all sorts of content. This is where profiles come in. On the NOOK HDs, up to six profiles can be created. Child profiles in particular offer customizable parental controls.

The NOOK Simple Touch is a simple-to-use device slightly bigger than a paperback book. Because it is not backlit, you can easily read a book in bright sunlight with little glare. If you have the NOOK Simple Touch™ with GlowLight™, however, you can turn on a built-in light that softly illuminates the screen, allowing you to read in dim light or complete darkness. Also, its E Ink screen is less than ideal for reading graphic-intensive books, but for reading the latest mystery or newspapers, it is an excellent device that can go anywhere and is easy on the eyes.

This book is intended to give you all the information you need to get the most out of your NOOK, whichever version you have, and the associated supporting applications. You not only learn how to use your NOOK, but you also learn all the best places to get books and other content. After you've learned all the great resources available for books, you'll quickly find that you need a way to organize your ebooks, so you also learn how to do that using a free tool called Calibre.

By the time you finish this book, you'll be comfortable with all aspects of your NOOK. Following are some of the many things you can learn how to do in this book:

- ▶ Add your own pictures for use as a wallpaper or screensaver.
- ▶ Use B&N's unique LendMe® feature to lend and borrow books.
- ▶ Play music, audiobooks, podcasts, and more.
- ▶ Watch video, including Netflix and Hulu Plus.
- ▶ Read your ebooks on your iPhone, iPod Touch, iPad, Android tablet, Android phone, and computer.
- ▶ Get books (many free) from many sources on the Internet, and load them onto your NOOK.
- ▶ Manage all your ebooks, and update author and title information if needed.
- ▶ Automatically download full-color covers for your books that display on your NOOK.
- ▶ Use your NOOK HDs to browse the web.
- ▶ Use your NOOK HDs to read enhanced books and children's books. You can even record your own readings of your child's favorite books.
- ▶ Use highlights, annotations, and bookmarks.
- ▶ Use the NOOK Friends™ app to see what your fellow friends are up to.
- ▶ Set up profiles.
- ▶ Build scrapbooks from pages of catalogs and magazines.
- ▶ Learn how to publish your books using B&N's PubIt feature.

This book is divided into three parts:

▶ Part I, "NOOK HD+ and NOOK HD," focuses exclusively on using the NOOK HDs. The NOOK HDs are identical except for their size. Thus, while reading this part, when you read about the NOOK, it is for either the NOOK HD+ or NOOK HD.

▶ Part II, "NOOK Simple Touch," focuses on using the NOOK Simple Touch.

▶ Part III, "Beyond the NOOKs," focuses on using the NOOK-related apps, Calibre, and B&N's PubIt.

Mixed in with all this, you can find plenty of tips and tricks to help you get the most from your NOOK.

> NOTE: Writing this book presents a unique challenge. The E Ink NOOK has some limitations with images. Although the images do appear, complex images or images with lots of information can be tedious to see. The NOOK HDs, however, present images in a much better fashion, as do the related NOOK Reading Apps™. Therefore, for all aspects of the NOOK HDs and NOOK Apps, the use of images will be more substantial than with the NOOK Simple Touch chapters. I used NOOK HD+ to create the images.

> NOTE: Throughout this book, you encounter the terms *ebook* and *NOOK Book*; ebook will be used generically. NOOK Books™ is what B&N calls its version of ebooks that it sells through B&N. These are still ebooks, and NOOK Book is more of a marketing piece, but the distinction is useful because only NOOK Books sync between devices and support social features. Also, only NOOK Books are visible in My NOOK® Library on BN.com.

It's my hope that you don't have any questions about using your NOOK after reading this book, but if you do, please don't hesitate to send me an email at NOOK@patrickkanouse.com. I'll gladly help if I can. You can also find me on Twitter at @patrickkanouse. Finally, my blog, http://patrickkanouse.blogspot.com/, has a section devoted to updates as I get them related to this book, so check in every so often.

Thank you for buying *The NOOK Book*!

CHAPTER 1

Getting Started with Your NOOK HDs

Before getting into the details of using your NOOK HD+ or NOOK HD, take a look at some of the basics: gestures, setup, and basic navigation. With these basics in place, you can then discover all the other incredible things your NOOK HD+ or NOOK HD can do.

> NOTE: I simply refer to these devices as NOOK. The two are identical in functionality. The only difference is screen size.

> NOTE: Barnes & Noble uses a lowercase *n* when it spells *NOOK* and for the NOOK's logo.

Understanding NOOK Gestures

You control the NOOK, excepting the Power button, Home button, and volume controls by gestures:

- ▶ **Tap**: This is the most common gesture. Just press your finger to the screen and raise it. Usually, you use this gesture with buttons and covers.

- ▶ **Press and hold**: This is the same as the tap gesture, but instead of raising your finger, you hold it to the screen for a couple of seconds. This often opens an additional menu from which to choose by a tap, but you can encounter other results from a press and hold.

- ▶ **Swipe left/swipe right**: The gesture is mostly for turning pages. Like a tap, touch your finger on the screen and quickly drag it to the left (or right) and lift your finger up.

▶ **Scroll**: Essentially the vertical version of the swipe gesture. You can control the speed of the scroll by swiping up or down more rapidly. You can slow down or stop the scroll by tapping the screen (to stop) or pressing and holding to slow the scroll.

▶ **Pinch and zoom in/pinch and zoom out**: This is a method to zoom in or out on pictures, PDFs, web pages, and so on. To zoom in or show part of the screen more closely, you place your index finger and thumb closely together on the screen (that is, pinch) and then spread them apart. To zoom out or show more of the screen, you do the pinch and zoom in gesture in reverse—this is also called unpinch.

Setting Up and Registering Your NOOK

When you first turn on your NOOK, you are asked if you are in the UK or United States. Tap the appropriate response.

The first step in getting started with your NOOK is to set up and register it with Barnes & Noble (simply B&N from now on).

The next step is to set up the Wi-Fi access (see Figure 1.1). You can go to a B&N store, and your NOOK will recognize its network and log on automatically. More likely, though, you are at home, so you need to set up the NOOK to access your wireless network. Enter the required information. Tap Continue with Setup.

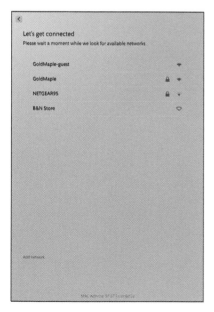

FIGURE 1.1　Pick your Wi-Fi network.

NOTE: Want Wi-Fi access on the go? The NOOK and NOOK Wi-Fi need only a wireless network to access the Daily (articles from B&N), subscription content, and so on. Many wireless companies such as Verizon offer mobile Wi-Fi hotspots at reasonable prices. A mobile hotspot uses the 3G or 4G cellular network but treats it as a Wi-Fi connection, so you never need to be without wireless access.

For more information on connecting your NOOK to a Wi-Fi hotspot after your initial set up, **see** "Using Wi-Fi Hotspots," later in this chapter.

Now you need to pick your time zone. Then you see a screen to set your time zone (see Figure 1.2). Choose your time zone and tap Next. The NOOK registers with B&N.

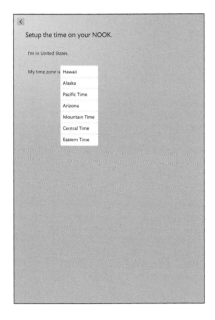

FIGURE 1.2   Pick your time zone.

You need to agree to the terms of service. Tap the check box for Yes, I Accept the NOOK Terms of Service and tap Agree. After this, you land at the Do You Have a NOOK Account screen. If you have an existing B&N account, tap Yes, I Have an Account and enter your account information. Tap Submit. If you don't have an account, you can create one by tapping No, I Need to Create an Account. Fill out the form and tap Submit (see Figure 1.3).

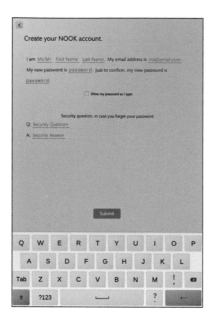

FIGURE 1.3   Create a B&N account if you do not already have one.

> NOTE: You can also set up a B&N account on your computer by visiting www.nooktablet.com/setup.

To register your NOOK, you also need to provide a default credit card with a valid billing address to be associated with your B&N account.

After you have an account, you are asked to enter your interests. These are used later by B&N to provide recommendations. You can select one or more. A screen about building your library appears offering some free sample content. You can skip this or tap the covers to receive the content.

You are then taken to the Home screen, and your NOOK is now set up for use.

Orienting Yourself to Your NOOK

Now orient yourself to the NOOK and the basic navigational features. You won't get the details about putting items on it and so on in the following sections, but you'll get there eventually. This is simply to orient you to common locations you revisit often in this book.

The Welcome Back Screen

After you set up your NOOK, whenever it goes to sleep or powers off, whenever you wake it up or power it back on, you must unlock it. This occurs on the Welcome Back screen. If the NOOK is asleep, pressing the Home button starts the Welcome Back screen. If you power the NOOK on, after it completes the start sequence, you go to the Welcome Screen.

From the Welcome Back screen, you can select the profile you want to start using (profiles are covered in Chapter 11, "Creating and Using Profiles and Your NOOK Today"). Click the icon of the profile and drag it toward the unlock icon in the middle. (The arrow from the profile icon points you in the correct direction.) If you set up a lock sequence, enter the PIN and tap OK. The screen that appears is the Home Screen.

Home Screen

This is the screen that appears after you unlock the NOOK. The Home screen is a central location, and you interact with it a lot. The screen is divided into several sections (see Figure 1.4):

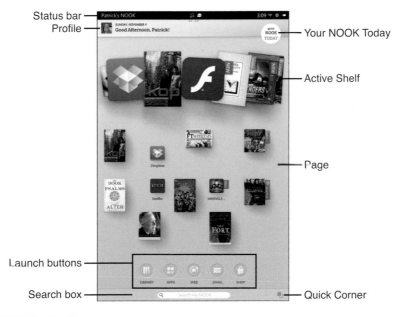

FIGURE 1.4 The Home screen.

▶ **Status bar**: This is the top of the screen. You see whatever you name your NOOK (Patrick's NOOK in Figure 1.4). Also, you see notifications in the middle of the screen. On the right side, you see the current time, Wi-Fi connectivity, settings (the gear icon), and battery monitor.

▶ **Profile**: This is the icon or image, the date, and a welcome greeting on the left side of the screen just below the status bar. You use this to change profiles outside of the Welcome Back screen.

▶ **Your NOOK Today**: This takes you to the Your NOOK Today screen (covered next).

▶ **Active Shelf**: This is a carousel of large icons of recently accessed items, new downloads and purchases, and so on. You can scroll through the Active Shelf by swiping your finger left or right across it. Tap one of the icons to launch the app, magazine, book, and such.

▶ **Pages**: You have five pages on the Home screen to do with as you please. The Home screen is the middle of the five (you can see which page you are on by looking at the dots immediately below the notifications in the status bar; the white dot is the current page). On these pages you can add apps, books, and more for quick access.

▶ **Launch buttons**: These are Library, Apps, Web, Email, and Shop. Tapping these launches new screens. Depending on the profile, some of these Launch buttons may not be visible.

▶ **Search box**: You can tap in here and begin typing for something you're searching for. This is an easy way to access your content.

▶ **Quick Corner**: By default, the Quick Corner action is the Recent Drawer. However, you can set it to be Continue Reading. The Recent Drawer icon is a filled in square overlapping the outline of a square. The Continue Reading icon is a spread open book with a clock on the bottom right.

If you press and hold an empty area of the Home screen, the Add to Pages screen appears. From here, you have a variety of options for accessing your content.

Recent Drawer

If your Quick Corner is set up for the Recent Drawer, if you tap the icon, the Home screen goes dark, and the bottom third of the screen presents a scrollable list of the 50 most recently used and accessed apps, videos, books, and so on (see Figure 1.5). When you tap Recent Drawer, you also have a magnifying glass to open a search page. If you tap the Recent Drawer icon again, it closes the Recent Drawer and returns you to the screen you were previously on. Use the Recent Drawer to quickly and easily access recent items without having to press the Home button and navigate where you want to go.

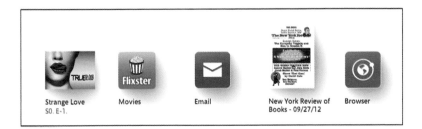

FIGURE 1.5   The Recent Drawer.

Add to Pages Screen

The Home screen enables you to access your library, app, and Internet bookmarks quickly for placing onto one of the pages; to do so, you need to access the Add to Pages screen (see Figure 1.6). To access this screen, press an area of the Home screen without an image, and tap Add to Pages from the pop-up menu. The Home screen shrinks and several options appear. For example of what you can do on this screen, from the Add to Pages screen, tap Bookmarks. When the list of bookmarks appears, scroll to the one you want, press and hold it, and drag it to the page. The bookmark is added to the page, which lets you quickly launch it. Tap Done when complete.

FIGURE 1.6   The Add to Pages screen.

The Wallpapers option here is different, as discussed in Chapter 2, "Customizing and Configuring Your NOOK HDs."

Using Wi-Fi Hotspots

Your NOOK can connect to Wi-Fi networks other than the one you initially set up. B&N offers free Wi-Fi access in all B&N stores. If you take your NOOK to a B&N store, it can automatically connect to the Wi-Fi hotspot in that store.

For more information on using your NOOK in a B&N store, **see** Chapter 13, "Shopping and Visiting B&N on Your NOOK HDs."

To connect your NOOK to a Wi-Fi hotspot other than one in a B&N store, follow these steps:

1. From the status bar, tap the Settings gear icon (see Figure 1.7).

FIGURE 1.7   Access your Wi-Fi settings here.

2. In the Wi-Fi section, tap Change. If Wi-Fi is Off, tap Off to turn it On.

3. Tap the Wi-Fi hotspot you want to use. Your NOOK displays the SSID for all Wi-Fi hotspots in range.

4. If required, enter the password for your Wi-Fi hotspot.

5. Tap Connect.

Your NOOK should now indicate that it is connected; you should see the Wi-Fi signal indicator on the status bar on the bottom right next to the battery indicator.

If your Wi-Fi hotspot isn't listed after you turn on Wi-Fi or is not in the list of Wireless Networks, follow these steps:

1. From the status bar, tap the Settings gear icon.

2. Tap All Settings.

3. Tap Wireless & Bluetooth.

4. Tap Find Other Networks.

5. Tap Scan to refresh this list, or tap Add Network.

6. Enter the network service set identified (SSID), select the type of security (if the Wi-Fi is secured), and enter the password for your Wi-Fi hotspot if necessary. If you don't know this information, ask the person who set up the Wi-Fi network.

Your NOOK can connect to a Wi-Fi hotspot that requires you to browse to a web page to authenticate yourself. For example, many hotel Wi-Fi hotspots require you to enter a room number or other information to connect. You can connect to a Wi-Fi hotspot that has this requirement by tapping the Web Launch Button from the Home screen after you join the Wi-Fi network.

Does My NOOK's Battery Drain Faster with Wi-Fi Connected?

I tested my NOOK's battery life using Wi-Fi hotspots. In my testing, the battery life was quite a bit shorter when using Wi-Fi than when not. However, Wi-Fi affects battery life only when your NOOK is actually connected to a Wi-Fi hotspot. Simply having Wi-Fi turned on doesn't affect battery life.

You can significantly improve battery life by turning off Wi-Fi.

Disconnecting and Forgetting a Wi-Fi Hotspot

If you want to stop using a Wi-Fi hotspot, you have two options: disconnect or forget. Disconnect just prevents your NOOK from connecting to that Wi-Fi hotspot. Forgetting the hotspot removes the information about the hotspot from your NOOK.

If you later want to reconnect to that hotspot, you must set it up again. To disconnect or forget a Wi-Fi hotspot, follow these steps:

1. From the status bar, tap the Settings icon.

2. If Wi-Fi is turned off, turn it on.

3. Tap the Wi-Fi hotspot. This displays a pop-up window.

4. Tap Forget to disconnect from the Wi-Fi hotspot.

For more information on configuring the settings on your NOOK (including turning off the Wi-Fi card), **see** "Your NOOK's Settings" in Chapter 2.

Charging and Caring for Your NOOK's Battery

Your NOOK uses a high-tech battery called a lithium polymer battery. You can charge your NOOK's battery either by plugging your NOOK into your computer's USB port or by plugging your NOOK into a wall outlet using the supplied AC adapter. Plugging your NOOK into a wall outlet charges the NOOK quicker.

> TIP: Just like any electronic device, your NOOK is susceptible to power spikes and other electrical anomalies. If you want to ensure that your NOOK is protected from electrical problems, plug it into a surge suppressor when charging the battery.

Unlike older rechargeable batteries, your NOOK's battery doesn't suffer from a charge "memory." However, you should still follow some basic rules to maximize the life of your battery:

> NOTE: Charge memory means that over time, a battery can store less power because it thinks it's full when it's not. Essentially, most people don't operate a battery-powered device until it reaches zero over time. So, as they recharge it over and over, the battery recalibrates what "zero" is—thus, the battery holds less charge. This explains the instructions on such devices to occasionally drain the battery completely.

▶ Try to avoid fully discharging your battery. Recharge it when it gets down to approximately 20% or so. Although charging it repeatedly is not necessarily a bad thing, the battery seems to function optimally if you charge it only when it drops down toward that 20% area.

▶ To maximize battery life, turn off Wi-Fi, and leave it off whenever you don't need it. Same goes with Bluetooth.

▶ Avoid high heat. Reading in sunlight is fine, but avoid storing your NOOK near a heat source.

▶ If storing your NOOK for a long period (a week or more), charge the battery to approximately 50% rather than giving it a full charge. The battery, even off, slowly loses its charge—very slowly, but loses nonetheless. By charging it to 50% only and then powering it off for a long time, it mimics how it was initially packaged and shipped. The 50% will go away slowly, and when you power it on again, it may have a low charge, but it is more like what the "factory" setting would have been.

By following these instructions, your NOOK's battery should last years. If you do need to replace the battery, contact B&N Customer Service.

When You Are Not Reading

When you finish reading, you should let your NOOK go to sleep instead of turning it off. You can force the NOOK to sleep by pressing and quickly letting go of the Power button.

By leaving your NOOK on with Wi-Fi on, it will occasionally download content from B&N such as subscription content and any books that you purchase from the B&N website. When you're ready to start reading again, simply press and release the power switch at the top of your NOOK to wake it up. Alternatively, you can press the Home button.

Your NOOK's Controls

Before you enjoy content on your NOOK, let's go over the controls on your NOOK (see Figures 1.8 and 1.9). In general, you can interact with your NOOK using the touch controls of tapping, pressing and holding, and swiping. The few physical buttons are minimal but provide some tactile controls. The most frequent button you are likely to use is the Home button.

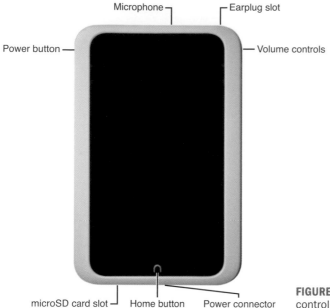

Microphone — ⌐ Earplug slot

Power button — — Volume controls

microSD card slot ⌐ Home button Power connector

FIGURE 1.8 Your NOOK HD's controls.

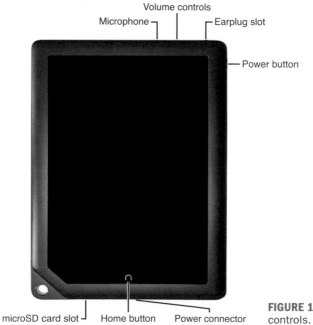

Volume controls

Microphone — ⌐ Earplug slot

— Power button

microSD card slot ⌐ Home button Power connector

FIGURE 1.9 Your NOOK HD+'s controls.

The Power Button

The Power button is the sole button on the top-right side of the NOOK. In addition to powering your NOOK on and off, the Power button can wake your NOOK when it's sleeping or put it to sleep when you finish reading.

To put your NOOK to sleep or wake it using the Power button, press and release the Power button quickly. To turn off your NOOK, press and hold the Power button for 5 seconds. To turn on your NOOK again, press and release the Power button quickly.

The Home Button

The Home button is identified by the NOOK logo (a lowercase n) and is located in the center of the black bar along at the bottom of the touchscreen display. Like the Power button, the Home button performs more than one function.

You can wake your NOOK by pressing the Home button. If the touchscreen is already illuminated, pressing the Home button twice takes you to your NOOK's Home screen.

The Volume Buttons

These two buttons on the top of the NOOK that control the volume. If no videos, music, or other sounds are playing, the Volume buttons control the Notification volume (that is, when something new arrives such as subscription content). When video, music, or other sounds are playing, the Volume buttons control the sound of the media.

How Should I Clean My NOOK's Touchscreen?

Your NOOK's touchscreen is going to get dirty and covered in fingerprints. The best way to clean it is using a dry, microfiber cloth like the one you would use to clean eyeglasses. If you must use a cleaning fluid, spray it lightly on the cloth and then wipe the touchscreen. Use only cleaning sprays designed for cleaning LCD screens.

The Microphone

Use the microphone to record voice narration for NOOK Kids^{TM} books. In the author's recordings, the microphone had an okay quality. When you speak into it for recording, use a strong voice and hold it close to your mouth if you can.

CHAPTER 2

Customizing and Configuring Your NOOK HDs

Your NOOK has many features that enable you to easily customize it and make it your own. There are also many settings that control how your NOOK operates. In this chapter, you examine how to customize and configure your NOOK.

Using Custom Wallpaper

You can customize your NOOK by using custom wallpaper images. Wallpaper appears on the Home pages when you are on the Home screen. (One image appears on all five pages.) Basically, it's the background that you always see when you press the Home button, so something nice is desirable. You also encounter the term *live wallpapers*, which are images that change over time, for example, a set of waves that a whale comes riding through.

If you do a Google search for **NOOK wallpaper**, you receive many results for where you can obtain wallpapers. You can also load them to your NOOK with the necessary images.

Choosing a Wallpaper

The easiest place to change your NOOK's wallpaper is to go to the Home screen. Here's how:

1. Make sure your NOOK is at the Home screen by pressing the Home button.

2. In an area of the Home page where a cover does not appear, press and hold until the Add to Pages screen appears (see Figure 2.1)—the Home screen seems to shrink and you get a set of options below the "shrunken" Home screen.

3. Tap Wallpapers.

4. Tap either Gallery, Wallpapers, or Live Wallpapers (see Figure 2.2). Wallpaper consists of images provided by B&N or images you have loaded into the Wallpaper folder. Gallery displays any photographs in JPG, PNG, or

GIF formats you have placed on your NOOK. Live Wallpapers are those that B&N has provided and others you have installed from BN.com

FIGURE 2.1   The Add to Pages screen appears when you press and hold on a blank area of the Home page.

FIGURE 2.2   Make use of B&N provided images, browse the Gallery, or choose from Live Wallpapers.

NOTE: Live Wallpapers are images that change over time (some quickly, some slowly). You can purchase Live Wallpapers from B&N—just type Live Wallpapers in the search box (**see** Chapter 13, "Shopping and Visiting B&N on Your NOOK HDs"). Live wallpapers are sold as apps and automatically appear in the Live Wallpapers options.

5. If you chose Wallpaper, choose the wallpaper you want. The screen shows you the image. Tap Cancel or Set Wallpaper. If you chose Gallery, choose the photo you want. An enlarged version of the photo appears with some outlined boxes and two buttons: Cancel and Crop.

> TIP: You can place images you want to use for wallpaper in the Wallpaper folder on your NOOK. (Plug your NOOK into your computer and navigate to that folder.) Because the Gallery displays every JPG, GIF, and PNG file on your NOOK, including cover images, the Gallery list can quickly become lengthy.

The outside box controls the sizing of the two interior boxes. Those two boxes represent the landscape and portrait layouts—basically making a nice image regardless of how you hold your NOOK (see Figure 2.3). Whatever is *inside* the interior boxes will be used for the wallpaper. To adjust the cropping size, press and hold the outer box, and then drag it around to wherever you want it. If you press and hold inside the outer box, you can drag the boxes around to a place you want to crop. Tap Crop to make it the wallpaper and return to the Add to Pages screen, or tap Cancel to exit to the Add to Pages screen.

FIGURE 2.3 Pick the area of the image you want to use for your Home screen.

If you chose Live Wallpapers, choose the Live Wallpaper you want. The screen shows you the animation. Tap Cancel or Set Wallpaper. You may also have a Settings option. If you tap this, you are provided settings specific to that Live Wallpaper. Adjust as you see fit. Tap the back arrow on the bottom left to apply the adjustments. To set the wallpaper with those configuration options, tap Set Wallpaper.

Should You Use a Specific File Format for Images?

Your NOOK supports JPEG, GIF, and PNG files. For images, using either JPEG or PNG is your best option. GIF isn't a good option for photographs, but if your image is line art or text, GIF can work fine. If you're unsure, stick with JPEG.

Your NOOK's Settings

Your NOOK offers configurable settings for controlling many of its features. If you tap the Setting icon in the status bar, you can gain access to the settings. Depending on what application you currently use, the top option (in Figure 2.4, it is Home Settings) changes. For example, if you browse the web and tap the Settings icon, Home Settings is replaced with Browser settings. Regardless, you can get to any setting at any time by tapping the Settings icon and then tapping All Settings (see Figure 2.5).

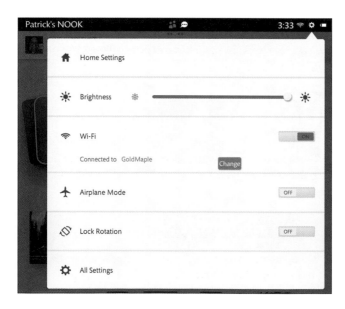

FIGURE 2.4 The Settings options that appear initially.

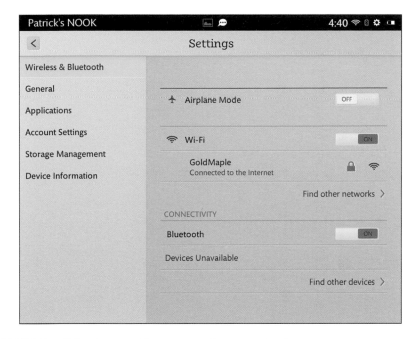

FIGURE 2.5   All Settings provides an extensive array of options.

For simplicity's sake, the following sections deal with all settings.

Basic Settings

At the top of the Settings screen, you have the specific settings for whatever task you are doing—for example, Browser, Home, Reader, and so on. Tap this to access those options. These specifics are discussed next.

The other options are

- ▶ **Brightness**: Press and hold the dot on the slider to adjust the brightness, which changes as you move the slider.

- ▶ **Wi-Fi**: Turn off or on Wi-Fi, and change which Wi-Fi you are connected to. **See** Chapter 1, "Getting Started with Your NOOK HDs," for more information about Wi-Fi networks.

- ▶ **Airplane Mode**: Turn this on to turn off Wi-Fi functionality quickly. Turn this off to allow the NOOK to connect to Wi-Fi networks.

- ▶ **Lock Rotation**: Turn this on to lock the NOOK's display orientation to however you have it at this current time. In other words, if you are in portrait orientation (the Home button is at the bottom or top) and turn Lock

Rotation to On, when you flip the NOOK into landscape orientation (the Home button is at the right or left), the image on the screen will not adjust.

▶ **All Setting**: Tap this to access more settings.

Wireless & Bluetooth Settings

You saw the Airplane Mode option earlier, and the Wi-Fi options are covered in Chapter 1. However, you also have Bluetooth connectivity options available. Bluetooth is Off by default. You can turn it on here. When you turn it on, you are taken to a new screen (see Figure 2.6), and you see a search begin. Your NOOK is looking for Bluetooth capable devices.

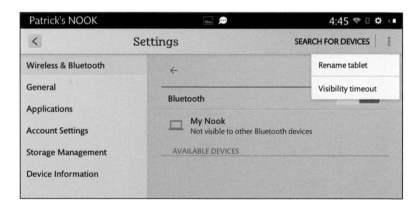

FIGURE 2.6   Bluetooth settings.

In this screen, you see the name of your device (My Nook) and also available devices. If you tap the Options button on the top right (the three squares next to Search for Devices, you see two options: Rename Tablet and Visibility Timeout. Rename Tablet is self-explanatory; this is a useful item to change for multiple NOOK households to easily distinguish between their devices.

If you tap Visibility Timeout, you can choose between 2 minutes, 5 minutes, 1 hour, and never. Essentially, you are setting the length of time that the NOOK remains visible to Bluetooth devices. If you stop using the Bluetooth device (with earbuds, for example) and power it off, your NOOK continues to look for Bluetooth connections to make for as long as the Visibility Timeout is set.

> NOTE: To connect a Bluetooth device, make sure you have your NOOK's Bluetooth setting turned to On. Follow the instructions that came with your Bluetooth device about pairing it with another device. When you have paired the Bluetooth device to your NOOK, you will see it in the list of Available Devices, and you can tap it to make the connection.

General Settings

A large number of options exist here (see Figure 2.7). So take them in order:

FIGURE 2.7 The General settings screen.

> ▶ **PowerSave Mode**: According to B&N, with Wi-Fi off and this feature on, you can read for 11 1/2 hours or watch video for 9 hours. Power Save just seems to dim the brightness on the screen a bit. After some discussion with

a B&N rep, the exact specifics of what Power Save does beyond that are a mystery. To maximize your battery time without charging, do turn on this feature.

▶ **Lock Rotation**: Turn this on to lock the NOOK's display orientation to however you have it at this current time. In other words, if you are in portrait orientation (the Home button is at the bottom or top) and turn Lock Rotation to On, when you flip the NOOK into landscape orientation (the Home button is at the right or left), the image on the screen will not adjust.

▶ **Brightness**: Press and hold the dot on the slider to adjust the brightness, which changes as you move the slider.

▶ **Screen Timeout**: This controls the time interval after which your NOOK puts itself to sleep. This timer is set to 2 minutes by default. To change the interval, tap Screen Timeout, and then tap the preferred time interval.

> TIP: If you set the sleep timer to a time interval that is shorter than the amount of time it takes you to read a page on the reading screen, your NOOK goes into sleep mode while you are reading. So, be sure you set the interval appropriately for your reading speed.

▶ **Language**: Tap this to change between UK English and US English.

▶ **Personal Dictionary**: Do you use shorthand in emails? Words that spell checkers always want to change? Personal names? Personal Dictionary can help with that. Tap Personal Dictionary, which shows a new screen. To add words to the dictionary, tap Add, enter the word, and then tap OK. This word is added to the dictionary.

▶ **Default**: This lets you know which keyboard you currently are using. For now, there's not much beyond giving you information here.

▶ **NOOK Keyboard**: Tap the gear icon to the right of this to see two options. First, you can change the keyboard input language. Tap Input Languages, and then tap the check mark for whichever language you want the keyboard to use for input. However, to change beyond English US, you need to turn off Use System Language at the top.

The other option you have here is Auto-Capitalization. This setting enables the NOOK to auto-capitalize while typing. For example, if you type a period, for the next letter you type, the NOOK capitalizes it. (If you don't want to capitalize that letter, tap the Shift key, which enables you to enter a lowercase letter.)

▶ **Text-to-Speech Output**: Tap this to see the options for text-to-speech output. When you do, a few options become available.

To change the settings for the engine (Pico TTS), tap the gear icon to the right. Tap Language to choose a different language. Tapping Settings for Pico TTS at this time just shows you a list of installed language packs.

To change the rate of speed at which text is spoken, tap Speech Rate and choose from Very Slow to Very Fast.

Tap Listen to an Example to hear a sample bit of text spoken at the selected rate of speed.

▶ **Pointer Speed**: Tap this to adjust the speed of the mouse/trackpad pointer (for when you have a mouse or trackpad connected via Bluetooth).

▶ **Set Volume for Music and Videos**: You can adjust the volume for these items here in addition to using the buttons at the top of the device.

▶ **Set Volume for Notifications**: Notifications, such as disconnecting the NOOK from your computer, emails received, and so on, can be accompanied by a sound. This slider controls the volume of that sound.

▶ **Alarms**: Tap this to adjust alarms for calendar reminders.

▶ **Screen Lock Sound**: When you press the Power button for a couple of seconds, the screen locks. If you'd like this to be accompanied with a sound, turn it on.

▶ **Security**: Tap this to turn on or off screen locks and change the PIN. If this is off, turn to On, tap Set Passcode, and enter a PIN. (It can be up to 16 numbers long.) Tap Continue. Re-enter the PIN and tap OK. The PIN is set.

To turn off the passcode, turn Screen Lock to Off. Tap Continue. Enter your PIN and tap Continue. A passcode is no longer required to access the NOOK.

To change the PIN, tap Change Passcode. Enter the existing PIN and tap Continue. Enter your new PIN and tap Continue. Re-enter the PIN and tap OK. The new PIN is set.

NOTE: Forgot your passcode? The good news is that you can get your NOOK back. The bad news is that you have to reset your NOOK to factory settings, which means you lose all content you placed on your device.

To reset your NOOK to factory settings, do the following:

1. With the NOOK off, hold the Home button and the Power button.
2. The NOOK starts up. Keep holding the buttons.
3. After a few seconds, you see a screen to reset your NOOK to factory settings with two options:
   ▶ Press Power to exit.
   ▶ Press Home to continue.
4. Press the Home button. You see the two options again.
5. Press the Home button.
6. Your NOOK erases the data, deregisters, and reboots the device.

▶ **Certificate Management**: When you go to secure websites, digital certificates are used to valid legitimate from nonlegitimate sites, thus ensuring security for your personal information. When you tap this, you can see which certificates have been approved by both the system (that is, what B&N has installed) and what you have approved (usually occurs when you visit a website and your receive that "trust this website's certificate" information.

If you have certificates you know about, have, and want to add to the NOOK device, you can place them on a microSD card, insert that card, and choose the Install from SD Card option here.

If you want to remove all certificates, tap Clear Credentials.

CAUTION: Be careful about Clearing Credentials. Do this only if you know what you are doing and why.

▶ **Select Time Zone**: This setting enables you to select your current local time zone. Your NOOK normally gets the current time using Wi-Fi access. However, if Wi-Fi service isn't available, it still displays the current time, provided you have configured your time zone. If you do not see the time zone you need here, tap Show All World Time Zones to see a longer list. (You can sort this list alphabetically by tapping the three button icon in the top right.)

▶ **Use 24-Hour Format**: This enables you to choose between a 12-hour time format and a 24-hour time format.

▶ **Select Date Format**: This enables you to choose how you want the day, month, and year to appear.

▶ **Notifications**: If you don't want to receive notifications when email arrives, a friend is offering a LendMe book, and so on, turn this option off.

Applications Settings

The options here (see Figure 2.8) are the ones that can be found contextually, but each is covered in turn.

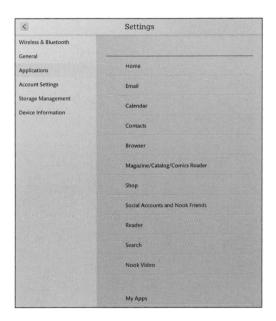

FIGURE 2.8   The Application settings screen.

Home Settings

The Home options (see Figure 2.9) control how the Home screen and Quick Corner Action work. The Quick Corner Action item determines if the Quick Corner Action either opens the Recent Drawer or opens what you were last reading.

Select Shelf Behavior defines how the Active Shelf operates. By default, what you see in the carousel of the Active Shelf shows recently purchased items, any apps, books, or videos you have recently viewed, and so on. If, however, you choose for Active Shelf to be Inbox, what you see in the carousel shows only new purchases and new subscription deliveries.

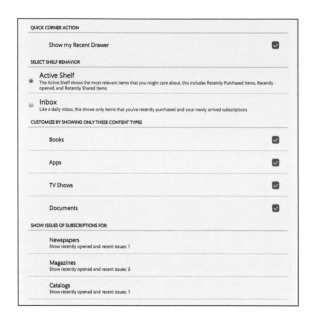

FIGURE 2.9   The Home Screen settings.

You can customize what you see in the Active Shelf by selecting from the options in Customize by Showing Only These Content Types. Turn off (that is, remove the check mark) for those items you don't want to appear in the Active Shelf. Documents are documents and files you have added to the NOOK outside of purchasing at the NOOK Store™.

You can also manage how many of each subscription appears in the Active Shelf. You can set up Newspapers, Magazines, and Catalogs individually. Tap each one and choose from none, 1, 2, 3, or all.

Email Settings

The options give you control over how the email application functions. You can also add and remove any accounts. See Chapter 9, "Using NOOK Apps and Surfing the Web," about setting up an email account. For the general email settings, you have several options:

▶ **Auto-Advance**: Tap this to choose between Newer Message, Older Message, and Message List. Whenever you open a message and delete it, the screen shifts to whichever option you select here.

▶ **Message Text Size**: Think of this as the font size for your email. Tap it and pick the size you want.

▶ **Reply All**: If Reply All is selected, when you click reply to a message, everyone who was on the original email is added to your reply. That said, so far I haven't seen this setting have any effect yet. When you click Reply Now, you get all reply options, including Reply and Reply All. For more about using email, **see** Chapter 9.

▶ **Ask to Show Pictures**: Emails take longer to download if the images are automatically downloaded. By default (and this is an option in the actual email application), you can choose to always show pictures from a particular sender. This setting enables you to clear those times when you said, "Yes, always show pictures from bn.com." Figure 2.10 shows an email where pictures are not automatically shown. Figure 2.11 shows that same email *after* showing pictures.

When you tap individual accounts, you get specific options related to that account (see Figure 2.12). First, you get some basic information. You can change the Account Name and Your Name. Just tap the option, enter the change, and tap OK.

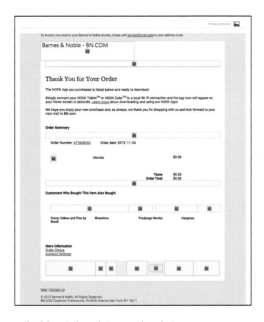

FIGURE 2.10   An email without the pictures showing.

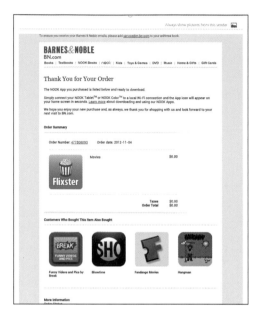

FIGURE 2.11   The same email as before but with images showing.

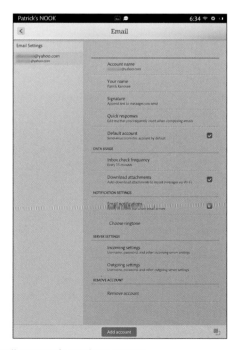

FIGURE 2.12   An email account's settings screen.

If you would like to add a signature to each email you write, tap Signature. The screen appears with a keyboard. Enter your signature and tap OK. Now, whenever you compose a new email or reply to an email, the signature is entered automatically, and your cursor is placed above it.

Quick Responses are items that you frequently type in emails: things like, **Hello! I hope all is well with you.** You can add quick responses by tapping the option and tapping Create New. Enter the message and tap Save. To delete a quick response, tap the trash can icon next to it.

If you have multiple email accounts, you can set one up as the default account. What this means is that when you respond or forward an email, the email address shown for you is the default.

Inbox Check Frequency determines how often you want your NOOK to check for new email messages. Tap it to see your options, which vary from every 5, 10, 15, 30, and 60 minutes to never. If you select Never, when you launch your email, you need to click the Check for New Messages button (see Chapter 9). The more often you check, the more power (albeit not that much) your NOOK uses. If you are an email junkie, you may opt for the lower settings, but if you don't get a lot of emails or you don't like distracting notifications, you may opt for the higher values.

The Download Attachments setting determines whether you want to automatically download the latest cat photo making the Internet rounds your cousin sent or whether you want to make that decision.

When a new email arrives, a notification appears on the status bar at the top of the screen. If you don't want to be informed when new email arrives (regardless of how often the NOOK checks for new email messages), clear the check mark for this option.

When those notifications arrive, they come with a notification sound. You can control that sound by tapping Choose Ringtone. You have a variety of options here. Tap the ringtone to hear what they sound like, and then tap OK after you have selected the one you want.

> TIP: You're an email junkie checking email every 5 minutes, and you get lots of emails, so you like to get the notification in the status bar but you don't want any ringtone? Choose Silent in the list of ringtones.

The Incoming and Outgoing Settings are advanced options covered in Chapter 9.

If the account you have selected is one you want to delete from this NOOK, tap Remove Account. You'll be asked to confirm the deletion, so either tap Cancel or OK. If you tap OK, the account will be deleted from the NOOK. You can always re-add it by tapping Add Account.

Calendar Settings

The NOOK features a powerful calendar option. The caveat is that it must be connected to a Microsoft Exchange account. Most people do not run Microsoft Exchange, which is typically an enterprise management system. If your company does use Microsoft Exchange, you still may not use the NOOK's calendar depending on security restrictions. The following settings are viable only if you have connected your calendar to a Microsoft Exchange account.

When you receive an invitation to attend a meeting, go to a play, and so on, you can decline those events. If you decline them, they still appear in the calendar. Tap Hide Declined Events to remove their visibility. Some people may like to keep those declines visible in case their time frees up and they can accept the invitation.

Each year has 52 weeks, and if you want to see in your calendar what week number it is, turn Show Week Number on.

Some people say the week starts on Sunday. Others like to make it Monday. Others think Saturday is the beginning of the week. All have good reasons to think so. The Week Starts On option enables you to adjust when the week starts, which adjusts how the calendar looks (That is, when you look at the calendar, what day it is appears on the far left beginning each week of the calendar.) The default option is set for Locale Default [*sic*]. So wherever your location is (and the NOOK is aware of it), the calendar adjusts accordingly.

If you are traveling, you may want to have the calendar show the local time zone for meetings. (You live in Los Angeles, but when you travel to New York, you may want to show meetings on New York time.) If, however, you would rather always show the calendar entries in your home time zone, check this option. In the example, regardless of where you are (New York, Chicago, or Paris) your calendar will always show Los Angeles time for the meetings. If you do elect to have the calendar always show your home time zone, the option below that becomes available. You can tap Home Time Zone and select it.

Clear Search History enables you to clear all searches you have made in the calendar. As you enter search items, your NOOK remembers what you have typed in calendar searches and attempts to assist you as you begin typing additional searches. For example, if in the past you searched for **Dinner Date** and in a new search you begin by typing **D**, the search box displays Dinner Date and any other search items that began with D. Clearing your search history basically tells the NOOK to forget all the calendar searches you have made.

The Reminder Settings category has a variety of information associated with how your NOOK reminds you that meetings are upcoming. Notifications can be turned on or off. If you turn it off, the other settings become unavailable, except for Default Reminder Time. If you choose to receive Notifications, you can choose the ringtone you want by tapping Choose Ringtone and then selecting from the available options and tapping OK. If you choose Silent, no sound accompanies the notification. Calendar notification can also appear (that is, pop up) on the screen, regardless if you are reading, watching a movie, and so on. Turn this off if you want notifications to appear *only* on the status bar. When you set up a meeting, it automatically has a default reminder time: so much time before a meeting that you receive the notification. Tap Default Reminder Time to adjust this. A new screen appears and offers a large number of options.

You can set up multiple calendars: a work one, a home one, your exercise calendar—whatever. Tap Calendars to Display to get a list of calendars. Select which ones you want to appear or not appear.

Contacts Settings

The options revolve around your contacts. First, you can choose which contacts to display. By default, all contacts display, which means whenever you interact with your contacts (sending recommendations, emails, and so on), you see all of them. You can choose to narrow the contacts to display by tapping the Contacts to Display option and tapping from the results.

In Display options, you can choose how you want contact to display. The Sort List By and the View Contact Names As options enable you to choose whether to use the Given Name or Family Name. Tap either option and select your preference.

You can import, export, and share you contacts. To do so, tap Import/Export. Import and Export is done using vCard files. If you have imports you would like to use, export from whatever system you are using into the vCard or VCF format and place on the microSC card, insert it, and come to this option. When you tap Import from Storage, your NOOK searches the microSD card for any vCard files. When it finds it, you are given an option to import one, multiple, or all the vCard files. (These latter two options are available only if more than one vCard file is found.) If you tap Import One vCard File or Import Multiple vCard Files and then tap OK, you are given the available options. Tap the one or multiple ones you want, and tap OK.

If you have only one vCard file on the microSD card, it finds the file and automatically adds it without any other prompting.

When you tap Import/Export, you have the option to Share Visible Contacts. When you tap this, you are provided a number of options depending on what apps you have installed. In Figure 2.13, the options are to share the contacts with Dropbox or Evernote (two apps the author installed) or via email. You always have the email option. When you select an option, you are provided a screen appropriate for that app (for email, an email message is opened). The file will be shared as a vCard file.

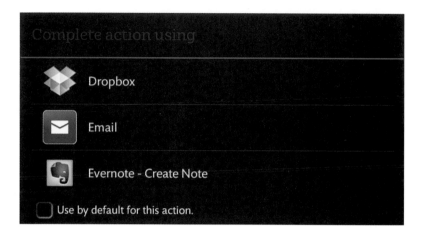

FIGURE 2.13   Sharing contacts.

Browser Settings

The options (see Figure 2.14) revolve around how your browser functions and are divided into several categories. For how to use your browser to surf the web, **see** Chapter 9.

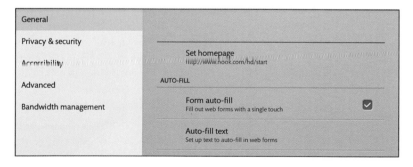

FIGURE 2.14   The Browser settings offer many options in a variety of categories.

General Browser Settings

These options, shown in Figure 2.14, are simple to use. Whenever you open your browser or a new tab, it defaults to a particular web page: the homepage. With the Set Homepage option, you can define what that page is. By default, it is http://www.nook.com/hd/start. Tap the option to see what you can do.

- ▶ **Current Page**: Tap this option to make whatever page your browser is on the homepage.

- ▶ **Blank Page**: Tap this option to make a blank web page the homepage.

- ▶ **Default Page**: Tap this option to make http://www.nook.com/hd/start the homepage.

- ▶ **Most Visited Site**: Tap this option to have the browser open a new page with a list of your most visited websites. From there, you can tap the site you want to go to.

- ▶ **Current Page**: Tap this option to make whatever page your browser is on the homepage.

- ▶ **Other**: Tap this option to enter a website's address and make it your homepage. When you tap Other, a box opens for you to enter the address. Tap OK when done and that is now your homepage.

When you visit a website that has forms, you can have the browser take a stab at filling out the information for you. Basically, your NOOK remembers your information, so when you start typing your name, it can go ahead and enter your email, address, phone number, and so on automatically. You can overwrite it, but it does save time. If you leave this option on, you can enter the information used by auto-fill by tapping Auto-Fill Text. Enter the information and tap Save.

Privacy and Security Browser Settings

These settings center around protecting your data. The cache is the browser's temporary memory. For example, if you buy something, the information in the shopping cart is in the cache. You may want to clear this out to prevent others from potentially having access to that information. Tap Clear Cache and then OK to confirm.

As you move from website to website, the browser maintains a history of sites visited. If you want to clear that information, just tap Clear History and tap OK to confirm.

If the NOOK's browser suspects issues with the website's security (for example, it doesn't use SSL security to protect your credit card data), the browser lets you know. If you don't want those warnings, just turn Show Security Warnings off.

Cookies are small files that many websites use to remember who you are. If you sign in at bn.com, shut down the browser, and then return at a later date and it remembers who you are, the browser is using a cookie to do that. Some sites require you to use cookies, but you can always remove them. (You just need to re-enter your account information when you visit bn.com again.) If you turn off Accept Cookies, websites cannot store cookies for reference later. If you tap Clear All Cookie Data, all cookies currently used by websites will be removed.

Earlier, you learned about forms and auto-filling information. Here is another way that the browser tries to make using forms on websites easier. Your browser remembers and tries to assist. If you turn this feature off, your browser won't remember form information that you enter. If you do have your browser remember but you want to clear it (perhaps you have moved and want it to forget your old address), tap Clear Form Data and then tap OK to clear out the information.

One other way your browser attempts to make your life easier is to offer to remember passwords. For example, if you visit bn.com and enter your account information, you must enter a password. The browser can remember this for you and keep you from needing to re-enter it in the future. You can turn this off, which means you must enter your passwords all the time.

Tap Clear Passwords and then OK to remove all remembered passwords.

Accessibility Browser Settings

These settings enable you to configure how the browser displays text and other options to make the website more readable. Some websites work to control how a person can zoom in and out from it. Your browser enables you to ignore the website's rules and zoom in or out as you want. Turn this on to give you complete control of zooming.

The Text Size set of settings has a preview option so that the options you select below it are represented and give you an idea of how the browser can display real content.

- ▶ **Text Scaling**: Use the slider to scale the text—that is, set how large the text will appear. As you use the slider, the text in the preview box adjusts.

- ▶ **Zoom on Double-Tap**: When you double-tap in the browser, it automatically zooms in on the area you tapped, or if you were already zoomed in, it zooms out and shows more of the page. Use this slider to determine how much that double-tap both zooms in and zooms out.

- ▶ **Minimum Font Size**: Use this slider to force all fonts on a web page to be at least a minimum size. As you change the slide, the fonts in the preview box will be adjusted.

The Inverted Screen Rendering settings basically enable you to have the website show inverted black and white renderings on screen. If you select this option, the Contrast slider becomes active, enabling you to control the contrast.

Advanced Browser Settings

These settings, shown in Figure 2.15, are primarily, but not exclusively, concerned with how your browser deals with certain types of content.

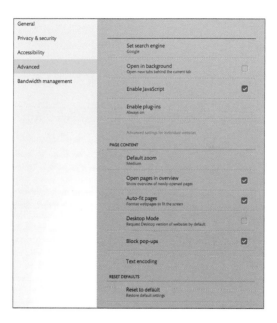

FIGURE 2.15   Advanced Browser settings enable you to control pop-ups and other things.

▶ **Set Search Engine**: Tap this to change the browser's search engine when you type in search criteria on the menu bar. You have three options: Google, Yahoo!, and Bing.

▶ **Open in Background**: When you tap to open a new tab, by default the browser assumes you want to go to that new tab. However, if you turn Open in Background on, the new tab appears behind existing tabs, leaving you on your current tab.

▶ **Enable JavaScript**: JavaScript is a widely used language for enhancing websites. You can forbid websites from running JavaScript in your browser by turning this feature off. However, you may be preventing some websites from being fully functional.

- ▶ **Enable Plug-Ins**: Many websites rely on small applications to assist with their websites. One of the more famous plug-ins is Flash, but you may also encounter Real Audio, Silverlight, QuickTime, and more. If you tap this option, you can choose from three options: Always, On Demand, and Off. With Always, you are never asked to start the plug-in. It just starts. If, however, you choose On Demand, the browser asks you first if you want the plug-in to play. If you choose Off, no plug-ins starts. You won't even be asked. However, you may be preventing some websites from being fully functional.

- ▶ **Default Zoom**: You have three options here: Far, Medium, and Close. This zoom feature determines how closely the zoom out on a double-tap goes. The browser uses the site of the web page to determine what is a Far, Medium, and Close zoom.

- ▶ **Open Pages in Overview**: Web pages can open in one of two ways. First, they can download everything, and you can see it when all the information is ready to display. Second, it can download the text to show you that while it then processes the larger files like images. The second option described here is Overview. If you elect to Open Pages in Overview, the page display the text for you to begin reading while it downloads the images and shows them when they are ready.

- ▶ **Auto-Fit Pages**: With this option on, the browser determines the size of the web page and fits it within the screen. With this option off, all web pages are loaded at the same size, regardless if it goes offscreen.

- ▶ **Desktop Mode**: Most websites have both a desktop and a mobile version. When you go to a website on your NOOK's browser, most treat it as a mobile site and offer you that. However, you may want those websites to treat your NOOK's browser like any regular laptop or desktop. Use this option to control that behavior.

- ▶ **Block Pop-Ups**: Some websites have pop-ups appear for ads and more. If you don't want those, keep this option turned on. If you don't mind pop-ups, turn this feature off.

- ▶ **Text Encoding**: Text encoding is the mechanism to display characters that are less common—for example, é and ÷. For reasons not mentioned here, computers need ways to represent this. You can change the text encoding by tapping this option. However, for the most part, just leave this as is.

- ▶ **Restore Defaults**: Tap this, and then tap OK to restore all the browser settings back to the way they were originally.

Bandwidth Management Browser Settings

You have two settings here: Search Result Preloading and Load Images. These options are particularly relevant for users who have bandwidth limitations. (That is, if you go over 5GB a month, you are charged for the extra.)

When you conduct a search, the browser thinks in the background about what are likely search results. For example, if you start typing in Barnes and Noble and conduct the search, it's probably likely that you want to go to bn.com. To help make that web page pop up faster, the browser starts to preload that in the background, which takes up a bit of bandwidth. If you tap Search Result Preloading, it gives you three options: Never, Only on Wi-Fi, and Always. If you choose Never, no preloading is ever done. The default is Only on Wi-Fi, so only when you connect to a Wi-Fi network is preloading done. If you choose Always, regardless if you are on a Wi-Fi network or using a 3G portable hotspot, preloading is always done, which could slow your Internet speeds a bit.

Load Images is on by default. If you turn this off, images do not display on pages. This saves a lot of bandwidth.

Magazine/Catalog/Comics Reader Settings

These three options relate to particular aspects of these types of content. Catalogs have hotspots that you can tap to be taken to a product page to potentially purchase the item. If you turn Hotspots off, these will not be enabled.

Comics feature ZoomView. For more details about that, **see** Chapter 3, "Reading on Your NOOK HDs and Beyond." ZoomView goes from panel to panel in the comic. By default, you see the other panels, but they are cut off. If you turn ZoomView Letterboxing to on, you do not see the other panels. Instead, black bars surround the panel zoomed in on.

Page Turn controls, when you turn the page, if the page curls or slides to the next page.

Shop Settings

These options (see Figure 2.16) relate to the NOOK Store:

▶ **Password Protect Purchases for Adult Profiles**: For adult profiles, you can require a password to be entered prior to making a purchase. If you tap this to turn it on, a dialog appears and asks you to enter your BN account password. Enter it and tap OK. To turn it off, tap Password Protect Purchases for Adult Profiles, enter your BN account password, and tap OK.

FIGURE 2.16   Use these settings to add gift cards.

▶ **Manage Credit Card**: Tap this to change your default credit card. If you have an expired credit card you need to change, use this feature as well. Tap Change Default Credit Card, enter the information, and then tap Next. The information is verified, and it now becomes your default credit card.

▶ **Gift Cards**: Tap this to enter a gift card (which is used first when making purchases). Tap Add Gift Card and enter the necessary information. Tap Submit and the Gift Card is added to your account.

▶ **Clear Recent Shop Searches**: This setting enables you to clear the shop searches. Whenever you search the NOOK Store on the NOOK, it saves the recent searches. The searches are saved to make it easier to conduct searches. For example, you can search for ebooks related to Sherlock Holmes but decide not to purchase now. When you go back to the NOOK Store on your NOOK, you can type **Sher**, and Sherlock Holmes appears below the search text. You can then tap Sherlock Holmes, and the search is performed.

▶ **Clear Recently Viewed List**: As you browse items, look at their details; those items are captured and kept in a recently viewed list. If you want to clear those and start fresh, tap Clear Recently View List and tap OK.

Social Accounts and NOOK Friends Settings

You have two initial options here: Manager Your Accounts and Add Facebook Friends as NOOK Friends. If you tap Manage Accounts, you see a screen like Figure 2.17.

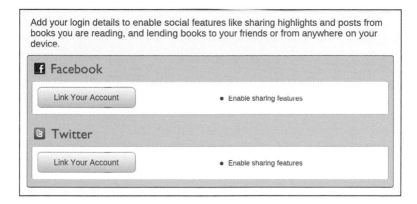

FIGURE 2.17   Link your Facebook and Twitter accounts to share and recommend books with friends.

▶ **Facebook**: This enables you to link your Facebook account to your NOOK. If you have already linked your Facebook account, you can unlink it. To link it, tap Link Your Account. Then enter the required information and tap Log In. The NOOK by Barnes & Noble screen appears. If you tap the friends image, you can choose with whom you share posts. Tap the group you want to see the posts. Tap Install and then tap Allow. Then determine if you want to allow access and actions by your NOOK. Tap the check box to uncheck the item. When you are ready tap Allow All or Allow Some. For more information about Facebook with your NOOK, **see** Chapter 12, "Using the Social Features of Your NOOK HDs."

▶ **Twitter**: This enables you to link your Twitter account to your NOOK. If you have already linked your Twitter account, you can unlink it. To link it, tap Link Your Account. Then enter the required information and tap Authorize App. For more information about Twitter with your NOOK, **see** Chapter 12.

Tap Add Facebook Friends as NOOK Friends. If any of your Facebook friends are also NOOK friends, you'll start seeing their updates in the NOOK Friends app, covered more in Chapter 12.

Reader Settings

These options (see Figure 2.18) relate to Reader app, which is where you read NOOK Books.

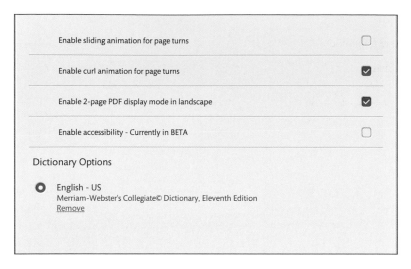

FIGURE 2.18   The Reader settings screen.

- ▶ **Enable Sliding Animation for Page Turns**: This is off by default. Tap the check box to turn it on. The default behavior when you tap to change a page in an ebook is for the text on the screen to simply disappear and be replaced by the next page of text. With this feature on, however, when you tap to change a page in an ebook, you see the text on that page slide either left or right and the next page of text slide into view. If you have this option on, you cannot have Enable Curl Animation for Page Turns on as well.

- ▶ **Enable Curl Animation for Page Turns**: This is off by default. Tap the check box to turn it on. Instead of having the page turn just be a sliding page to page, page curl can lift up the edge of the page and "curl" it over more like reading an actual paper book. If you have this option on, you cannot have Enable Sliding Animation for Page Turns on as well.

- ▶ **Enable 2 Page PDF Display Mode in Landscape**: When reading PDFs, when you switch to landscape mode, you can either see two pages of the PDF or a single page of the PDF. Here is where you control that. If this option has a check mark, when you move to landscape mode, you see two pages of the PDF.

- ▶ **Enable Accessibility**: This feature is currently in beta mode, so it still has bugs. But when on, when you open a book, a voice reads the text.

The Dictionary Options show which dictionary is currently installed or gives you an option to install one if needed. To look up definitions when reading, a dictionary must be installed.

Search Settings

You have two options here.

▶ **Searchable Items**: This enables you to adjust what searches are conducted on (see Figure 2.19). When you conduct a search from the Home screen, you can search a variety of different categories, which you define here. By default, Apps, Web, Contacts, Music, Library, and Shop are searched. You can turn any of these off. In addition, you can add other categories, which are dependent on the apps you have installed.

FIGURE 2.19   Adjust search functions on your NOOK.

▶ **Clear Search Shortcuts**: This setting enables you to clear the list of recent searches. Whenever you search your NOOK, it saves the recent searches. The searches are saved to make it easier to conduct searches.

NOOK Video Settings

The single option here is Authorized Device List. From here, you can remove devices (other NOOKs, laptops using the NOOK Video app, and so on) from viewing B&N purchased NOOK Videos.

My App Settings

What appears here is ultimately dependent on what apps you have installed. However, you can tap the app and generally see a screen like that in Figure 2.20.

FIGURE 2.20   A typical app's settings.

If the app is running, tap Force Stop to stop it. Tap Uninstall to uninstall the app from the NOOK. (You can always reinstall it later.) If you tap Clear Data, you remove any information that app has kept. This may include usernames, passwords, scores, and so on.

Account Settings

The options here revolve around UltraViolet and Adobe Digital Editions. UltraViolet is a system when you purchase some Blu-ray items that you also receive a free digital copy of that item. For example, if you buy *Blade Runner: 30th Anniversary Edition*, it comes with an UltraViolet copy of the movie, which you can access with a code provided in the package. To use UltraViolet, you must set up a separate account at www.uvvu.com. You can use the UltraViolet option in Account Settings to link your UltraViolet account to watch your movies on your NOOK. As of November 2012, linking your UltraViolet account ability is not available.

Adobe Digital Editions is software released by Adobe that many libraries and publishers use to secure their ebooks from piracy. Getting an Adobe Digital Editions account is free at http://www.adobe.com/products/digital-editions.html. Getting one enables you to read library books and books from other publishers that use Adobe Digital Editions security but that you do not buy from BN.com. **See** Appendix B, "Sources for ebooks Other than B&N," to learn how to use Adobe Digital Editions with your NOOK. In Account Settings, tap Adobe Digital Editions to authorize this device by adding your Adobe Digital Editions account information. You can have more than one user's information.

Storage Management Settings

Come here (see Figure 2.21) to see how much space you have left on your NOOK or its microSD card.

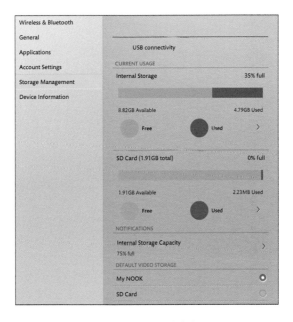

FIGURE 2.21 Seeing how much space you have left is easy.

The top feature, USB Connectivity, enables you to determine how your NOOK acts when you are connected to a computer. When you tap USB Connectivity, you have two options: Media Device (MTP) and Camera (PTP). By default, Media Device (MTP) is selected, and this works for the vast majority of people. When you plug your NOOK into the computer and have Media Device (MTP) selected, the computer treats the NOOK as a hard drive. If, however, you have Camera (PTP) selected, your computer treats your NOOK as a camera instead. When the author plugs it into his Mac, iPhoto launches and wants to import images.

For all practical purposes, either setting enables you to put files onto your NOOK and take them off of your NOOK. Media Device (MTP) is typically the easiest way to do this.

Current usage displays the amount of free space (gray) versus used space (blue) for both the NOOK's internal storage and microSD card (assuming one is installed). If you tap the arrow next to Used, you see something like Figure 2.22, which gives you a breakdown of what takes up the used space.

FIGURE 2.22   Find out how different types of content take up your storage space.

Your NOOK warns you when the internal storage is getting full. By default, you are notified when you reach 75% full. You can adjust this by tapping Internal Storage Capacity and choosing between 75% full, 90% full, and 95% full.

Finally, you can decide where NOOK videos are stored when you download them. By default, they are stored on the NOOK's internal storage. However, by tapping SD Card, you can have downloaded video stored there instead.

Device Information Settings

Most of the information here is informative rather than applicable, so focus on the applicable.

The Software Version (also called firmware) gives you the current version of the NOOK software installed on this NOOK. B&N releases periodic updates to the NOOK to improve performance and fix known issues. As long as your NOOK has a connection to a Wi-Fi connection, your NOOK Tablet can automatically download any updates that B&N releases.

Not all NOOK owners receive new firmware updates at the same time. B&N rolls out new firmware over a period of approximately 1 week. You can also check for any updates that haven't been rolled out to you yet by tapping Software Version and then tapping Check for Updates. Your NOOK checks with B&N, and if it finds an update, it begins installing it.

Battery gives you the current charge on your battery. If you tap it, a screen gives you more details about what's going on with your battery (see Figure 2.23). Here you can see an estimated time of battery life based on what is used, which you can see in the details below the estimated time left. You can see that maintaining the screen illumination accounts for 62% of battery usage.

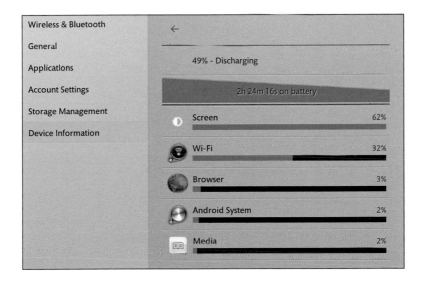

FIGURE 2.23 What is drawing the most power from the battery?

The Legal Information option provides more options to review the terms and conditions and such.

The Developer Options are for those who develop NOOK apps to be sold by B&N.

If you tap Erase & Deregister Device, you will be warned that doing so removes all books and files, including sideloaded content, and deregisters the device. Then you have a button to do just that. You should not do this except for potentially severe problems with the NOOK. More likely, you use this if you finish with the NOOK and want to give it to a friend.

Adding and Using a microSD Card to Your NOOK

Your NOOK has approximately 8GB, 16GB, or 32GB of built-in memory depending on the model you purchased. You have a lot of memory, but music and videos can begin to eat that space up. Therefore, your NOOK's memory is expandable using a microSD card.

> TIP: A microSD card is not the same as an SD memory card like the kind typically used in digital cameras. A microSD card is approximately the size of your fingernail.

> NOTE: You will see both microSD and microSDHC. Your NOOK can use either format—they are the same for all intents and purposes. The HC is used for microSD cards greater than 2GB in size.

Installing a microSD card in your NOOK is easy—you don't even need to turn off your NOOK:

1. Flip your NOOK so that you are looking at the bottom where the power connector connects (see Figure 2.8 or 2.9). To the left of the connector, you see a little plastic flap. Pull that flap out to expose the microSD slot.

2. The microSD slot is the small opening. With the metal connectors of the microSD card facing the back of the NOOK, slide the microSD card in, and push until it locks into place. The NOOK automatically recognizes the card. Close the flap.

3. If the microSD card has not yet been formatted, a screen appears letting you know that formatting it will erase everything on the disk. Tap Format Now. Tap Format Now again to confirm.

In the Device Information settings, tap SD Card (only available to tap if a microSD card is installed). This opens the SD Card screen (see Figure 2.24). Here, you can unmount the SD card (which you should do before removing it).

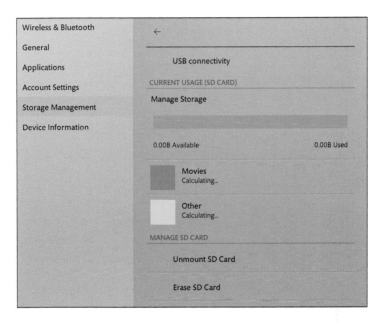

FIGURE 2.24   The SD Card menu where you can safely dismount the card before removing it from your NOOK.

If you tap Erase SD Card, you can format the microSD card, which erases everything on the card. A confirmation screen to format and erase all data on the microSD card appears. Tap Format SD Card to do so. Tap Format Everything. Tap OK when done.

To remove a microSD card, follow these steps:

1. From the SD Card screen, tap Unmount SD Card.

2. Flip your NOOK so that you are looking at the bottom where the power connector connects. To the left of the connector, you can see a little plastic flap. Pull that flap out to expose the microSD slot.

3. The microSD slot is the small opening. With the metal connectors of the microSD card facing the back of the NOOK, slide the microSD card in, and push until it locks into place. The NOOK automatically recognizes the card. Close the flap.

4. With your finger, push the microSD card further into the slot. The microSD card partially pops out, letting you get a grip on it to pull it out completely. Close the metal plate.

When you connect your NOOK to your computer, you now see your microSD card as a folder titled SD Card.

> NOTE: You can add a microSD card that already has items loaded on it, but the NOOK folder structure is necessary, so it is easiest to install a blank microSD card into the NOOK and then plug the NOOK into your computer and load files into the appropriate categories (documents, videos, and so on).

Now that you have a microSD card installed, how do you access those files? From the Home Screen, tap Library, and tap My Files. You see two options near the top that you do not see if you do not have a microSD card installed: Device and SD Card. By default, you are looking at the Device files. Tap SD Card to switch to seeing the files on the microSD card. (Tap Device to go back to the files on the NOOK's internal storage.) You can then tap the folders to navigate deeper as necessary. (For basic instructions to interact with these files, **see** "Reading Microsoft Office and Other Documents on Your NOOK" in Chapter 3.)

CHAPTER 3

Reading on Your NOOK HDs and Beyond

Although your NOOK has many unique features and capabilities, its primary purpose is for reading ebooks and other content. One of the benefits of owning a NOOK is that you can carry a complete library with you everywhere you go. If you don't have your NOOK with you, you can also read your ebooks on your PC, Mac, iPhone, iPad, iPod touch, Android phone, or Android tablet.

Various forms of content are available to read on your NOOK—NOOK Books and other EPUB files, along with PDFs; Microsoft Word, Excel, and PowerPoint files; and plain text files. Appendix A, "Understanding ebook Formats," explains more about the details of ebook formats. You are probably already familiar with Microsoft documents, although you can use either the DOC or DOCX formats (and the corresponding XLS or XLSX and PPT or PPTX formats) used in all versions of Word.

Browsing Your Library

The two main places for content on your NOOK are the Home screen and Library. The Home screen is a quick-and-easy way to see content that you are reading now or access often. When I am reading a book, I make sure it appears on the Home screen, but when I finish it, I go to the Library to find my next read.

The Home Screen

The Home screen includes the Active Shelf, covers you have placed on the Home pages, and other ways to access your content. (**See** the section "Home Screen" in Chapter 1, "Getting Started with Your NOOK HDs," for a complete review of the options.)

The Active Shelf shows the most recent downloads and opened items. Swipe left or right to view the items.

To open an ebook, magazine, or newspaper from the Home screen, tap the cover—you can do this in the active shelf or on the Home screen. The ebook, magazine, or newspaper opens to the last page that you were on when you closed it. However, NOOK Kids books always open from the beginning.

The Home screen has five Home pages. (You can see which page you are on at the top. Just beneath the notifications are three dots—the white one is the Home page you are on.) You can add icons to the Home pages (not the Active Shelf) by tapping and dragging a cover from the Active Shelf. In the Library, you can press and hold a cover and then tap Add to Home from the menu that appears.

To remove an item from a Home page, press and hold the cover. Tap Do Not Show on Home from the menu that appears. This also works for the Active Shelf.

To place an item on a different Home page, press and drag the cover to the far right or left edge of the screen. The cover slides to the next page. Release the cover.

The Library

The Library contains all the content you've purchased from B&N and the content you have sideloaded (see Figure 3.1). This includes not only ebooks you've purchased, but also magazine and newspaper subscriptions, sample books, videos, music, Microsoft documents, PDFs, ebooks purchased from other sources, and free books downloaded from B&N and other sites.

FIGURE 3.1 The Library where all your books and content are stored.

To go to the Library, tap Library on the Home screen. When at the Library, you see a list of large categories. Next to each category is a small arrow. Tap it to show the covers, which you can scroll through by sliding across them left or right. To see only your Books or Apps, tap Books or Apps (or whatever):

- ▶ **Books**: Tapping this displays the full list of ebooks on your NOOK, whether from B&N or other sources.

- ▶ **Magazines**: Tapping this displays the full list of magazines on your NOOK, whether from B&N or other sources.

- ▶ **Movies and TV**: Tapping this displays the full list of movies and TVs on your NOOK or available for streaming, whether from B&N or other sources.

- ▶ **Apps**: Tapping this displays the apps you have installed on your NOOK.

- ▶ **Kids**: Tapping this displays the apps and books categorized for kids.

- ▶ **Catalogs**: Tapping this displays the catalogs on your NOOK.

- ▶ **Newspapers**: Tapping this displays the full list of newspapers on your NOOK, whether from B&N or other sources.

- ▶ **My Scrapbooks**: Tapping this displays the full list of scrapbooks you've made on your NOOK.

- ▶ **My Files**: Tapping this gives you access to the files you have added to your NOOK that don't fit neatly into one of the existing categories or are downloaded via the browser, Dropbox, and so on.

> NOTE: For more information on using My NOOK Library on bn.com, **see** Chapter 25, "Using My NOOK Library."

If you purchase a book using the Shop on your NOOK, that book is automatically downloaded to your NOOK within a few minutes. If you purchase an ebook from B&N using your computer, the ebook is added to My NOOK Library on bn.com, but it isn't downloaded to your NOOK automatically—although the cover appears. You can tell it was *not* downloaded because a white cloud with a green down-pointing arrow icon appears on the upper left of the cover. Tap the cover to download the NOOK Book.

> CAUTION: If you plan to be away from Wi-Fi hotspots, you should make sure that the items that appear in My NOOK Library have actually been downloaded to your NOOK.

Many options exist here, so work your way through each button and the myriad of
actions you can take in interacting with the Library.

Books

Note that all files placed in the microSD card's My Files\ Books folder are shown
here along with all NOOK Books and documents in the NOOK's My Files\ Books
folder or NOOK's Digital Editions folder.

At the bottom of the screen, you have the Options and View buttons. Tapping Options
gives you four choices:

▶ **Create New Shelf**: Tapping this lets you create a shelf. **See** the "My
   Shelves" section later for more details.

▶ **Manage Content for Profiles**: Tapping this lets you manage what content
   appears in which profile. **See** Chapter 11, "Creating and Using Profiles and
   Your NOOK Today," for more information.

▶ **View Archive**: Tapping this displays the full list of archived materials. To
   remove something from the archive, simply tap the cover to download it.

▶ **Refresh**: Tapping this gives updates the content appearing here.

Tapping the View button enables you to sort your ebooks by Title, Author, or Most
Recent, which means either read or added and determine what view you want to see
your content (see Figure 3.2). By default, these are Grid and Most Recent. List view
(see Figure 3.3) shows smaller covers with the text to the right.

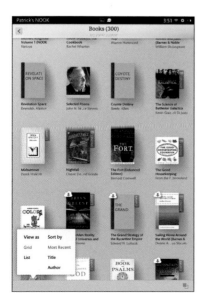

FIGURE 3.2   Sort your library by one of these
choices.

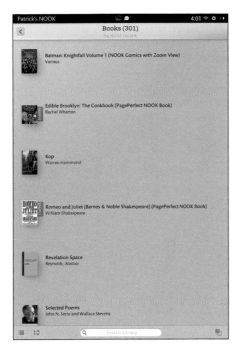

FIGURE 3.3   Your library in List view.

From the Books part of the Library, you can interact with your ebooks in two ways. First, you can just tap the cover to open the ebook. Second, if you tap and hold the cover, a pop-up menu appears (see Figure 3.4) with several options:

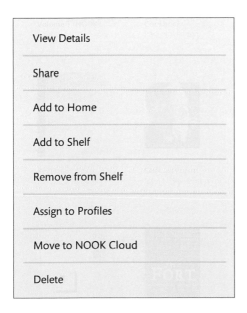

FIGURE 3.4   The pop-up menu that appears after pressing and holding a cover.

▶ **View Details**: Tapping this option opens a screen with many options (see Figure 3.5). **See** "The View Details Screen" section for more about this screen and its options.

FIGURE 3.5   The View Details screen.

▶ **Full Version Available**: This option appears for NOOK Book samples. Tapping it takes you to the View Details screen.

▶ **Share**: This enables you to recommend, rate and review, like on Facebook, or lend. For more about recommending and liking, **see** Chapter 12, "Using the Social Features of Your NOOK HDs." For more about lending, **see** Chapter 6, "Lending and Borrowing Books with LendMe on Your NOOK HDs."

▶ **Add to Home**: This option lets you add it to the Home page with a single tap.

▶ **Add to Shelf**: This option lets you add it to a shelf. A Select Shelf screen appears. You can tap an existing shelf to add that ebook to that shelf. Alternatively, you can tap Add to a New Shelf. The Create New Shelf screen appears. Type in the shelf name and tap Save. The shelf is created and that ebook is added to that shelf. You can add ebooks to multiple shelves.

▶ **Remove from Shelf**: This option lets you remove the ebook from a shelf. If you tap Remove from Shelf, the Select Self screen appears and displays all the shelves this ebook is in. Tap the shelf you want to remove this ebook from.

▶ **Move to NOOK Cloud**: This option enables you to remove the content from your device and into the NOOK Cloud (essentially, an archive).

▶ **Delete**: This option enables you to delete items. If it is B&N content (for example, a NOOK book), the content will be deleted from your NOOK Library—meaning you *cannot* redownload it or read it on other devices. If the content is additional content that you added (for example, a Project Gutenberg ebook), the content is deleted from the device—you can put it back on later. In short, be careful with this option. When you tap Delete, you are asked to confirm that you do indeed want to delete it.

Books, magazines, and newspapers purchased from B&N often have notices on the cover regarding them:

▶ **New**: This is a recent NOOK Book you have purchased and not yet downloaded.

▶ **LendMe**: This NOOK Book can be lent to a friend.

▶ **Borrowed**: You have borrowed this NOOK Book from a friend. The number of days left (out of 14) is in a small, gray circle at the bottom right of the cover.

▶ **Lent**: You have lent this NOOK Book to a friend. The number of days left (out of 14) is in a small, gray circle at the bottom right of the cover.

▶ **Sample**: This is only a portion of the NOOK Book to give you a chance to review before you buy.

The View Details Screen

The View Details screen for B&N content has a number of options. If it is a NOOK Book, you see the star rating from B&N. Tapping the Read button opens the ebook for reading. (Alternatively, if you have not downloaded the NOOK Book yet, you can tap Download to download the NOOK Book.)

Tap LendMe to see the LendMe screen. For more information on the LendMe feature, **see** Chapter 6.

Tap Share (the thought bubble icon) to see options for Recommend, Rate and Review, Like on Facebook, and LendMe (if available for that particular title). For more information on the Recommend, Rate and Review, and Like on Facebook features, **see** Chapter 12. For more information on the LendMe feature, **see** Chapter 6.

Tap Profiles (the person's head icon) to manage which profiles on this NOOK have access to that content. **See** Chapter 11 for more information about profiles.

Overview provides a description of the ebook. Tap More Like This to see other available B&N content by other customers who have purchased the same item, by the same author, or in the same series (see Figure 3.6). Tap a cover or icon to go to a View Details screen for that item (including an option to purchase or sample the content).

FIGURE 3.6   The View Details screen showing what other customers have purchased.

If the NOOK Book is a sample or borrowed (for more information related to shopping and sampling NOOK Books, **see** Chapter 11), you can tap Read Sample (or just Read for borrowed NOOK Books) to read the sample or tap the Price button and then tap Confirm to purchase the NOOK Book.

Tap Reviews to see what reviewers have written or what other customers have posted about the NOOK Book (see Figure 3.7). From here you can read what others have to say. You can sort the comments by tapping the drop-down list and choosing from among the options. If you find any of the reviews helpful (or not), you can tap Yes or No for that review. If you think the review is off base for any number of reasons (see

Figure 3.8), tap Report This Review, tap the reason, and then tap Send to report the review to B&N, who may remove the review.

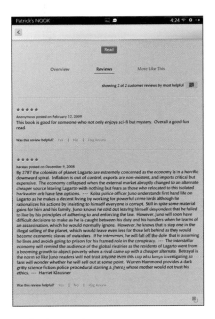

FIGURE 3.7   The Customer Reviews tab.

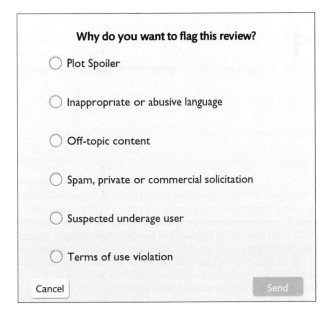

FIGURE 3.8   The options when you flag a review as problematic.

Tap Editorial from that drop-down list to see what professional reviewers say (for example, excerpts from *The New York Times Book Review* or *Kirkus Reviews*).

Magazines

This is where B&N places all your magazines (as opposed to newspapers) that you purchase from B&N (see Figure 3.9). Also, if you placed any files in either the NOOK's Magazines folder or in the microSD card's My Files\Magazines folder, those documents are shown here as well. You have the same options here as you do with the Books section.

FIGURE 3.9   The Magazines screen.

For magazine subscriptions, you probably have multiple issues here. (More than one cover is stacked on top of the other.) To open and read an issue, tap the cover, which opens a screen and shows all available issues. Tap the cover of the issue you want to open and read.

Movies and TV

This is where B&N places all the videos that you purchase or rent from B&N (see Figure 3.10). Also, if you have placed any files in either the NOOK's Videos folder or in the microSD card's My Files\Videos folder, those videos are shown here as well. **See** Chapter 8, "Watching Videos on Your NOOK HDs," for more information on videos.

FIGURE 3.10   The Videos screen.

Note that if you have rented a movie, a banner indicates the amount of time left to watch.

Apps

This is where B&N places all your apps that you purchase from B&N (see Figure 3.11). Tap the Options list and Check for Updates to see if any apps have been updated and install those updates. **See** Chapter 8 and Chapter 9, "Using NOOK Apps and Surfing the Web," for more information on apps and the video apps specifically.

FIGURE 3.11   The Apps screen.

Kids

This is where B&N places all your content (apps, books, whatever) that you purchase from B&N (see Figure 3.12) related to kids. **See** Chapter 5, "Reading and Using NOOK Books for Kids Features," for more information about NOOK Books for kids.

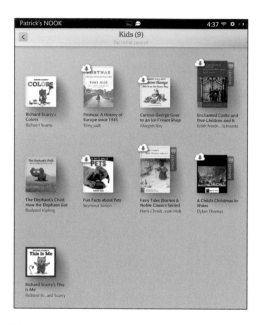

FIGURE 3.12   The Kids screen.

Catalogs

This is where B&N places all your catalogs that you purchase from or subscribe to at B&N (see Figure 3.13). You have the same options here as you do with the Books section.

Newspapers

This is where B&N places all your NOOK Newspapers™ (as opposed to magazines) that you purchase from B&N (see Figure 3.14). Also, if you have placed any files in either the NOOK's Newspapers folder or in the microSD card's My Files\Newspapers folder, those documents are shown here as well. You have the same options here as you do with the Books section.

For newspaper subscriptions, you probably have multiple issues here. (More than one cover is stacked one on top of the other.) To open and read an issue, tap the cover, which opens a screen and shows all available issues. Tap the cover of the issue you want to open and read.

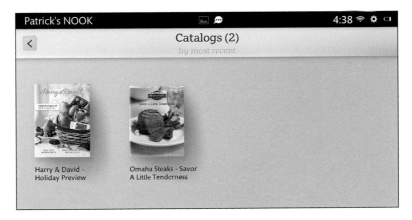

FIGURE 3.13 The Catalogs screen.

FIGURE 3.14 The Newspapers screen.

My Shelves

The NOOK enables you to organize your ebooks into categories (or shelves) that you can name (see Figure 3.15). If you have a lot of ebooks and you want to categorize them beyond just author name, title, and most recent, this is how you can do it.

My Shelves shows you any existing shelves. You can use the View option at the bottom left to show your shelves as a grid or list and to sort by either shelf name or most recently created.

To add a shelf, from the bottom-left Options menu, tap Create New Shelf. The Create New Shelf screen appears. Type the name of the shelf and tap Save.

You can also edit existing shelves by pressing and holding a shelf's covers. When you lift your finger, you get three options. Tap Manage Content in Shelf to see the Library options. Expand each category by tapping the small circle to the right of the content type (see Figure 3.16). Here you can do several things. A listing of titles appears. To add titles to this shelf, tap the check box next to the title so that a check mark appears. Removing check marks remove that title from that shelf. Tap Save make the changes.

FIGURE 3.15   The My Shelves screen.

FIGURE 3.16   Edit existing shelves.

To rename a shelf, press and hold the shelf's covers. Choose Rename Shelf from the resulting pop-up menu. Enter the new name and tap Rename.

To delete a shelf, press and hold the shelf's covers. Choose Remove Shelf from the resulting pop-up menu. Your NOOK asks you to confirm. Tap Remove to delete the shelf.

> NOTE: When you delete a shelf, you are not deleting the content in the shelf.

My Scrapbooks

When you are reading magazines or catalogs, you can save advertisements in scrapbooks. This way, you don't need to remember what catalog or magazine you saw that ad in. When you create a scrapbook, here is where you access it.

My Files

My Files enables you to access files on the NOOK internal memory or on the microSD card. The view defaults to the files on your NOOK. Tap SD Card (which appears only if a microSD card is installed) to access the files there.

The folder structure on the NOOK and on the microSD card is straightforward, as shown in Figure 3.17.

> NOTE: Adobe Digital Editions (ADE) ebooks also appear in the Books section of the Library. For more information about ADE ebooks, **see** Appendix A.

Tap the folder icon to go into there. You can drill down to documents you have downloaded or other items to open the directly.

Reading NOOK Books on Your NOOK

If you open a NOOK Book or sideloaded EPUB file for the first time, after you select it, you are taken to the starting point that the publisher has chosen for that item. This might or might not be the first page. For example, some ebooks open on the first page of Chapter 1. Other ebooks open on the cover or title page. The publisher of the book decides which page is visible when you first open an ebook.

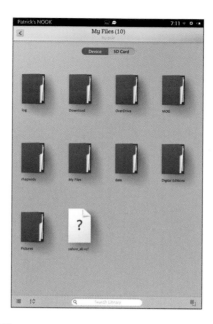

FIGURE 3.17 The My Files screen.

If you open a NOOK Book that you have read on the NOOK before in any of the NOOK Apps, NOOK Study™, or NOOK device, you are taken to the last location you were reading. If you open a sideloaded EPUB file you have read on the NOOK before, it opens to the last page you were on in the NOOK. In other words, non-B&N content does not sync across applications.

> NOTE: In August and September of 2012, B&N experienced server issues that prevented, delayed, or otherwise interrupted synching between devices and apps. So the synching is by no means perfect, although it works well for the vast majority of the time.

As you're reading, swipe right across the page to go to the previous page, or swipe left across the page to go to the next page.

Of course, there's more to reading books than just reading, right? Figure 3.18 shows the reading screen and the Reading Tools available. To see the Reading Tools, quickly tap the reading screen.

FIGURE 3.18 The reading interface.

Following are features of the Reading Tools:

- ▶ **Bookmark**: Tap this to add a bookmark. Chapter 4, "Using Highlights, Bookmarks, and Annotations," covers using bookmarks in detail.

- ▶ **Scroll Bar**: Drag this to quickly slide through the book.

- ▶ **Go to Page**: Tap this to enter a specific page number to go directly to that page.

- ▶ **Go Back**: When you use the Go to Page option, after you have advanced to that page, you can tap Go Back to take you back to the location where you just were—kind of like flipping back and forth between two channels on your TV remote.

- ▶ **Reading Tools Bar**: This bar has five options: Details, Content, Text, Share, and Find. You see each of these buttons in action in the following sections.

To exit the Reading Tools, tap anywhere on the reading screen where those tools do not appear.

Finally, while reading, you can press and hold on a word. The Text Selection toolbar appears (see Figure 3.19). If you want to select more than that single word, drag the selection highlight to the end of the block of text you want to select. For the Highlight, Notes, and Look Up buttons, **see** Chapter 5. For the Share button, **see** Chapter 12. Looking up and finding words is discussed in the "Looking Up Words" section of this chapter.

FIGURE 3.19 The Text Selection toolbar.

Fixing Reading Orientation

With your NOOK, you can read in either portrait or landscape mode. The NOOK switches between these two modes depending on how you hold the NOOK—flip it sideways to have it shift to landscape, or flip it upright to display in portrait mode. However, if you want to fix the mode so that even if you flip the NOOK on its side or upright it remains in the same mode, tap Settings from the status bar and then turn Lock Rotation to On. To unlock, tap Settings in the status bar and turn Lock Rotation to Off.

Changing the Text Font and Text Size

Your NOOK enables you to easily change the text font and text size while reading. To change the font or the text size, tap the reading screen, and then tap Text on the Reading Tools bar (see Figure 3.20).

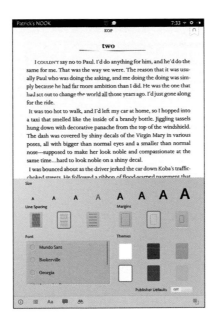

FIGURE 3.20   Use this screen to adjust the font size among other things.

Your NOOK supports eight text sizes, represented by the A. The current text size A is colored teal. Tap the A for the size you want. You can see the text size adjust behind the text menu. Adjust the text size to whichever size you want.

The current font selected has the button next to it filled in. To change the text font, tap the Font you want. The text adjusts to the new font behind the text menu. You have six fonts to choose from, and you can see a representation of them in the Font selection. (Scroll to see all the fonts.)

▶ You cannot change the text font if the publisher created the content with a specific font embedded in it.

▶ You cannot change the text font for PDF files. If the creator of the PDF file embedded a particular font, your NOOK uses that font. Otherwise, it uses the default font.

▶ Some ebooks consist of pages scanned as images, usually as PDF files. You cannot change the text font for these ebooks.

NOTE: Tapping Publisher Defaults to On changes all settings on this screen to the options chosen by the Publisher for all content that you read. You can toggle that back to Off at anytime.

Changing the Color Theme, Line Spacing, Margins, and Brightness

Your NOOK enables you to change the color scheme, space between lines, and margins while reading. To change these, tap the reading screen, and then tap Text on the Reading Tools bar. The current theme selected is highlighted in teal.

Tap the Theme box to change the color settings for the background and text. You have six options, top row from left to right first:

- ▶ Bright white page with black text

- ▶ Dark gray background with white text

- ▶ Gray background with black text

- ▶ Cream background with black text (this author's favorite)

- ▶ Brown background with white text

- ▶ Light yellow (butter) background with black text

Tap your choice. The reading screen changes to reflect what you chose.

The Line Spacing options are similar to using single-space, single-and-a-half-space, or double-space. The current selection is highlighted by a teal box, and you have three options. Tap the option you want. The reading screen adjusts.

The Margin options determine the amount of white space on the right and left sides of the text. The current selection is highlighted by a teal box, and you have three options. Tap the option you want. The reading screen adjusts.

To adjust the Brightness of the screen, tap Settings from the status bar and use the Brightness scroll bar.

Looking Up Words

One of the most convenient features of your NOOK is to quickly look up the definitions of words you don't know. If you're reading a book and encounter a word you don't know or are curious about, press and hold on that word until the Text Selection toolbar appears. Tap Look Up. A window appears with a dictionary entry (see Figure 3.21). You can also tap Wikipedia or Google. Tapping takes you to the browser, opens up the corresponding website, and enters that word as the search criteria. (Use the Recent Drawer to return to reading your book.) If you want, you can look up another word by tapping in the Edit Your Search box and editing the word and tapping Search.

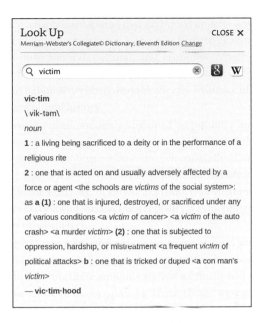

FIGURE 3.21 Your dictionary goes wherever your NOOK goes.

NOTE: Looking up words is not supported for certain types of ebooks:
- Magazines (Although magazines that "function" more like newspapers or books enable you to look up words.)
- NOOK Comics
- NOOK Books for Kids

To search your ebook for a specific word or phrase, tap the Find button, and then type the text you want to search. A keyboard and text entry box appear. Type your search words and tap Search. If it finds your word, your NOOK displays the locations of that word in a scrollable window (see Figure 3.22). The scrollable window provides a bit of context. Tap the location of the word you want to go to. You are taken to that location, the word is highlighted, and the scrollable window disappears, but you still see the search text box (see Figure 3.23). You can tap the button immediately to the right of search box to redisplay the scrollable window, or you can tap the left or right keys next to the search word to go to and highlight the next appearance of that word. Tap the X or tap the reading screen to exit search mode. If you want to search for a different word or phrase, tap in the box that contains your original search term, type in the new word, and tap Search.

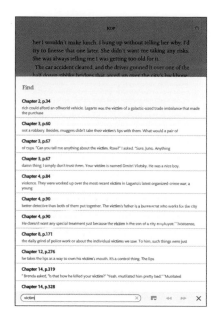

FIGURE 3.22   A scrollable list of search results.

FIGURE 3.23   Searching your ebook is easy.

Finally, if you select a word while reading, from the Text Selection toolbar, you can tap Find in Book. Your NOOK performs a search for that word or phrase in that ebook, displaying the results like any other search.

> TIP: Need to type lots of uppercase letters? Tap the Shift key twice. This enables you to enter only uppercase letters. Tap the Shift key again to release the caps lock.

Reading Enhanced NOOK Books

Enhanced NOOK Books feature video and audio directly within the ebook. When shopping for these ebooks at BN.com, look for the NOOK Book enhanced™ designation. The cover of the NOOK Book also shows Enhanced Edition at the bottom of the cover.

When reading one of these enhanced NOOK Books, you will encounter the enhanced material, as shown in Figure 3.24.

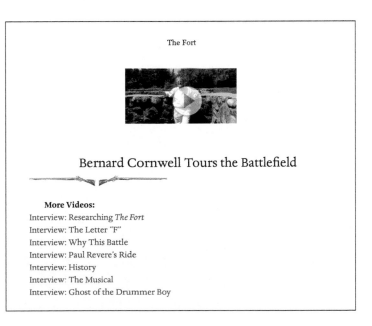

FIGURE 3.24 Here's a page with enhanced content.

Tap the Play button on the content. When you do, the screen adjusts to offer more control (see Figure 3.25). Tap the Pause button to pause the video, and tap the Play button to restart the video. Use the scrollbar to scroll to a specific location. Tap the Expand button (four arrows pointing away from each other) to make the video full screen; then you can switch between portrait and landscape mode for viewing if you want.

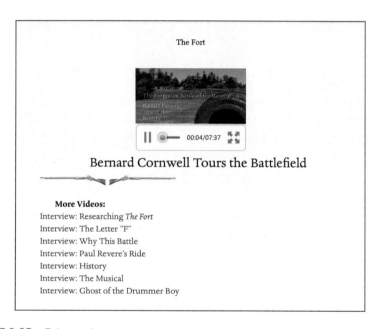

FIGURE 3.25   Enhanced content playing in your ebook.

NOTE: You cannot sample enhanced NOOK Books from B&N.

NOTE: Enhanced NOOK Books at this time work *only* on your NOOK HD+ or NOOK HD. If you own a NOOK Simple Touch, you can see it listed in the Everything Else list, but you cannot download it. On the NOOK App for iPad, you can see it as a title, but when you try to download it, you are informed that it is not yet supported on the iPad.

Reading Magazines and Comics on Your NOOK

In addition to books, B&N provides magazine subscriptions and comics for your NOOK. B&N automatically delivers subscription content to your NOOK if a Wi-Fi connection is available. (For now, you purchase comics individually.) For more information on subscribing to content on your NOOK, **see** Chapter 11.

B&N recognizes that many magazines and comics are more image-intensive than ebooks, and the NOOK takes full advantage of that to display a rich reading environment for magazines. Often, magazines are read in landscape mode, although portrait mode works as well.

NOTE: Some magazines function more like newspapers (for example, *The New York Review of Books* or *Analog Science Fiction and Fact*), so if you encounter a magazine like that, use the "Reading Newspapers on Your NOOK" section for more appropriate instructions.

Because magazines differ, you might encounter a range of reading interfaces. The "standard" interface described for *National Geographic* is quite common. However, many magazines feature enhanced content such as videos, interactive graphics, and so on. These activities (see Figure 3.26) use standard gestures to interact with, but the "standard" magazine reading options may not be available. Fortunately, many emagazines that differ from the standard magazine reading experience offer instructions in the first page or so.

When you open a magazine or comic, you can use pinch and zoom techniques to narrow in on pages. If you tap the page, you see the Thumbnail view at the bottom of the page (see Figure 3.27). This is a thumbnail of each page that you can scroll through. Tap the thumbnail to go to that page.

Pinching and zooming and dragging can be tedious for reading articles, and this is where the Article View is handy. When you see that button, tap Article View, and a secondary reading window opens on top of the magazine (see Figure 3.28). This is the text of the article (with an opening image) that you can scroll through to read more easily. Tap the Magazine View to close Article View. The good news is that your NOOK remembers where you were in the article, so if you tap Article View again for that article, it takes you to where you last stopped reading. You can also swipe left and right to navigate from article to article.

FIGURE 3.26   A magazine with enhanced content.

FIGURE 3.27   Scroll through a magazine's pages in Thumbnail view.

NOTE: Reading comics is best in portrait mode.

While in Article View, if you tap the screen in the article, a Reading Tools bar appears (see Figure 3.28). This functions the same.

> NOTE: Comics do not have an Article View.

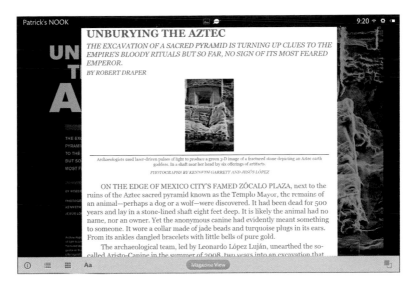

FIGURE 3.28   The Reading Tools bar in a magazine.

The Content option provides a table of contents for the magazine with brief descriptions of each article (see Figure 3.29). The Text options are identical, excepting the Publisher Default option, as the Text options for ebooks.

With magazines, you have a Grid view that is available in the Reading Tools bar. Tap it, and all the pages appear in a scrollable grid in the reading screen (see Figure 3.30). Tap the Grid view icon to exit this view, or tap the page you want to go to, which takes you to that page and exits Grid View.

With magazines you also have the Scrapbook function. **See** Chapter 10, "Using Catalogs and Scrapbooks," for more about these features.

NOOK Comics come with ZoomView. You can choose to not use ZoomView, and if so, the previous description for reading a magazine applies equally well to NOOK Comics. But those with ZoomView have a bit more you can do. As you can see in Figure 3.31, you have a Zoom View button at the bottom of the screen. When you tap this, the screen zooms in to the first panel of that page. You can then use normal page turning gestures to move from panel to panel on the page in the order specified by the publisher. This is a nice feature so that you do not need to pinch and zoom on your own. To turn off ZoomView, just tap Comic View.

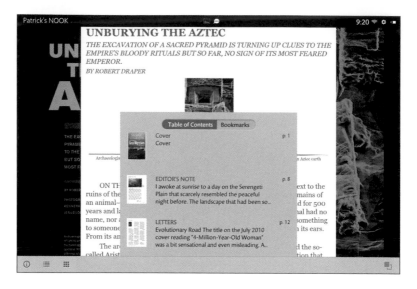

FIGURE 3.29   The contents of a magazine.

FIGURE 3.30   A magazine in Grid View.

FIGURE 3.31 Reading a page in a comic.

Reading Newspapers on Your NOOK

In addition to books, B&N provides newspaper subscriptions for your NOOK. B&N automatically delivers subscription content to your NOOK if a Wi-Fi connection is available.

For more information on subscribing to content on your NOOK, **see** Chapter 13, "Shopping and Visiting B&N on Your NOOK HDs."

Unlike books, newspaper content isn't presented in a linear format. Content is often presented in major sections with article headlines and possibly followed by a small synopsis of each article (see Figure 3.32). To read the specific article, tap the headline for that article. After an article is open, use swipe left and right gestures to navigate between pages just as you do when reading a book.

Tapping the screen displays the Reading Tools, which are the same as the ebook Read Tools (see Figure 3.33).

To navigate back to the list of sections and their articles, tap the left-pointing arrow button on the top right.

For more information on subscription content, including when your NOOK automatically deletes subscription content, **see** Chapter 11.

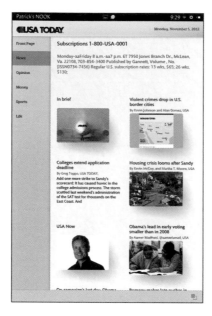

FIGURE 3.32   Reading a newspaper.

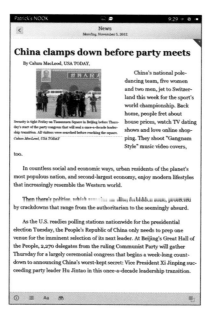

FIGURE 3.33   The Reading Tools bar is the same for ebooks and newspapers.

Reading Microsoft Office and Other Documents on Your NOOK

Beyond the NOOK Books, magazines, ebooks from other sources, and newspapers you can read, on your NOOK you can also read Microsoft Office documents, HTML files, and PDFs.

Reading Microsoft Office Documents

Your NOOK has OfficeSuite installed, which is an application running on your NOOK that can open and read Microsoft Office documents.

> NOTE: You cannot edit the content of Office documents on your NOOK.

A great thing about this is you don't need to worry about which version of Word or Excel you have; you can open them up so long as they are valid Office documents. Have Word 2010 DOCX files? You can open these as easily as you open Word 2003 DOC files. No worries either between Mac or PC.

To open an Office document, from the Home screen, tap Library, and tap My Files. You can then navigate to the location on either the NOOK or microSD card where your Office document is located. (Generally, these are in the My Files\Documents folder.)

> TIP: If you use a file hosting service such as Dropbox.com or Box.com, you can download their free apps from B&N, store your Word, Excel, and other files directly there, and open them through the app on your NOOK.

You see a listing of files. You have two options at this point. Tapping the File icon opens the file. Pressing and holding the File icon displays a pop-up menu with Add to Home, Add to Shelf, and Delete options, which are familiar options previously described in the chapter.

The different types of Office documents have some similar and some different options available when you open them, so now look at them individually.

Word

After the Word document opens, just below the status bar you have a few options (see Figure 3.34).

FIGURE 3.34   Reading Word documents on your NOOK.

TIP: You can also read RTF and TXT documents in this viewer.

You scroll the document up and down to change pages. Tap the three vertical squares to see a menu:

- ▶ **View**: Tapping this offers some more options:

  - ▶ **Page View or Web View**: You either read the document in either view. (I cannot tell any difference between the two.) In both views, you can use pinch and zoom gestures.

  - ▶ **Go to Top**: Tapping this takes you to the top of the document.

  - ▶ **Go to Bottom**: Tapping this takes you to the end of the document.

  - ▶ **Go to Bookmark**: Tapping this displays a list of bookmarks, which you can tap to jump to that location. Bookmarks must have been inserted in Word; you cannot add bookmarks on your NOOK.

  - ▶ **Zoom**: Tapping this lets you choose a zoom option. Tap the percentage, and the screen zooms to that choice.

▶ **Full Screen**: Tapping this hides the menu options and status screen, maximizing the real estate devoted to reading.

▶ **Settings**: Tapping this displays a screen for dictionary configuration. A dictionary is not automatically installed, so the value of this menu is limited.

▶ **Help**: Tapping this opens the browser to a help page for this app.

▶ **About**: Tapping this displays information about OfficeSuite.

While reading Word documents in either Page or Reflow view, you can use pinch and zoom to zoom in and out of the document. If you tap the reading screen, two zoom control buttons appear at the bottom of the page.

Tap Word Count to displays a screen that shows the word count of this document. Tap Find to search for specific text. Enter the text in the search box, and as you type items found that match the criteria are highlighted. Tap the forward and backward buttons to advance back and forth in the findings. Tap Done to exit search.

Excel

After the Excel document opens, just below the status bar you have a few options (see Figure 3.35).

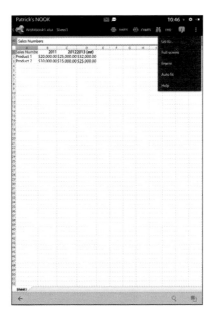

FIGURE 3.35   Reading Excel documents on your NOOK.

You scroll the document up and down to change pages. Tap the three vertical squares to see a menu:

▶ **Go to Cell**: Opens a text entry screen. Type the cell (for example, D1) that you want to go to. The cell is then selected.

▶ **Full Screen**: Tapping this hides the menu options and status screen, maximizing the real estate devoted to reading.

▶ **Freeze**: Tapping this provides a pop-up to choose Freeze Row, Freeze Column, and Freeze Row and Column. Where you select in the spreadsheet determines the row and column that is frozen. If you freeze the spreadsheet, when you scroll through cells, it hold the row, column, or both that you freeze.

▶ **Auto Fit**: Tapping this adjusts the selected cell to fit the text, thus widening or shrinking the cell to fit the content.

▶ **Help**: Tapping this opens the browser to a help page for this app.

While reading Excel documents, you can use pinch and zoom to zoom in and out of the document. If you tap the reading screen, two zoom control buttons appear at the bottom of the page.

The FX row at the top shows the formula or text in the selected cell. You cannot modify it, but you at least can see what is going into that cell.

The Information button displays information about OfficeSuite.

The Find option enables you to search for specific text. In the dialog that appears, enter the text and you can choose whether the search is case-sensitive, should match the entire cell, or whether to search in results of formulae.

Tap Charts to see charts built in the spreadsheet (if any). If the spreadsheet has more than one sheet, tap the Sheets and then tap the sheet you want to go to. Alternatively, you can tab the sheet tab you want to see at the bottom of the page.

PowerPoint

After the PowerPoint document opens, just below the status bar you have a few options (see Figure 3.36).

Along the left side, you can see thumbnails of the individual slides. You can scroll through these to advance quickly to the slide you want to see. You can also scroll through the sides.

FIGURE 3.36   Reading PowerPoint documents on your NOOK.

Tap the three vertical squares to see a menu:

- ▶ **Zoom**: Tapping this lets you choose a zoom option. Tap the percentage and the screen zooms to that choice.

- ▶ **Full Screen**: Tapping this hides the menu options and status screen, maximizing the real estate devoted to reading.

- ▶ **Find**: Tapping this opens the Find search box. Enter the text in the search box, and as you type, items found that match the criteria are highlighted. Tap the forward and backward buttons to advance back and forth in the findings. Tap Done to exit search.

- ▶ **Help**: Tapping this opens the browser to a help page for this app.

- ▶ **About**: Tapping this displays information about OfficeSuite.

While reading PowerPoint documents, you can use pinch and zoom to zoom in and out of the document. If you tap the reading screen, two zoom control buttons appear at the bottom of the page.

If you tap Outline View, the screen changes to show you just the text associated with each slide in a single page. The slide associated with the text is listed in gray boxes to the right. Tap Slide View to get back to seeing slides.

Tap Slide Show to start the slide show. Before it begins, you have two options. You can advance slides by manually touching the advance arrow, or you can set each slide to advance to the next one after so many seconds. Tap Start to start the slide show. When the show starts, if you tap the screen, you get four options in each corner. The bottom right and left advance or retreat the slide show one slide. The top left exits the slide show. The top right allows you to draw on the slide. (It's not permanent.) Tap the drop-down arrow to select the color. Tap the pencil icon, and use your finger to draw on the slide.

Tap Go to Slide to enter the specific slide you want to jump to.

Reading HTML Files

After you tap to open an HTML file, the HTML file is opened in the web browser. For more information about using the web browser, **see** Chapter 9 for more information.

Reading PDFs

This section is specifically about PDFs outside of Adobe Digital Editions PDFs (ADE PDFs). ADE PDFs operate like regular ebooks.

On the NOOK, when you open a PDF, you have two options for reading that PDF (see Figure 3.37). If you have installed an app that also reads PDFs (for example, ezPDF Reader Pro), the option to open the PDF appears here as well. The Reader and OfficeSuite offer different reading options, so you can explore both.

FIGURE 3.37   Which app do you want to read your PDF in?

Reading PDFs with OfficeSuite

Similar to Office documents, when a PDF opens, just below the status bar you have a few options (see Figure 3.38).

Tap the three vertical squares to see a menu:

▶ **Zoom**: Tapping this lets you choose a zoom option. Tap the percentage and the screen zooms to that choice.

▶ **Full Screen**: Tapping this hides the menu options and status screen, maximizing the real estate devoted to reading.

▶ **Help**: Tapping this opens the browser to a help page for this app.

▶ **About**: Tapping this displays information about OfficeSuite.

FIGURE 3.38   Reading a PDF document.

While reading PDF documents, you can use pinch and zoom to zoom in and out of the document.

Tap Go to Page, to enter a specific page number and jump to it.

Reading PDFs with Reader

When you use Reader to read PDF documents, it mirrors reading NOOK Magazines™ and NOOK Books.

If you tap the page, you display the Reading Tools (see Figure 3.39):

- ▸ **Thumbnails**: You can scroll through the PDF like you can a magazine. Tap the thumbnail of the page you want to go to.

- ▸ **Scroll Bar**: Drag this to quickly slide through the PDF.

- ▸ **Go to Page**: Tap this to enter a specific page number to go directly to that page.

- ▸ **Go Back**: When you use the Go to Page option, after you have advanced to that page, you can tap Go Back to take you back to the location where you just were—kind of like flipping back and forth between two channels on your TV remote.

- ▸ **Reading Tools Bar**: This bar has two buttons: Content and Find. The buttons function just like they do for NOOK Books except that Share and Discover are not "options" you can select.

FIGURE 3.39   Reading a PDF document with Reader.

While reading PDF documents, you can use pinch and zoom to zoom in and out of the document. Finally, while reading, you can press and hold on a word. The Text Selection Toolbar appears (see Figure 3.40). If you want to select more than that single word, drag the selection highlight to the end of the block of text you want to select. For the Highlight, Notes, and Look Up buttons, **see** Chapter 6. The "Looking Up Words" section of this chapter discusses looking up and finding words.

FIGURE 3.40   Highlight text in a PDF.

The options function just like the corresponding functions in the NOOK Books. In addition, you can freeze the orientation of a PDF just like a NOOK Book.

Reading Page Perfect Books

When you download the latest thriller, normally, the presentation of the text on the page is not all that important. But some ebooks require that the presentation in ebook format not shift based on the size of the text the reader wants, where images fall, and so on. Thus, Page Perfect books preserve exactly how the book is supposed to appear. These books function in many ways like the PDFs read with the Reader in the previous section.

You open a Page Perfect book like any other. If you double-tap the screen, it zooms into that portion of the book. Double-tap again to zoom out to the original size. If you tap once, you see the Reading Tools along with a thumbnail of the pages like a magazine (see Figure 3.41).

FIGURE 3.41   Reading a Page Perfect book.

All other functions of a Page Perfect book mirror reading a PDF in Reader. The only additional feature is the Share button next to the Contents button. **See** Chapter 12 for more about the social features of your NOOK.

CHAPTER 4

Using Highlights, Bookmarks, and Annotations

Take a look at one of your favorite books, and you can likely find notes in the margins and perhaps dog-eared pages. Jotting down notes about passages that impact you or marking pages you want to come back to visit later is how you make books a personalized possession. Fortunately, you don't have to forgo these things when it comes to ebooks, because your NOOK lets you easily highlight passages and add bookmarks and notes to pages.

Using Highlights, Notes, and Bookmarks on Your NOOK

When you think of highlighting something in a book, you typically think of using a yellow highlighter marker to draw attention to portions of the text. Highlighting on your NOOK is similar to that…but with a highlighter that has multiple colors all in one.

> TIP: Highlighting and notes are not supported for magazine content. You can add only highlights and notes in ebooks that support them. Caveat: Magazines that are more like newspapers (for example, *The New York Review of Books*) do support highlighting and notes.

A note in an ebook is simply a highlighted area with a message attached. Therefore, the steps necessary to add, view, edit, and delete notes are the same as the steps for using highlights.

Adding a Highlight or a Note

To highlight text or add a note in an ebook, follow these steps:

1. Press and hold a word. The word appears in a bubble, and that is your signal to raise your finger. The word is highlighted and the Text Selection toolbar appears.

2. If you want to highlight only that word, move to step 3. If you want to highlight a block of text, notice the highlighted word is bounded by two blue bars. Press, hold, and drag one of the blue bars to the location you want to end the highlight (see Figure 4.1).

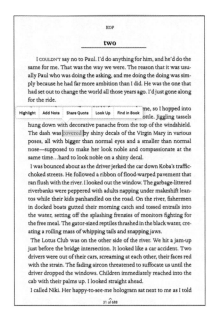

FIGURE 4.1   Highlight the text you want to add a note to.

NOTE: The initial word highlighted must always be the first or last word in the highlight.

3. Tap Highlight to just add a highlight. Tap Note if you want to add a note. If you chose the former, the text is highlighted. If you chose the latter, the Add Note screen appears (see Figure 4.2).

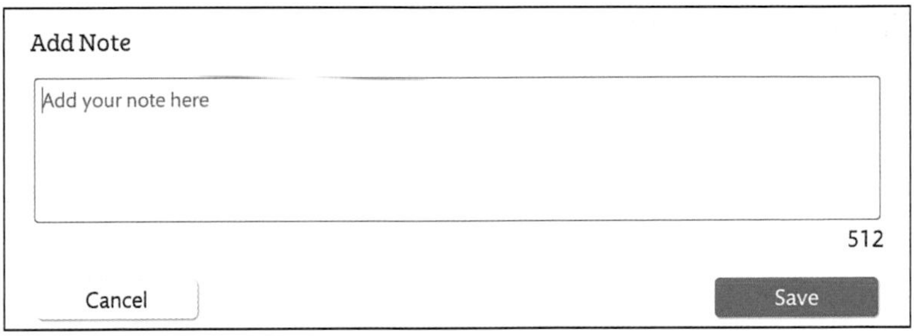

Add Note
Add your note here
512
Cancel
Save

FIGURE 4.2 Enter your note.

4. Type your note and tap Save.
5. The highlight is added, and a Note icon appears next in the margin (see Figure 4.3).

KOP

two

I COULDN'T say no to Paul. I'd do anything for him, and he'd do the same for me. That was the way we were. The reason that it was usually Paul who was doing the asking, and me doing the doing was simply because he had far more ambition than I did. He was the one that had set out to change the world all those years ago. I'd just gone along for the ride.

It was too hot to walk, and I'd left my car at home, so I hopped into a taxi that smelled like the inside of a brandy bottle. Jiggling tassels hung down with decorative panache from the top of the windshield. The dash was covered by shiny decals of the Virgin Mary in various poses, all with bigger than normal eyes and a smaller than normal nose—supposed to make her look noble and compassionate at the same time...hard to look noble on a shiny decal.

I was bounced about as the driver jerked the car down Koba's traffic-choked streets. He followed a ribbon of flood-warped pavement that ran flush with the river. I looked out the window. The garbage-littered riverbanks were peppered with adults napping under makeshift lean-tos while their kids panhandled on the road. On the river, fishermen in docked boats gutted their morning catch and tossed entrails into the water, setting off the splashing frenzies of monitors fighting for the free meal. The gator-sized reptiles thrashed in the black water, creating a roiling mass of whipping tails and snapping jaws.

The Lotus Club was on the other side of the river. We hit a jam up just before the bridge intersection. It looked like a car accident. Two drivers were out of their cars, screaming at each other, their faces red with the strain. The fading aircon threatened to suffocate us until the driver dropped the windows. Children immediately reached into the cab with their palms up. I looked straight ahead.

I called Niki. Her happy-to-see-me hologram sat next to me as I told

31 of 688

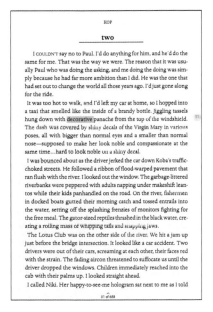

FIGURE 4.3 Your note is added.

Viewing, Editing, and Deleting Highlights and Notes

The simplest way to edit a note is to tap the highlighted text. A pop-up menu appears (see Figure 4.4), giving you several options:

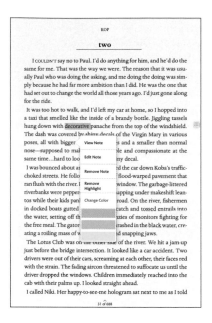

FIGURE 4.4   Your options after you have added a highlight and note.

▶ **View Note**: Tap this to view the note. This appears only if a note is attached to that highlight. After you are in the note, you can tap Edit to edit the note.

▶ **Edit Note**: Tap this to edit the text of the note. This appears only if a note is attached to that highlight.

▶ **Add Note**: Tap this to add a note to highlighted text. An Add Note screen appears. Type in your note and tap Post. This appears only if no note is attached to that highlight.

▶ **Remove Note**: Tap this to remove the note. The highlight remains. This appears only if a note is attached to that highlight.

▶ **Remove Highlight**: Tap this to delete both the note and highlight.

▶ **Change Color**: Tap the color you want to change the color of the highlight for that particular one. You can use all three colors for highlights in the same ebook.

TIP: You can view the note text by tapping the Note icon on the page. From there, you can then tap Edit to edit the text of the note.

To navigate or jump to notes throughout an ebook, from the Reading Tools toolbar (tap the screen), and tap Content. Then tap Highlights and Notes. You see a listing of the notes in the ebook (scroll if you need to see more), as shown in Figure 4.5. You see the text that was highlighted, the page number of the note, and the date and time it was last edited. Tap the particular note you want to jump to. The contents screen disappears, and you are taken to the page with the highlight or note you tapped.

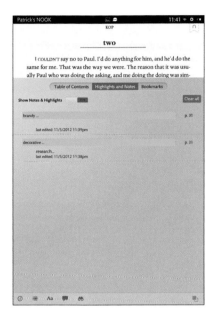

FIGURE 4.5 Jump to a specific note.

Two other options exist on the screen shown in Figure 4.5: Clear All and Show Notes & Highlights. If you tap Clear All, you delete all notes and highlights in the ebook. If you turn Show Notes & Highlights to Off, you turn off the visibility of the highlights; although, the Note icon stays in the margin. You can turn Show Notes & Highlights back to On to have the highlights reappear.

Using Bookmarks

Bookmarks enable you to easily return to a particular page. Unlike notes, bookmarks do not have any text associated with them. Bookmarks work in all your ebooks, magazines, and newspapers.

For ebooks and newspapers (and magazines that read like books), to add a bookmark on the page you're reading, tap the reading screen, and then tap the icon that looks like a bookmark in the top-right corner. It drops down a bit and changes to blue. Tap it again to remove the bookmark. Alternatively, you can tap the upper-right corner of the screen to place a bookmark or tap the bookmark to remove it.

For magazines, comics, catalogs, scrapbooks, and newspapers, to add a bookmark on the page you're reading, tap the reading screen and then tap the + icon in the top-right or top-left corner (see Figure 4.6). It folds down. (Think of flipping the corner of a page in a book.) Tap it again to remove the bookmark.

FIGURE 4.6   Bookmarks in newspapers.

To return to a bookmark, from the Reading Tools toolbar, tap Content and then tap Bookmarks. A list of pages containing bookmarks appears (see Figure 4.7). Tap the bookmark you want to go to; your NOOK immediately takes you to that page.

To remove a bookmark, tap Clear All to remove all bookmarks in that ebook, magazine, or newspaper.

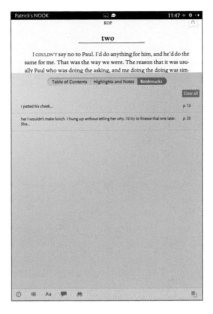

FIGURE 4.7   Jump to a specific bookmark in an ebook.

Page Perfect Books

Page Perfect books function identically to regular ebooks. You can select text and receive the same Text Selection options. To make selecting text easier, double-tap to zoom into the section you want, and then press and select the text.

CHAPTER 5

Reading and Using NOOK Books for Kids Features

The NOOK has several features geared specifically to kids, and the device takes full advantage of the landscape reading mode and touch technology to offer an immersive and entertaining experience for kids.

Some kids books have prerecorded readings (those labeled as Read to Me), and others have interactive features (those labeled Read and Play). The NOOK also has a microphone that enables you to record your own reading of the story.

> NOTE: For more information about setting up a child's profile, **see** Chapter 11, "Creating and Using Profiles and Your Nook Today."

Reading NOOK Books for Kids on Your NOOK

One of the exciting things about the NOOK is the NOOK Books for Kids; many of them (and growing) feature Read to Me or Read and Play. In addition, the NOOK enables you to record your own reading of children's books; a feature called Read and Record for NOOK Books for Kids. When you shop for NOOK Books for kids, you see four formats for children's books:

▶ **NOOK Kids Read to Me**: The books have the enhanced Read to Me experience.

▶ **NOOK Kids (eBook)**: The regular NOOK Kids book lacks the Read to Me or Read and Play features, although it functions in every other way as a NOOK Book for Kids. If you have a NOOK, you can use the Read and Record feature.

▶ **NOOK Kids Read and Play**: These books feature not only the Read to Me feature but also interactive activities. (For example, the narrator asks the child to tap the pig that is running; the child does so, and the running pig, well, runs.) These books have the most options of all the NOOK Books for Kids.

▶ **NOOK Kids Interactive**: These are Read and Play books but with a different designation.

NOOK Books for Kids function differently than other content you read (or listen to) on the NOOK. The books open in landscape mode. The first page you are presented with has at least Read by Myself buttons, although it can also have a Read to Me or a Read and Play buttons (see Figure 5.1). In addition, it has the Read and Record button.

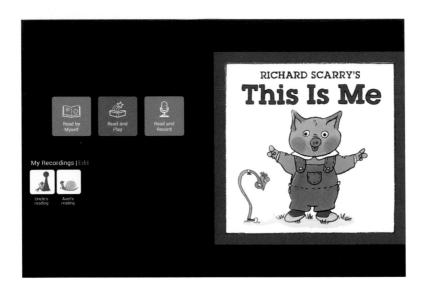

FIGURE 5.1   Tap Read and Play to have your NOOK read to you.

Read to Me and Read and Play open the next page of the book, and you hear a voice reading the title (and not a mechanical voice). Each time you swipe to the next page, the voice reads the text on that page.

Read by Myself opens the next page of the book, but no voice begins reading. Instead, you can choose to have segments of the text read to you while you're reading if you want.

If you have already made a Read and Record book, you can tap the recording you want to listen to. (You can have more than one.) The book functions like a Read and Play or Read to Me book.

Picking any of the choices does not limit you to that choice again when you next open the book or return to the cover page. Also, Read and Play books do not have a specific choice to activate that option. When you open the book in either Read to Me or Read by Myself mode, the Read and Play activities are available.

NOOK Books for Kids features a Thumbnail view much like magazines (see Figure 5.2). Tap the upward pointing arrow to display the thumbnails. You can then scroll through these and tap the thumbnail you want to advance directly to that page. If you chose Read to Me, after that page opens, the reading begins. Tap the downward pointing arrow to hide the thumbnails.

FIGURE 5.2   NOOK Book for Kids' Thumbnail view.

If you tap a block of text, the text displays in a whitish balloon for easier reading. In addition, you see a right-pointing yellow arrow. Tapping that arrow reads to you that particular bit of text in that balloon. This works whether you chose Read to Me or Read by Myself earlier and does not alter what happens on the next page. In other words, if you chose Read by Myself, choosing to have a balloon of text read to you does not then activate Read to Me for the rest of the NOOK Book for Kids.

If you are reading a Read and Play NOOK Book, tap the Star button at the top of the page to begin the activities for that page. Just follow the instructions.

Tapping the Home button takes you back to the Home screen.

> NOTE: NOOK Books for Kids are only available to read on the NOOK HD, NOOK HD+, NOOK Tablet, NOOK Color, or NOOK Kids for iPad™ app.

Using Read and Record

When you tap the Read and Record button, the book advances to the title page with the controls onscreen, as shown in Figure 5.3. You can record page by page, and don't worry about keeping up; the NOOK has made it easy to record that page.

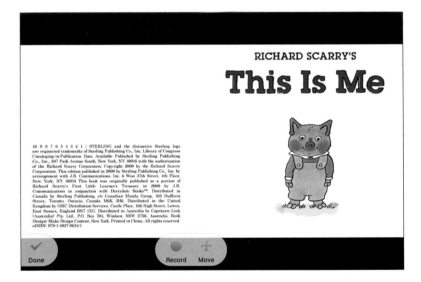

FIGURE 5.3   The Record button.

> NOTE: All NOOK Books for Kids have the option to Read and Record.

Follow these instructions to record your narration:

1. Tap Record.

> NOTE: If you don't like the location of the controls, press and hold the Move button, and drag the Record button out of your way.

2. Read the text.

3. Tap Stop.

4. Tap Play to hear the recording.

5. If you are unhappy with the recording, tap Re-Record and repeat the process. If you are happy with the recording for that page, swipe advance to the next page, and repeat the process.

> NOTE: You do not need to record the entire narration in one sitting. You can save the recording (described in the following steps) and return to continue the recording later.

6. When you finish recording, tap Done.

7. Choose a picture to associate with that recording (see Figure 5.4).

FIGURE 5.4 Choose the image you want to associate with this recording.

8. Type a name for the recording (see Figure 5.5). If you type nothing there, the default recording name is My Recording.

9. Tap Save.

Now when you open a NOOK Book for Kids, your recording appears as an option (refer to Figure 5.1). Just tap the icon for your recording rather than the Read to Me or Read and Play buttons. The NOOK Book for Kids functions identically as it did without your recording, with the added bonus that it is your recording.

If you need to edit an existing recording, tap Edit and then tap the Edit button on the icon of the particular recording you want to modify to see your editing options (see Figure 5.5). If you choose Edit Recording, you perform the same steps as previously described (rerecording or recording for the first time). You can also change the name and picture associated with that recording or delete it outright. Tap Done to save your changes.

FIGURE 5.5   You can edit your recording.

CHAPTER 6

Lending and Borrowing Books with LendMe on Your NOOK HDs

To keep readers from sharing ebooks with all their friends, publishers usually protect ebooks with digital rights management (DRM), which ties an ebook to an individual, and unless that individual can prove that he is an authorized reader, the ebook will not open.

DRM is one of the reasons some people don't like ebooks. After all, when readers find a good read, they like to pass it on to friends and family. The number of people with whom you can share a physical book is fairly limited, but because ebooks are digital copies of a book, they can be shared with millions of people quite easily via email, Facebook, and any number of other methods.

One of the unique features that B&N added to your NOOK is the ability to lend some NOOK Books to other readers using the LendMe feature. Although there are some restrictions when lending and borrowing books, the LendMe feature is a step in the right direction.

TIP: If you receive a LendMe offer, the LendMe logo appears in the notification area of the NOOK. You can tap the logo, and then tap the You Have a New LendMe Item link. From here, you can cancel the item (that is, make a decision later), decline the offer, or accept the offer.

Lending Books with LendMe

To lend a book to someone, the book must support LendMe. Not all books do. If a book does support lending, you see the LendMe logo on the book's page in My NOOK Library on bn.com, as shown in Figure 6.1. You also see the LendMe logo banner on the top-right corner of the cover on the NOOK.

FIGURE 6.1   The LendMe logo appears on a book's page at bn.com if the book is lendable.

The NOOK has many methods for lending books to your friends.

Lending from Your Library

If you are at the Home screen or in your library:

1. Press and hold the cover, and then tap View Details. The details screen appears.

2. Tap LendMe. The LendMe screen appears (see Figure 6.2).

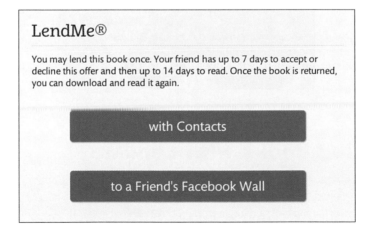

FIGURE 6.2   Tap With Contacts or To a Friend's Facebook Wall to pick a friend to lend to.

3. Tap With Contacts or To a Friend's Facebook Wall. Either option gives you a similar screen (see Figure 6.3). The primary difference is the method the lend offer is communicated. If you choose With Contacts, the person is sent an email. If you choose To a Friend's Facebook Wall, the offer is posted on the person's wall (see Figure 6.4).

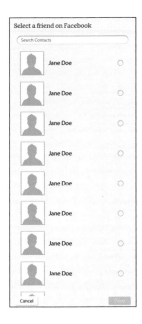

FIGURE 6.3 Select one of your Facebook friends.

FIGURE 6.4 The loan offer appears on your friend's wall.

4. Select a contact, or select Add Contact to add someone not currently in your contact list. Tap Done.

   If you use the To a Friends Facebook Wall option, tap Select Friend to see a list of your Facebook friends. Type in the Search field to narrow your search, select your friend, and tap Done.

5. Type a message to send with the lend invitation. (The message is optional.)

6. Tap Post.

Your NOOK sends the offer and lets you know when it is successfully sent. The cover banner LendMe changes to Lent.

Rules for Lending

Choose carefully when lending a book because after you lend a NOOK Book, you can never lend that particular NOOK Book to anyone again. However, a NOOK Book is considered to be on loan only if your friend accepts the LendMe offer. If your friend rejects the offer or if she allows the offer to expire without accepting it, you can lend the NOOK Book again after it's returned to your library.

I Want to Lend a NOOK Book to One of My Friends. Does My Friend Have to Own a NOOK for Me to Lend Her a NOOK Book?

No. Your friend can read a NOOK Book you've lent to her using the NOOK Apps, NOOK Color, NOOK Simple Touch, or original NOOK. However, your friend cannot read the book unless the email address you used to send the LendMe offer is associated with her B&N account.

The person to whom you've loaned the NOOK Book has 7 days to accept the loan offer. If she doesn't accept within 7 days, the book is returned to your library. The loan offer can also be rejected, in which case the book is returned to your library immediately.

A NOOK Book is loaned for 14 days, and while it is on loan, Lent appears on the cover, and you cannot read the book. When you loan a book, you also loan your DRM rights to the book. Only one person can possess the DRM rights to a book at any one time, so you need to wait until the book is returned to your library before you can read the book again.

CAUTION: There is no way to cancel a LendMe offer.

Borrowing Books

When a friend lends you a book, you receive a notification of the offer (see Figure 6.5). You have 7 days to either accept the offer or reject it. You can accept or reject the loan offer from your NOOK device or any of the NOOK Apps.

FIGURE 6.5   Versions of the LendMe offers on different NOOK devices: NOOK for Mac™ app, My NOOK Library, NOOK HD/HD+, and NOOK Simple Touch.

If you accept a loan offer from your NOOK, that book is also available for the loan period in NOOK Apps or NOOK device, and vice versa.

Lending and Borrowing Using the NOOK Friends App

You need to understand that the NOOK Friends app is closely related but separate from the LendMe program. This section covers the LendMe features of the NOOK Friends app; for the social features of the NOOK Friends app, **see** Chapter 12, "Using the Social Features of Your NOOK HDs," for more information about this app.

If you have a circle of NOOK friends, you can see what NOOK Books they have available to lend and make a request. Here's how you do this:

1. Press the Home screen; tap Apps. Then tap NOOK Friends, and then tap LendMe. A screen show items related to LendMe appears (see Figure 6.6).

   This tab shows several shelves that you can swipe to see all or tap See All to see a vertical representation of the list:

▶ **My Lendable Books**: Shows the NOOK Books you can lend

▶ **Friends Books to Borrow**: Shows the NOOK Books your friends have available for borrowing

▶ **Offers from Friends**: Shows NOOK Books friends have offered to lend you

▶ **Requests**: Shows NOOK Books your friends have requested to borrow

FIGURE 6.6 The NOOK Friends app on the LendMe tab.

2. If you tap a book on the My Lendable Books shelf, you begin the LendMe process. Tap With Contacts or To a Friend's Facebook Wall to open a screen to select the person. Enter a message if you want and tap Post.

3. If you tap a book from the Friends Books to Borrow shelf, you can request to borrow that book. Tap Request to ask to borrow this NOOK Book. Enter a message if you want and tap Send. Your friend sees a LendMe request.

4. If you receive a lend offer, you can open the NOOK Friends app, tap LendMe, and review the Offers from Friends shelf, where you see what NOOK Books are offered you. Tap the cover to see the over. Here you can cancel (thus, postponing the decision until later), decline the offer, or accept it (see Figure 6.7).

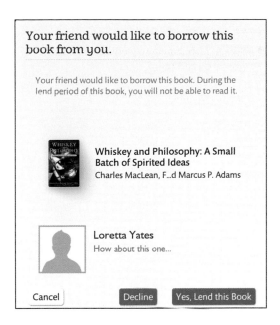

FIGURE 6.7   A friend is requesting to borrow a book.

If you tap the Privacy button, you can choose to show certain NOOK Books to your friends (see Figure 6.8). If you want to hide a NOOK Book from lending, clear the check mark. You can change this back by tapping the check box.

FIGURE 6.8   Hide books from your friends so they cannot borrow them.

NOTE: You must be connected to a Wi-Fi hotspot to refresh the available books or alter the LendMe visibility. If you are not connected to a hotspot, tapping either button opens a Network Settings screen for you to choose a hotspot, if available.

Why would you want to hide a book from lending? You may be reading it at this moment and don't want to decline a request, or you may have a friend you know wants to borrow the book. Because the book can be lent only once, you want to remove it from view so that others cannot request it and you, again, have to decline.

CHAPTER 7

Playing Music, Audiobooks, and Podcasts

For those of you who love to read, almost nothing stirs up as much nostalgia as the thought of listening to some nice music while reading a good book and maybe sipping a nice glass of wine. Your NOOK can't make wine, but it can provide the other two ingredients to this nostalgic scene.

> NOTE: You can also listen to music via the online music service, Rhapsody. To learn more about using Rhapsody, **see** Chapter 9, "Using NOOK Apps and Surfing the Web."

Adding Audio Files to Your NOOK

The Music folder on your NOOK is used specifically for audio files (whether on the NOOK or on the microSD card). When you add audio files to this folder, your NOOK recognizes the files and enables you to play the audio using its built-in audio player.

> NOTE: Your NOOK supports the following audio file types: MP4, MP3, AAC, WAV, FLAC, OGG, 3GP, and AMR. The best options are MP3 and AAC given their ubiquitous presence.

Playing Audio on Your NOOK

To play audio on your NOOK, you first need to copy the music files to its memory or to a microSD card in your NOOK. Audio files should be copied into the Music folder (My Files\Music). If your microSD card does not have a Music folder, create one before copying audio files to it.

> TIP: If you haven't done so already, first load your music into a music player on your desktop or laptop (iTunes, Media Player, and so on). Doing so enables you to set album and artist name, and so on, which affects how easy it is to navigate your music in the Music Player on your NOOK.

After you copy your audio files to the Music folder, you can play them using the music player on your NOOK.

Using the Music Player

The Music Player on your NOOK is a basic music player. So, if you're expecting an iPod on your NOOK, you'll be disappointed. However, for playing background music while reading and for listening to audiobooks and podcasts, your NOOK's Music Player is a great feature.

To launch the music player, from the Home screen, tap Apps, and then tap Music Player. The Music Player opens with four ways to browse your music (see Figure 7.1).

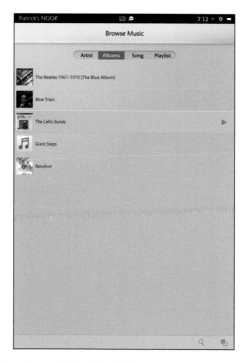

FIGURE 7.1   Browsing albums in the Music Player.

TIP: The speakers on your NOOK are stereo and much touted by B&N. Honestly, they are adequate in my opinion. You'll hear better audio if you use headphones or ear buds plugged into the mini-jack at the top of your NOOK or through a Bluetooth headphone.

The following browser options are available:

▶ **Artist**: Displays your music according to artist. Tapping the artist name shows the albums associated with that artist. Tapping the album takes you to a song list of tracks in that album. Tap a track to begin playing.

▶ **Albums**: Displays your music by albums in alphabetical order (by the name of the album). You can scroll through this list. Tapping the album takes you to a song list of tracks in that album. Tap a track to begin playing.

▶ **Song**: Displays your music in alphabetical order (by the name of the song). You can scroll through this list. If you scroll to the top and try to scroll beyond, a small, blue icon appears with up and down arrows. If you press and hold that, you can drag between the songs faster, jumping from A to B to Z (based on the song title) faster. Tap a song to play it.

▶ **Playlist**: Displays your music by playlists in alphabetical order (by the name of the playlist). You can scroll through this list. Tapping the playlist takes you to a song list of tracks in that album. Tap a track to begin playing.

If you press and hold a song title, artist name, album name, or playlist, you see a menu with several options: Play, Add to Playlist, Delete, Search (see Figure 7.2). Tapping Play plays the song, album, artist, or playlist.

Tapping Add to Playlist displays two options: Current Playlist and New. If you want to add the selection to the Current Playlist you are playing, tap Current Playlist. Tap New to create a new playlist. New, type in the playlist name, and tap Save.

Tap Delete to delete the song from your NOOK.

If you tap Search, the screen changes and gives you a breakdown of your music (see Figure 7.3). When you tap from the results here, you get one of two results. First, if the result you tapped had multiple albums and songs, you see a screen that shows just those results. Second, if you tap a single track, it begins playing.

To search your music, tap the magnifying glass on the bottom bar and begin typing. Album, artist, and so on results appear.

Blue Train

Play

Add to playlist

Delete

Search

FIGURE 7.2   Your options when pressing a track in the list.

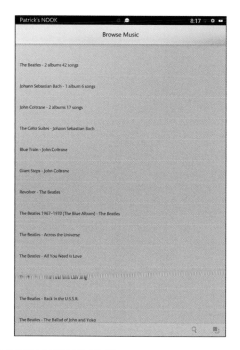

FIGURE 7.3   Search results in the Music Player.

NOTE: For search on your music to work, ensure that you have allowed searching on music. From All Settings, tap Applications, and then tap Search. Ensure that the check box next to Music is selected.

When you tap a song or album to play, the screen changes to the player. You also have your typical music player controls (see Figure 7.4):

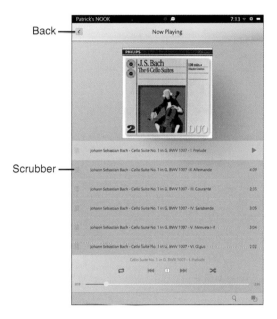

FIGURE 7.4   Now Playing view in the Music Player.

- ▶ **Location in Track/Total Track Time**: Informational items only. The time listed on the left shows the time location within the track. The time on the right shows the total track time.

- ▶ **Play/Pause**: If the Music Player is playing audio, tapping this button pauses the audio. Otherwise, it resumes playing the audio.

- ▶ **Previous/Next Track**: Tapping this button takes you either to the previous or next track.

- ▶ **Scrubber**: The scrubber enables you to change the position in the current audio file quickly. Drag your finger on the scrubber to change the position. When you lift your finger from the touchscreen, the track plays from that location.

- ▶ **Shuffle**: Toggles shuffle mode on or off. Each time shuffle is toggled on, a new random order is created for the currently playing tracks.

- ▶ **Repeat**: Tapping once repeats that playlist, album, or set of songs you see in the player. Tap Repeat again. A 1 appears. This song is now set to repeat until you turn off repeat by tapping the Repeat button again.

▶ **Back**: Tapping this takes you back to browsing your music. However, you see the currently playing track displayed at the bottom. Tap the play button to go back to the player.

While playing audio, exit the Music Player by pressing the Home button. Your audio continues playing, but you can interact with other items on your NOOK. To stop the audio from playing, you can navigate back by starting the Music Player in Apps or tapping the Notification area in the status bar. You'll see an item there describing the current album playing. Tap that notification to go back to the Music Player.

> TIP: Don't want to mess with opening up the Music Player, and such? From the Home screen, tap Library, tap My Files, and tap Music. Find the track you want to play, and tap that file. The Music Player opens and begins playing that track.

Playing Podcasts and Audiobooks on Your NOOK

In addition to listening to music, you can also use the audio player on your NOOK to play podcasts and audiobooks.

Podcasts

Podcasts are audio programs released on a regular schedule. You can subscribe to a podcast using any number of software applications, and when a new episode is released, it's automatically downloaded to your computer.

Podcasts are available that cover just about every topic of interest that you can think of. For example, podcasts can help you use your computer or help you take better pictures. Some podcasts deliver the news daily or weekly and some podcasts cover entertainment gossip. Other podcasts enable you to listen to your favorite radio shows on demand whenever you want.

If you own an iPhone, iPad, or iPod, you almost certainly already have iTunes on your computer. iTunes lets you easily subscribe to podcasts. You can search or browse for podcasts in the iTunes store. If you don't already have an application that you can use to subscribe to podcasts, you can download Juice, a free podcast receiver that makes finding and subscribing to podcasts easy. Juice is available from http://juicereceiver.sourceforge.net.

When you subscribe to a podcast, each time you launch your podcast application (whether that's iTunes, OneCast, Juice, or some other application), it checks for new episodes. If it finds a new episode, it downloads it automatically to your computer. You can then copy that episode to your NOOK. You need to check the documentation and options for the software you use to determine where it stores podcasts it downloads.

> TIP: Be sure that you subscribe to podcasts in a NOOK compatible format (most podcasts are in MP3 format). Some podcasts offer an MP3 version and versions in other formats.

Podcasts should be copied to the Music folder on your NOOK. The podcast will be available when you start the Music Player on your NOOK.

Audiobooks

Audiobooks are recordings of someone reading a book out loud. They are the digital version of books on tape. The most popular source of audiobooks is Audible.com, but your NOOK is not compatible with Audible audiobooks. However, you can enjoy plenty of sources of MP3 audiobooks on your NOOK.

Following are sources of MP3 audiobooks you can use on your NOOK:

▶ **Audiobooks.org**: Free audiobook versions of some classic books. There aren't many books here, but the ones they offer are of good quality.

▶ **Podiobooks.com**: Free serialized audiobooks. This site is run by volunteers and features a large number of indie authors. Podiobooks are free to listen to, though you can donate to an individual audiobook and 75% of that donation goes to the author or creator. You can download episodes via iTunes and move them to your NOOK.

▶ **Simply Audiobooks (www.simplyaudiobooks.com/downloads)**: For a few dollars per month, you can download as many audiobooks as you want. Simply Audiobooks offers both MP3 and WMA audiobooks, so be sure you choose the MP3 versions for your NOOK.

▶ **B&N Audiobooks (www.barnesandnoble.com/subjects/audio)**: B&N offers a wide assortment of audiobooks. If you're a B&N member, you can get some great deals for your NOOK.

▶ **Google Product Search**: Google Product Search (www.google.com/prdhp) is an excellent way to locate MP3 audiobooks. Simply search for "mp3 audiobook," and you can find a vast assortment from many merchants.

After you download an audiobook, copy it to the Music folder on your NOOK. You can then play it by selecting the file from the Media Player playlist.

> TIP: You can listen to most MP3 tracks in your music player. Check out the Teaching Company's (www.teach12.com) courses, many of which are available as audio downloads. As noted, always choose files that are compatible with your NOOK.

CHAPTER 8

Watching Videos on Your NOOK HDs

Just as ebooks are changing the way you interact with books, streaming video is changing the way you consume TV shows and movies. As of November 2012, B&N has introduced streaming video and downloading to their content. You now have multiple options to view video content on your NOOK.

B&N Video Content

B&N offers movies and TV shows via the NOOK Store. You can buy videos in either Standard Definition or High Definition. Usually, Standard Definition is cheaper. Many movies are also available as rentals, which means when you buy the rental, you have up to 30 days to begin watching it and, after you have begun watching it, you have 24 hours to finish watching the video. You can watch it as many times as you want within that 24-hour period. When either time period ends, the video is removed from your NOOK.

> NOTE: B&N has indicated that in the near future, it will release a NOOK Video App that you can install on your computer, iPad, or Android tablet. So, you can, eventually, watch video content you purchase or rent from B&N regardless if you have your NOOK.

Regardless whether you rent or buy a video, the functionality works the same. To access your videos, from the Home screen tap Library and then tap Movies & TV (see Figure 8.1). If the video has not been downloaded to your NOOK, you see the typical download option. In addition, if the movie is a rental, you see the number of days left you have to start watching the video. Alternatively, if you have begun watching the rental, you see the amount of time left in the 24-hour period.

FIGURE 8.1   Your videos in the library.

Tap the cover image to open the Details screen for the movie or TV show (see Figure 8.2). If you have not downloaded the video, you have two options: Stream and Download. If you have downloaded the video, you have the single option, Watch.

FIGURE 8.2   The video's Details screen.

> NOTE: If you move a video to the NOOK Cloud, the video is removed from the
> NOOK and the options when you tap Details become Stream and Download.

If you have an active Wi-Fi connection and don't want to download a video to your
NOOK, tap Stream to start watching. Tap Download if you want to download the
video to your NOOK. When the video is downloaded, tap Watch to begin watching
the video. If you stop watching a video and come back to it later, the NOOK offers to
let you resume playing from where you stopped or to start over.

The video player controls are standard controls: pause, play, fast forward, rewind, and
volume control. To see the controls (if you do not see them), tap the screen. To hide
the controls (if you do see them), tap the screen. At the bottom left of the screen, you
see an i in a circle. Tap this and you are taken back to the Details screen for that
video. Similarly, if you tap Close in the upper right, you are taken back to the Details
screen.

Netflix Versus Hulu Plus

Netflix and Hulu Plus are two of the most popular streaming video services available,
but how do they compare? What are the differences? First and foremost, neither
Netflix nor Hulu Plus have all the movies and TV shows you may want to watch via
streaming, so you are likely to want to watch a show that is not available. Still, both
have impressive libraries.

Both Netflix and Hulu Plus cost $7.99 per month to access their content; although
Hulu does offer free content in the form of clips or a few episodes of a show (typically the three to five most recent). Those subscriptions enable you to watch unlimited video on your NOOK, iPhone, iPad, Android tablets, and any Hulu Plus or
Netflix-enabled device (for example, TiVos, many Blu-ray players, Xbox, Roku
boxes, and Internet-ready TVs).

> NOTE: Some content may be prevented from appearing on mobile devices
> because of rights-related issues—that is, the broadcaster or distributor may
> now allow it.

The main difference between the two is that Hulu Plus is devoted to TV shows and
Netflix is devoted to both TVs and movies. Netflix has a substantially higher quantity
of movies than Hulu Plus, whereas Hulu Plus has many TV shows available a few
days after their original broadcast. (You'll have to wait months or more for Netflix to
make TV shows available.)

One other difference is that Netflix is ad-free, whereas Hulu Plus videos start with an ad and have ads interspersed throughout the video.

Both services stream video to your device at the highest quality possible (although Hulu Plus lets you designate a lower level if you want when you start the video). What this means is that the Netflix and Hulu Plus apps "sense" how fast your network connection is operating while it plays the video. If the network is heavily used and going a bit slowly, the quality of the video will be adjusted downward to keep the video running. So, seeing fluctuations in the quality of the video as it's playing is not unusual. In general, the quality of both is excellent.

If you are debating between the two, try the free trials to see what you think. Browse around a bit to see what's available and what matches most with your interests.

Streaming Netflix and Hulu Plus Videos to Your NOOK

Both the Netflix and Hulu Plus apps start out almost the same. You need to sign in with a username and password. If you don't have one, you can request one from the Start screen. If this is the first time using Netflix or Hulu Plus, you can sign up for a free trial. With Netflix, the opening screen provides a link to Netflix.com to sign up for an account. The Hulu Plus app enables you to set up an account within the app. After you enter your username and password, the two apps—while offering streaming content—do operate differently, so now take a look at each.

NOTE: To use Netflix on your NOOK, you need to install the Netflix app from BN.com.

Using Netflix

Using the Netflix app is a straightforward thing. When you sign in, you see a screen divided into rows like the NOOK Library shelves (see Figure 8.3). If you have started watching any video, it appears at the top under Continue Watching. Just tap the red play arrow to start watching where you left off. The video player has the standard pause, play, fast forward, and reverse options. In the bottom right of the player, you may see a little bubble. Tap it to get options for subtitles and language options (if available). Tap the return arrow to go back to the main Netflix app.

FIGURE 8.3 The opening Netflix screen after you sign in.

If you tap a cover without the red play button or the i button, you see an informational screen (see Figure 8.4). Here, you can tap a star rating on how much you liked (or didn't like) the video. You can tap to Add or Remove from Instant Queue to do just that. Finally, you can also choose a season (if a TV series) and a specific episode to play.

> NOTE: The queue is a place for you to place videos that you want to watch later, sort of a wishlist for videos.

Netflix likes to recommend videos based on what you've liked or disliked in the past and shows you these recommendations in the Top 10 list. Tapping a title brings up a screen that lets you add the series or movie to your Instant Queue. You can also tap the red play button in that screen to start playing the show or movie.

The Instant Queue shelve consists of shows or movies that you have added to that queue. Swipe left and right to view it. Tap the title to see the now familiar informational screen.

The shelves below the Instant Queue offer a variety based on subjects or themes (for example, Mysteries, Dark Science Fiction, and Crime TV Dramas). You can scroll through them to see if there's anything of interest.

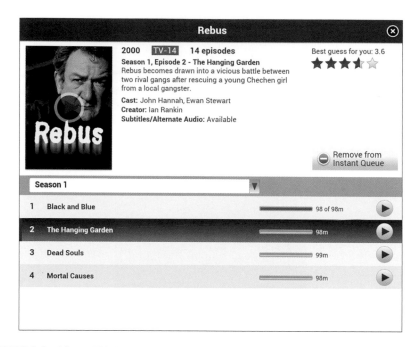

FIGURE 8.4   View a TV show's details.

Alternatively, you can tap Search in the upper right and search for a specific title, series, actor, or director. What is found displays below the Search box. Tap the item to see more information, add to the queue, and so on.

Finally, you can browse by tapping Browse in the upper left. Tap the category that interests you. (Home always takes you to the initial Netflix screen after you have signed in.) You are presented with a series of shelves, further categorized to browse.

Using Hulu Plus

After you sign into Hulu Plus, your opening screen presents you with several options (see Figure 8.5):

- ▶ **TV**: Takes you to a featured list of shows
- ▶ **Movies**: Takes you to a featured list of movies
- ▶ **Trailer**: Takes you to a featured list of trailers
- ▶ **Queue**: Takes you to your queue
- ▶ **Search**: Opens a text box into which you can type your search terms

In addition, you see lots of featured clips and shows, recommendations, and other lists.

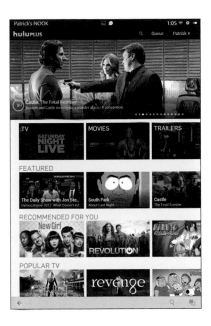

FIGURE 8.5   Hulu Plus's opening screen.

Hulu Plus TV and Movies Screens

Tapping any of these options on the startup screen takes you to a common interface used for both the TV and movies screens. However, if you tap TV, you land on the TV tab. Tap Movies, and you land on the Movies tab, and so on. TV shows, movies, and trailers screens are divided up into even more categories. Eventually, you get down to actual shows or movies (see Figure 8.6). You can add or remove the show as a favorite. If you tap More Details, you get a brief description. For TV shows, you can see individual episodes, clips, and similar shows. If you tap an individual show, you see a screen like that in Figure 8.6. You can add this to your queue (**see** the later section, "Hulu Plus Queue" for more information), play the video, and even share it with friends via email. When you play a video, you have the standard video player controls. Movies lack the Favorites feature that TV shows have.

Tap Queue, and you end up on the Queue tab.

FIGURE 8.6   A set of episodes for a TV show.

> NOTE: As you tap your way around Hulu Plus, to go back a screen (like clicking the Back button on a browser), tap the Back arrow down at the bottom of the screen.

Tap Search to enter text and search for videos that meet that search criteria.

Hulu Plus Queue

Tap Queue and you are taken to the Queue screen (see Figure 8.7). These are the items that you have added to your Queue, so you can minimize searching and save them for later. You can view this by the order you have placed them in the queue (Position) or by airdate (tap Position and then tap Airdate). In addition, you can view all videos as individual episodes or show grouped together by show.

Tap the episode cover and then tap Remove Queue to remove the video for the queue. Or you can tap Play Video to watch the video.

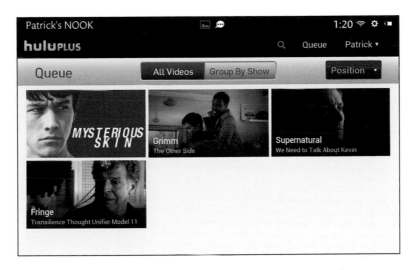

FIGURE 8.7 The Queue screen.

Watching Hulu Plus Videos

When you play a Hulu Plus video, an ad plays (and others play occasionally during the video). You may be asked to pick a quality level; if so, choose whichever quality level you want. After the video begins playing, you can tap the Back button to go back to the Hulu Plus app location you were just at. Tap More to learn more about the product advertised. From there, the video controls are the familiar controls.

CHAPTER 9

Using NOOK Apps and Surfing the Web

The NOOK includes a web browser and several pre-installed NOOK Apps, which include the Music Player you learned about in Chapter 7, "Playing Music, Audiobooks, and Podcasts," the Hulu Plus app you learned about in Chapter 8, "Watching Videos on Your NOOK HDs," the Contacts app, and other items.

Using NOOK Apps

If you have an iPhone, iPad, or Android phone, you are familiar with these download-able programs you can add to those devices. Well, a NOOK App is an app created specifically for the NOOK.

> NOTE: Though it is an Android-based device, you cannot download and use apps from Google Play.

You can get to your NOOK Apps by tapping Apps from the Home screen. B&N pre-loaded several NOOK Apps to your NOOK (see Figure 9.1):

- ▶ **Contacts**: Tap this to see the list of your contacts.

- ▶ **Email**: A full-featured email application.

- ▶ **NOOK Friends**: Tap this to open this social networking app, which includes LendMe options. **See** Chapter 12, "Using the Social Features of Your NOOK HDs," for more information about this app.

- ▶ **Music Player**: Tap this to open the Music Player (**see** Chapter 7 for more details about using the Music Player).

- ▶ **Rhapsody**: Tap this to open the Rhapsody application and listen to music.

- ▶ **Hulu Plus**: Tap this to open Hulu Plus (**see** Chapter 8 for more details about Hulu Plus).

- ▶ **Calendar**: Tap this to access your calendar.

NOTE: The NOOK features a powerful calendar option than ever before. The caveat is that it must be connected to a Microsoft Exchange account. Most people do not run Microsoft Exchange, which is typically an enterprise management system. If your company does use Microsoft Exchange, you still may not use the NOOK's calendar depending on security restrictions.

FIGURE 9.1   The NOOK Apps on your NOOK.

To see what apps are available, visit the NOOK Store or BN.com. (For more information about shopping for apps, **see** Chapter 13, "Shopping and Visiting B&N on Your NOOK HDs.")

If you tap the Options button, you can tap Check for Updates to see if any of your apps have had some tweaks and changes. After you tap Check for Updates, the Available Updates screen appears. You can choose to update all, some, or none of your apps. If no updates are found, the Available Updates states that all apps are up-to-date.

For apps you have added beyond the standard, if you press and hold the app, you see some options similar to ebooks (see Figure 9.2).

FIGURE 9.2   The Options for nonstandard apps.

Using Contacts on Your NOOK

If you imported contacts as described in Chapter 2, "Customizing and Configuring Your NOOK HDs," you see them here. Tap Contacts to open the Contacts app.

Here, you can filter your contacts by Groups, All Favorites, and Favorites (see Figure 9.3). By default, all are shown. To use Groups, you must have a Microsoft Exchange account. Most people do not run Microsoft Exchange, which is typically an enterprise management system. If you're company does use Microsoft Exchange, you still may not use the NOOK's calendar depending on security restrictions.

Use the Search Contacts box to search for a specific person, or you can scroll through your list.

If you want to add a contact, tap Add Contact (see Figure 9.4). You have a wide variety of options and ways to fill this in. Figure 9.4 shows the default fields. Fill in the Name and so on. When you enter a phone number, email, or street address, you can tap the arrow beneath Mobile or Home and select a more appropriate name (see Figure 9.5). If you tap Custom, a text box appears that lets you enter a custom label. When you type in one phone number, email, or street address, Add New appears. Tap that to add another phone number, and so on.

FIGURE 9.3   Filter your contacts to narrow your list.

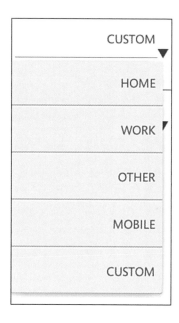

FIGURE 9.4   Adding a contact is easy.

FIGURE 9.5   Adding alternative email accounts.

If you have a photo of the contact on your NOOK, tap the image, and then tap Choose Photo from Gallery. Browse to the image you want and tap it. You'll be asked to crop it if the photo is too large. Drag the boundary box until it is the size you want and then tap Crop.

If you tap the down-pointing arrow next to Name, a more detailed set of options for the name appear, including Given, Middle, and such.

Tap Add Another Field to add a Phonetic Name, instant messaging information, notes, nicknames, website address, and Internet call information.

Tap Done when you have entered in all the information.

If you need to later edit that contact, find it in your Contacts, tap it, and tap the Edit button. Adjust as necessary and tap Done.

You can also email a contact. Find it in the list, tap it, and then tap Share. Tap Email from the list. Enter the email information.

Using Email on Your NOOK

Email is a full-featured email app. Start Email by tapping Email from the Home screen. Then tap Email. The Email app appears. If this is the first time you are starting Email, you see the Welcome screen (see Figure 9.6).

FIGURE 9.6   The Email app Welcome screen.

Type in your email username and password. Your NOOK connects with the email provider. After a few seconds, you receive a Congratulations screen.

Update the Account Description if you want. Also, adjust the Email Account Name, which makes it easy to find whose email account it is if you share your NOOK. Tap Done.

The NOOK downloads your email in the Email app interface (see Figure 9.7).

FIGURE 9.7   The Email app interface.

Now let's become oriented to this interface (which is the screen you see initially, if you have already set up an account and then start the Email app):

- ▶ **Compose**: Tap this to compose an email.
- ▶ **Folders**: Tap this to see a different folder (Inbox, Sent, ToKeep, and so on).
- ▶ **Email Check box**: Tap this to select an email to delete or move to a folder.
- ▶ **Delete**: Tap this to delete any selected emails.
- ▶ **Email**: Tap this to open the email.
- ▶ **Sync**: Tap this to connect with the email server to see if you have any new emails.
- ▶ **Folders**: Tap this to move selected emails to a folder.
- ▶ **Search**: Tap this to search your email.

Now look at a few of these items in more detail.

Compose

Tapping the Compose button opens up the Compose Email screen (see Figure 9.8).

FIGURE 9.8   The Compose Email screen.

In the To box, either type the email address you want to send the email to, or tap the Contacts button and select a contact (or contacts). If you want to CC or BCC an email address, tap CC/BCC. This expands into two separate text boxes: one for CC and one for BCC.

If you want a subject line for your email, tap the Subject text box, and type in the subject.

To begin typing your message, tap the large text box that states, Compose Email. (If you have a signature that automatically gets inserted, you'll see that instead of Compose email.) Type the email. If you want to attach a file (an image from the gallery, something from your linked Dropbox account, and so on), tap the paper clip, and browse to the attachment. The item is attached. Tap the x to remove the attachment.

When you are ready to send, tap Send. If you want to cancel your email, simply tap Cancel. Canceling saves the message as a draft in the Draft folder.

Account

Tapping the Account button displays your existing accounts. Tap the account you want to shift to (see Figure 9.9). Note that the numbers next to the account name are the number of unread messages in that inbox.

FIGURE 9.9   The Accounts screen.

If you have more than one account and want to see all emails for all accounts in one screen, tap Accounts and then tap Combined View.

Email

After you tap an email, the email opens (see Figure 9.10). You have a number of options here, but the options are typical of most email applications. Tap the Reply button; then tap Reply, Reply All, or Forward. Tap Move To and then select a folder.

If an attachment is included, tap the attachment. Tap Open or Save. If you tap open and your NOOK has the required software to open it, the attachment is opened (Gallery for images, Reader for PDFs, QuickOffice for Word, and so on). If you tap Save, the attachment is saved to your My Files\ Downloads folder.

When you open an email, its status changes automatically to Read. If you want to mark it as Unread, tap the Read button. It changes to Unread If you want, you can tap this to change the status back to Read.

While typing an email, if you need to make changes in another part of the email, you can tap the area, which moves the cursor to that point. In addition, you can press and hold a word, which highlights that word with two large blue bars on either side. You can drag either of those blue bars to select more text. Also, when the text is highlighted, you see several options at the top of the screen:

> ▶ **Done**: Tap to remove the highlight and blue bars. Your cursor appears where the ending blue bar was prior to tapping done.

▶ **Select All**: Tap to select all the text in the email. If you are replying or forwarding an email, Select All selects only your reply or forward text.

▶ **Cut**: Tap to remove the selected text and place it in the clipboard.

▶ **Copy**: Tap to copy the selected text to the clipboard.

▶ **Paste**: Tap to paste whatever is in the clipboard.

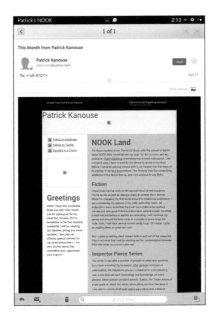

FIGURE 9.10   A typical email.

> NOTE: If you already have something in the clipboard (perhaps copied text from a website), when you initially select text in your email, a small gray Paste button appears just above the blue selected text. You can tap Paste there as well.

Tap the star if you want to mark this as a favorite email, which makes finding it easier.

If pictures are included in the email, you may have the Show Pictures option. (In Figure 9.10, the pictures were not downloaded.) Tap Show Pictures to show the pictures (see Figure 9.11). The option changes to Always Show Pictures from This

Sender. Tapping that tells your NOOK to remember this sender, and every time you get an email from them, the pictures automatically display.

FIGURE 9.11   An email with Show Pictures.

The top right has two arrows: one down and one up. Use these to navigate from email to email without going back to the inbox.

Tap Delete to delete the email.

Browsing the Web with Your NOOK

The NOOK comes with a full-featured web browser (see Figure 9.12). Unlike some mobile browsers, the NOOK browser supports Flash content (when you download and install the Flash app from BN.com). Flash content often appears on web pages in the form of videos or interactive animations and images. (Not all such images you see on web pages are Flash, but many are.) One concern with Flash content is that it is power hungry and uses more battery power than standard web pages. Nonetheless, much content on the web is in Flash, though the number is decreasing.

> NOTE: To access web pages, you must be connected to a Wi-Fi hotspot.

FIGURE 9.12 The NOOK's web browser.

An Overview of Browsing on Your NOOK

Browsing the web on your NOOK is easy. From the Home screen, tap Web to open the browser. The browser opens to the homepage or last page you were on.

At the top, you see a typical-looking web browser interface:

- ▶ **Back button**: Tap to go back to the previous web page.

- ▶ **Forward button**: Tap to go to the web page you were on prior to clicking the Back button.

- ▶ **Address bar**: Tap to enter a new web address or search the web. Tapping gives you the keyboard, and you can either enter a specific web address, or you can type a search term. As you type, a series of tappable links appears below the bar. This displays previously searched terms and websites. You can continue typing and tap Enter, which performs a Google search.

- ▶ **Stop button/Refresh page:** Tap the X button to stop the current page loading. When the page is loaded, it change to a circular arrow. Tap that to refresh the page.

- ▶ **Make Bookmark button (star)**: Tap to make a bookmark to this page.

► **Bookmarks**: Tap to access bookmarks, most visited sites, and your history. For more information about the Bookmarks options, **see** "Using the Bookmarks Screen."

► **Share**: Tap to share the website via email.

► **Find on Page**: Tap to search for text on the visible page.

► **Save page**: Tap to save the page for later reading

► **ArticleView**: Tap to convert the page to more of a book-like reading experience.

> NOTE: You can view web pages in either portrait or landscape mode.

When you are at a web page, press and hold, and then drag to maneuver the page. You can zoom into an area of the page by using the pinch and zoom gesture, or tapping twice quickly on that area of the screen.

To zoom back out, unpinch, or tap twice on an area of the screen.

> NOTE: To do a lot of the functions in the web browser, you must wait for the page to load completely.

Tap a link to go to that link if it is a regular hyperlink (for example, going to another web page). Some links download items to your NOOK. For example, if you press and hold on an image, you can get a menu to save or view the image (see Figure 9.13). However, if you are at Project Gutenberg, go to the download section for a specific book, and tap the EPUB link; the file downloads to your NOOK and opens in the chosen application (see Figure 9.14). These downloads go to the My Files\Downloads folder.

If you press and hold a hyperlink (see Figure 9.15), a menu appears with these options:

► **Open**: Opens the link. This is the same as tapping the link.

► **Open in New Tab**: Opens the link in a new tab, thus leaving your existing tab in place.

► **Save Link**: Adds a bookmark to the link you are pressing.

▶ **Copy Link URL**: Copies the link to the Clipboard.

▶ **Select Text**: Selects the hypertext's text.

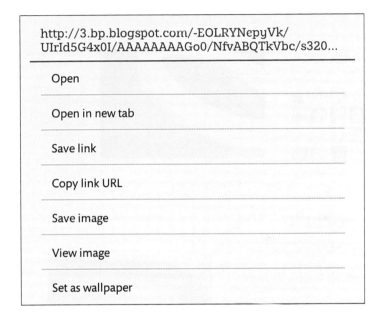

http://3.bp.blogspot.com/-EOLRYNepyVk/
UIrId5G4x0I/AAAAAAAAGo0/NfvABQTkVbc/s320...

Open

Open in new tab

Save link

Copy link URL

Save image

View image

Set as wallpaper

FIGURE 9.13   Some links offer you an opportunity to save or view the file.

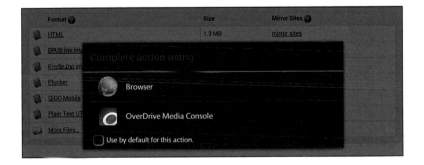

FIGURE 9.14   Some links download the file to your NOOK.

NOTE: In the browser, copying text or links is allowed in a couple places. However, I have yet to find a place where I can paste the said text.

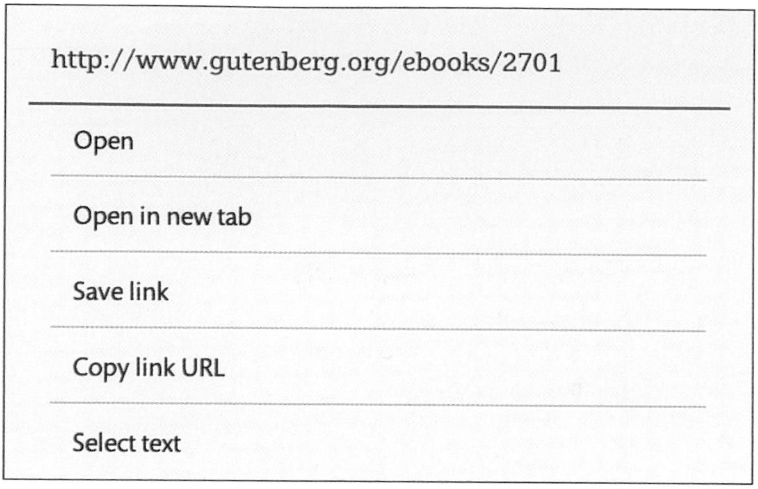

http://www.gutenberg.org/ebooks/2701

Open

Open in new tab

Save link

Copy link URL

Select text

FIGURE 9.15   Your options after you press and hold a hyperlink.

If you press and hold in a nonlink area of the web page, the text you select appears similar to an ebook, and a series of option appears at the top of the screen (see Figure 9.16):

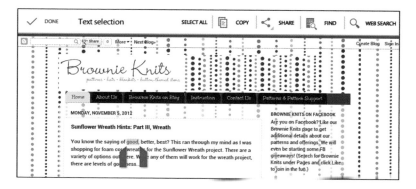

FIGURE 9.16   Your options after you press and hold a nonhyperlink area on a web page.

▶ **Select All**: Selects all text on that web page.

▶ **Copy**: Copies the selected text.

▶ **Share**: Lets you share the text via email or other compatible apps.

▶ **Find**: Tap this to search for specific text on this page. The keyboard appears. Type in what you want to search for. Tap Search. The keyboard drops away, and the number of occurrences found on the page is shown. If more than one appearance is on the page, use the back and forward buttons to highlight the word.

▶ **Web Search**: Tap this to open a new tab, in which the selected text is used to perform a Google search for the selected text.

Using the Bookmarks Screen

The Bookmarks screen, shown in Figure 9.17, enables you to add bookmarks, modify existing ones, and perform other options. The screen opens with three tabs: Bookmarks, History, and Saved Pages.

FIGURE 9.17 The Bookmarks screen.

To get to the Bookmarks screen, tap the Bookmarks button. The Bookmarks screen opens at the Bookmarks tab. The bookmarks are thumbnails of the web pages. The top-left thumbnail, with the plus button overlaid on it, is actually not yet a bookmark. You can make this a bookmark by tapping it.

The other thumbnails are your bookmarks. Tap the thumbnail to open that web page. If you press and hold the thumbnail, a pop-up menu provides these options (see Figure 9.18):

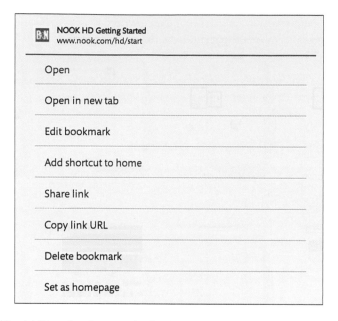

FIGURE 9.18   Additional options on the Bookmarks screen.

> ▶ **Open**: Opens the link. This is the same as tapping the link.

> ▶ **Open in New Tab**: Opens the link in a new tab, thus leaving your existing tab in place.

> ▶ **Edit Bookmark**: Opens the Edit Bookmark window. Here you can adjust the name and location (that is, the hyperlink address) of the bookmark.

> ▶ **Add Shortcut to Home**: Adds a shortcut to the Home screen, where you can tap it to automatically open the browser to that page.

> ▶ **Share Link**: Enables you to share the web page via email.

> ▶ **Copy Link URL**: Copies the link to the clipboard.

> ▶ **Delete Bookmark**: Deletes the bookmark. You will be asked to confirm that you want to delete it.

> ▶ **Set as Homepage**: Sets this bookmark as your homepage.

The History tab lists the web pages you have visited. A star appears to the right of the link. Green means that it is a bookmark. Gray means that it is not a bookmark. Alongside the left side, you have options for Yesterday, Last 7 Days, and Most Visited. Tapping one of those reveals more sites.

You can tap a link to go to that web page. If you press and hold the link, you see a set of options similar to the previous list of options. Tapping Remove from History removes the web page from the history.

The Saved Pages tab lists the web pages you have saved. Each saved page is a thumbnail. Tap the thumbnail to open the page. Press and hold the thumbnail, and tap Delete Saved Page to delete that page from the Saved pages list.

Using ArticleView

When you view a page in ArticleView (see Figure 9.19), you can adjust the text size. Tap the A, and then pick the text size you want. Tap Browser View to return to the normal browser view.

FIGURE 9.19 Reading a web page in ArticleView.

Using Gallery

The Gallery is a listing of all your images. You can access it by tapping Gallery from the Apps screen. You have several things you can do with your images in the Gallery (see Figure 9.20):

FIGURE 9.20   Looking at an image.

▶ If you tap Slideshow, the images in that folder automatically cycle through each image. Tap the screen to stop the slideshow.

▶ Tap the Share button to send the image via email or to an app (including Twitter if you have it installed).

▶ Tap Delete to delete the image.

▶ Tap Rotate to rotate the image 90 degrees clockwise.

▶ Tap Crop to crop the image. Drag the lines to the location and size you want and tap Crop.

▶ You can cycle through the images by swiping left or right.

CHAPTER 10

Using Catalogs and Scrapbooks

New to the NOOK reading experience are catalogs and scrapbooks. Catalogs are digital editions of those you get in the mail. L.L. Bean, Harry and David, and Pottery Barn are just three of the more notable. Now you get those delivered to your NOOK.

Scrapbooks take the idea of ripping pages from catalogs for saving to reference later and adds that experience to the NOOK. In addition, you can make scrapbook pages from magazines.

> NOTE: **See** Chapter 13, "Shopping and Visiting B&N on Your NOOK HDs," to find and download catalogs.

Reading Catalogs on Your NOOK

Catalogs are image-intensive and the point is to find something to buy. The NOOK takes full advantage of the visual richness of catalogs and a connection with the Internet to make digital catalogs a fun experience.

When you open a catalog, it has a lot of familiarity to the magazine reading experience. You can use pinch and zoom techniques to narrow in on pages. If you tap the page, you see the Thumbnail view at the bottom of the page (see Figure 10.1). This is a thumbnail of each page that you can scroll through. Tap the thumbnail to go to that page.

Catalogs feature hotspots, which you can tap (see Figure 10.2). When you do so, you see an expanded version of that product (see Figure 10.3). If you tap Shop Online, your browser launches and displays the webpage for that product, which you can then purchase. If you tap Add to Scrapbook, the Clip This Page window appears (see Figure 10.4). Tap an existing scrapbook to add it to that scrapbook. Tap New Scrapbook to enter a scrapbook name, tap OK, and create the first page of that scrapbook.

Add to Scrapbook

FIGURE 10.1   Scroll through a catalog's pages in Thumbnail view.

Hotspots

FIGURE 10.2   Hotspots on a catalog page.

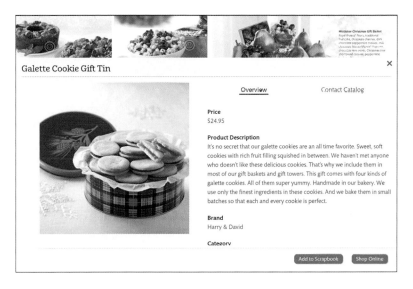

FIGURE 10.3 More information about a product.

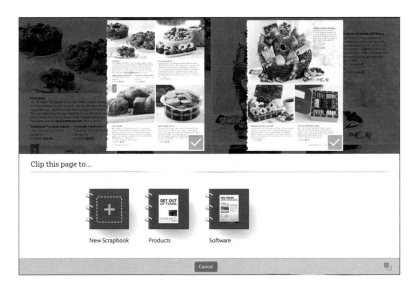

FIGURE 10.4 Adding a page to a scrapbook.

You can also add a page to a scrapbook by tapping the Add to Scrapbook button on the Reading Tools bar.

> NOTE: When reading magazines, you probably have seen the Add to
> Scrapbook button on the Reading Tools bar.

With catalogs, you have a Grid view available on the Reading Tools bar. Tap it and all
the pages appear in a scrollable grid in the reading screen (see Figure 10.5). Tap the
Grid view icon to exit this view, or tap the page you want to go to, which takes you to
that page and exits Grid View.

FIGURE 10.5   Viewing a catalog's pages in Grid View.

To add a bookmark, tap either the top-right corner or top-left corner to folder over the
bookmark.

Using Scrapbooks

You can access your scrapbooks from the Home screen by tapping Library and then
My Scrapbooks. When you open a scrapbook (see Figure 10.6), it functions like a catalog, without the Add to Scrapbook option.

FIGURE 10.6   Viewing a scrapbook.

CHAPTER 11

Creating and Using Profiles and Your NOOK Today

The NOOK introduced NOOK Profiles™, which enable more than one user to use the same NOOK. Of particular interest are children's profiles, where an adult can control what appears in the child's profile. In addition, you have probably seen the Your NOOK Today on the Home screen. This chapter explores profiles and Your NOOK Today.

Understanding Profiles

Three types of profiles exist on the NOOK:

▶ **Primary**: This is the profile to which the NOOK is registered. This profile has access to all content and can create and modify profiles. If something is bought on this NOOK, this profile's credit card is charged.

▶ **Adult**: This profile has only slightly fewer options than the primary. It can control what content it sees, it can make purchases, and it can alter child profile settings.

▶ **Child**: This profile is more severely restricted. Unless otherwise altered, a child's profile can see only what has been assigned to that profile. A child's profile cannot override parental controls or alter or add any profiles.

Your NOOK can support a maximum of six profiles (including the primary).

Creating a Profile

This section focuses on the Adult and Child profiles because the Primary is created when the NOOK is registered. Now let's create an adult profile first:

1. Tap your profile image at the top of the screen, which shows the Your NOOK Profiles screen (see Figure 11.1).

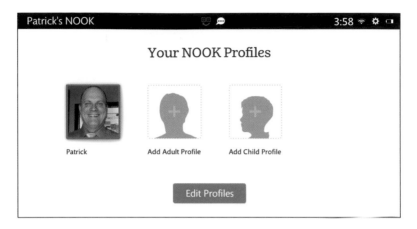

FIGURE 11.1   The Profiles screen.

2. Tap Add Adult Profile. The first page to create a profile appears (see Figure 11.2).

FIGURE 11.2   Creating a profile.

3. Tap His/Her to indicate if this is a His, Her, or Their.

4. Tap First Name and enter a name.

5. If you want all content on this NOOK to be available to this profile, tap the Add All Content in This Account to This New Profile's Library option.

6. If you want to change the image, tap the image. You can choose from any images in the Gallery. The default profile icons are in the Avatars folder.

7. Tap Next. The Interests screen appears (see Figure 11.3).

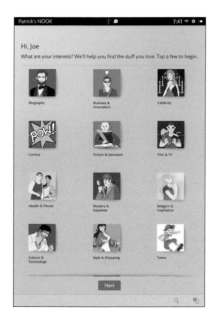

FIGURE 11.3   Pick some interests for this profile.

8. Pick one or more category of interest. This is a required action. The selection you pick here helps B&N focus content for that profile.

9. Tap Next. The Start Building Your Library screen appears.

10. Select any of the free content here by tapping the cover, and then tap Next. Or you can tap Skip without selecting any of the content. The new profile is created and the NOOK switches over to it. This refreshes the Home screen, which can be different for this profile from all other profiles.

Now let's create a child profile:

1. Tap your profile image at the top of the screen, which shows the Your NOOK Profiles screen.

2. Tap Add Child Profile. The first page to create a profile appears.

3. Tap Boy/Girl to indicate if this is a girl, boy, or child.

4. Tap First Name and enter a name.

5. Tap Age, and enter a month and year when the child was born. B&N uses this to help define age-appropriate material. Tap Done after you enter the month and year.

6. Tap the check box for the terms and conditions.

7. If you want to change the image, tap the image. You can choose from any images in the Gallery. The default profile icons are in the Avatars folder.

8. The Parental Controls screen appears (see Figure 11.4). You see a lot of options here. Set them to what you are comfortable with.

FIGURE 11.4   Parental controls for a child's profile.

9. Tap Next.

10. Pick one or more category of interests. This is a required action. The selection you pick here helps B&N focus content for that profile.

11. Tap Next. The Start Building Your Library screen appears.

12. Select any of the free content here by tapping the cover, and then tap Next. Or you can tap Skip without selecting any of the content. The new profile is

created and the NOOK switches over to it. This refreshes the Home screen, which can be different for this profile from all other profiles.

13. If you have not set a passcode, your NOOK recommends you do so and gives you an option to do so at this time. Tap Set Device Passcode to do so. When a child tries to switch to a different profile and a device passcode is set, the child must enter the passcode.

> CAUTION: If you do not set a device passcode, the child's profile can switch to any other profile and use it like a normal profile.

After you complete creating a child's profile, B&N sends an email to the primary profile's email to alert her of the new profile.

Editing a Profile

Editing a profile is simple:

1. Tap your profile image at the top of the screen, which shows the Your NOOK Profiles screen.

2. Tap Edit Profiles. The profiles you are eligible to modify appear with a pencil icon in the image.

3. Tap the profile image you want to edit. You see a list of options (see Figure 11.5):

- ▶ **Change Interests**: Tap this to modify the interests. Tap Done when complete.

- ▶ **Change Image**: Tap this to access the Gallery and change the image.

- ▶ **Manage Content**: Tap this to manage what content is visible to this profile. **See** the next section, "Managing Content Visible to a Profile," for more details about this.

- ▶ **Remove This Profile**: This deletes the profile from the NOOK.

That's all there is to editing a profile.

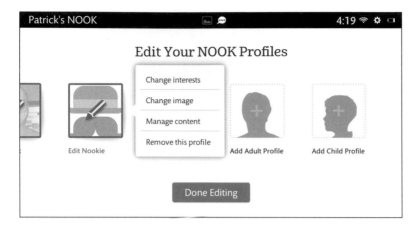

FIGURE 11.5   Options when managing a profile.

Managing Content Visible to a Profile

One of the reasons to use profiles is to control the content visible to individual profiles. You have two primary ways to do this.

From the Edit Profiles screen, you can choose Manage Content. This opens the Manage Content screen for that profile (see Figure 11.6). You can also access this screen in the Library by choosing Manage Content for Profiles from the Options menu.

FIGURE 11.6   Managing content for a profile.

From this screen, you can select whole categories. (Tap the check box next to the category.) You can also choose individual titles in each category. Tap the category to expand it. Tap the check box for items. If you want to remove items, tap the check box to remove the check mark. Tap Save when you finish, and the changes are made.

The other location you can manage content for profiles is on the View Details screen. Tap the Profiles to see which profiles have this title assigned to it (see Figure 11.7). Tap the profile images to select or deselect it. Tap Save.

FIGURE 11.7   Seeing a specific title's profile assignments.

The final location you can control visibility is from the cover pop-up menu. Press and hold a cover, tap Assign to Profile, and tap the profile you want to assign this content to. Tap Save when done.

Using Your NOOK Today

Your NOOK Today provides some weather information and provides B&N the opportunity to inform you about content you might be interested in (see Figure 11.8).

FIGURE 11.8   Your NOOK Today.

To change the location for the weather, tap Change Location, enter the city and state, and tap OK. Choose the resulting list. Your location is updated.

The three sections below feature items for sale at B&N based on library activity, interests, and so on. Tap the covers to go to the View Details screen.

CHAPTER 12

Using the Social Features of Your NOOK HDs

As you probably know, Facebook and Twitter are big deals these days—everyone is sharing everything. The NOOK makes this sharing even easier. You can share your reading status, share quotes, and rate and recommend books. You can share with specific contacts on BN.com, Facebook, and Twitter. Because many of these options overlap and at the same time are scattered across the interface, this chapter focuses on Facebook sharing and the NOOK Friends app.

Although the locations for the sharing features are scattered, they make sense in their location. Basically, B&N provides many locations for the sharing features to make it easy to share.

> NOTE: For LendMe coverage, **see** Chapter 6, "Lending and Borrowing Books with LendMe on Your NOOK HDs."
>
> Using Facebook and Twitter features requires that you link your Facebook and Twitter accounts to your NOOK. **See** Chapter 2, "Customizing and Configuring your NOOK HDs," for linking your accounts.

You can access the Facebook social features by

- ▶ Pressing and holding a cover image and tapping Share
- ▶ Pressing and holding a cover image, tapping View Details, and tapping Share
- ▶ Tapping Share from the Reading Tools toolbar
- ▶ Tapping Share Quote from the Text Selection toolbar

Now look at these contexts in turn.

Using Recommend from the Cover Menu or View Details Screen

Pressing and holding a cover either on the Home screen or in the Library displays a menu. Tap Share and then tap Recommend to see your recommend options (see Figure 12.1). Tap To My Facebook Wall or To a Friend's Facebook Wall to see the Facebook Recommendation screen (see Figure 12.2)—if you are not currently connected to a Wi-Fi hotspot, the Network Setting screen appears for you to connect to one.

FIGURE 12.1   Where do you want to recommend this NOOK Book?

To post to your Facebook wall

1. Press and hold a cover. From the pop-up menu, tap Share and then tap Recommend. From the View Details screen, tap the Share button, tap Recommend. Tap To My Facebook Wall.

2. Type your message that will appear. As you type, you see the number of available characters (max of 420) go down, giving you an indication of how much space you have left.

3. Tap Post. Your NOOK sends the recommendation to your wall.

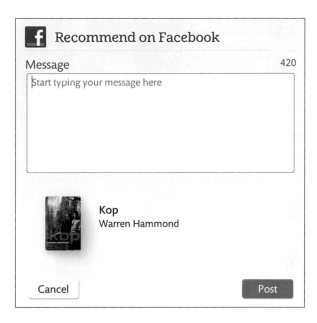

FIGURE 12.2   Use this screen to post a recommendation to your wall.

If you want to post to a friend's wall, tap To a Friend's Facebook Wall, tap the name of the lucky friend, and then tap Done. Type your message and then tap Post (see Figure 12.3). Your NOOK sends the recommendation to your friend's wall.

FIGURE 12.3   Use this screen to post a recommendation to a friend's wall.

> TIP: When you go to select friends, if you use the search box to narrow the list down, you may find that you now have a way to leave the screen. Actually, it's just hidden. Tap the hide keyboard key to get to the Done button.

You can recommend a title to a specific contact or via Twitter. The methods are essentially the same.

Using Social Features from the View Details Screen

Pressing and holding a cover either on the Home screen or in the Library displays a menu. If you tap View Details, you see the View Details screen, which contains many options. To access the social features, tap Share, which displays a menu with several options (see Figure 12.4).

FIGURE 12.4   The Share menu.

From here, you can recommend a book, rate and review the book on BN.com, and like the book on Facebook. (If you have previously liked this on Facebook, the final menu option is Unlike on Facebook.)

If you tap Recommend, the steps are exactly the same as in the preceding section.

If you tap Rate and Review, the Rate and Review screen displays (see Figure 12.5). The main purpose of this screen is to post your feedback on this title to BN.com. You can give it an overall star rating by tapping the star you want to give it. (For example, tap the middle star to give it a three-star rating.) Type in a brief headline for the review (for example, **Awesome history**). You can then type in your full review, for which you have plenty of space to do (3,500 characters). At the top, you have two options: Facebook and Twitter. You can choose both, one, or neither. If you choose to send it to either Facebook or Twitter, a link to your review is posted to Facebook or Twitter. This alerts your friends and followers that you have posted a review on BN.com for the book. Tap Post to post the review to BN.com.

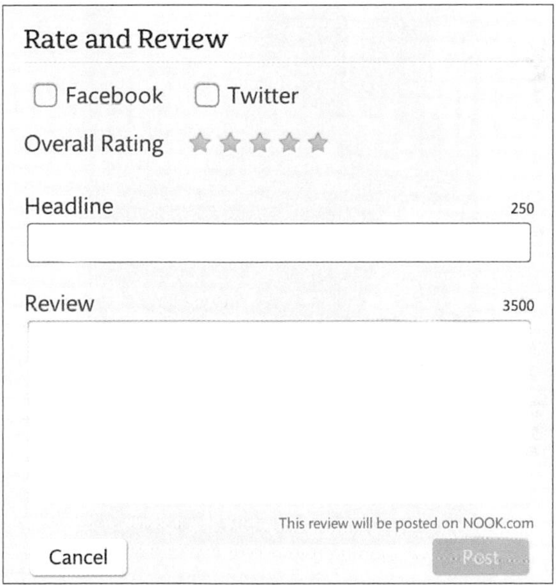

FIGURE 12.5 The Rate and Review screen.

To like the book on Facebook, from the Share menu, tap Like on Facebook.

If you press and hold a cover and choose Share from the pop-up menu, you have the Recommend, Rate and Review, and Like on Facebook options as well.

Using Share from the Reading Tools Toolbar

While reading a NOOK Book or newspaper, you can tap the Share button on the Reading Tools toolbar. You have four options (see Figure 12.6):

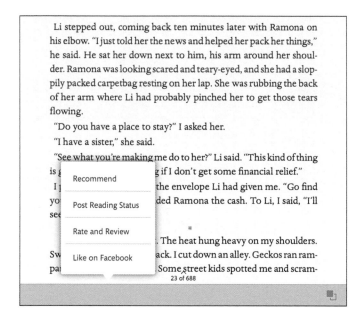

FIGURE 12.6   Tap the Share button to access the social features for NOOK Books.

> ▶ **Recommend**: This functions exactly as the earlier section, "Using Recommend from the Cover Menu or View Details Screen," functions.

> ▶ **Post Reading Status**: This option enables you to post how far along you are in reading this NOOK Book to Facebook and Twitter. You can find a brief headline indicating how far you are into the NOOK Book, and its title is followed by the synopsis of the NOOK Book on BN.com (see Figure 12.7). You can choose to post your status to Facebook or Twitter or both.
>
> After tapping Share and tapping Post Reading Status, tap the check box for Facebook or Twitter (or both) and then tap Post. The update is sent.

> ▶ **Rate and Review**: Tapping this allows you to rate and review the book on BN.com, which appears on the B&N book's specific web page (see Figure 12.8). You must provide both a rating and either a headline or review before you can post. After you tap Post, the information is sent to BN.com.

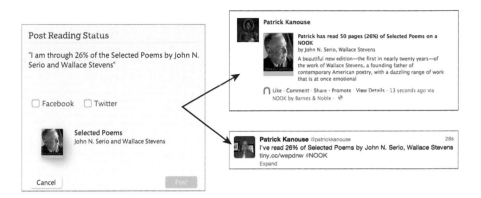

FIGURE 12.7   Sharing the reading status posts how far you are into that NOOK Book on Facebook and Twitter.

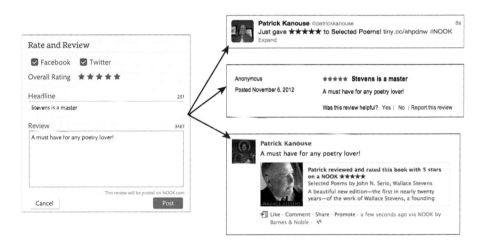

FIGURE 12.8   Rating and reviewing a NOOK Book posts that rating and review on BN.com.

> ▶ **Like on Facebook**: This option enables you to post to your Facebook wall that you like this book. Tap this link, and your NOOK posts on Facebook that you like the book. (If you have previously liked this book on Facebook, the option changes to Unlike on Facebook.)

Using Share from the Text Selection Toolbar

Use this share function when you have a quote you want others to see:

1. Press and hold the word you want to start the quote.

2. When the Text Selection toolbar appears, finish highlighting the quote by dragging the ending blue bar to where you want.

3. Tap Share Quote (see Figure 12.9).

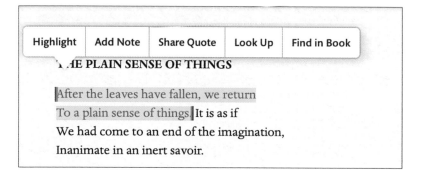

FIGURE 12.9   Highlight a quote and tap Share Quote.

4. Tap To My Facebook Wall.

5. Type your message. Tap Post.

The appropriate wall or walls are updated (see Figure 12.10).

FIGURE 12.10   Sharing a quote.

Table 12.1 quickly shows you where you can find which social action.

TABLE 12.1 Quick Chart of Where You Can Find Social Actions

	Library/Home Page Details Screen	Store Details Screen	Cover Pop-Up Menu	Ready Tools Toolbar	Text Selection Toolbar
Recommend	YES	YES	YES	YES	NO
Rate and Review	YES	YES	YES	YES	NO
Like on Facebook	YES	YES	YES	YES	NO
Post Reading Status	NO	NO	NO	YES	NO
Share Quote	NO	NO	NO	NO	YES

So What About Twitter and Contacts?

NOOK's support for Twitter and Contacts functions identically to Facebook, except that you share with specific contacts via email or your Twitter feed. Twitter has a more limited character count, however, than does wall posts on Facebook (140 character, to be exact). To share to Twitter, on the Home screen, press and hold the cover. When the menu appears, tap Recommend and then tap Via Twitter. Alternatively, if you are reading the book, tap Recommend from the Reading Tools and tap Via Twitter.

> TIP: If you have a WordPress blog, check out the NOOK widget at http://wordpress.org/extend/plugins/nook-color-widget/. This widget displays the cover of the book you are reading.

Using the NOOK Friends App

NOOK Friends is, to quote B&N, "the place for people who love to share their love for reading!" Here, you can connect with friends to lend and borrow books, see what your friends have been doing, and other things.

You access the NOOK Friends app by tapping Apps from the Quick Nav Bar. Then tap NOOK Friends. You are already set up with an account. The NOOK Friends screen is divided into Friends' Activities, About Me, and LendMe. In addition, you have two buttons at the top of the screen: Add Friend and All Friends.

Friends' Activities displays what your friends have been reading, what they recommend, how far along they are in a book, and so on (see Figure 12.11). You can tap the cover or price to see details about the item and purchase it if you want. If you tap the cover, the View Details screen appears. If, on the other hand, you tap the price in the Friends' Activities screen, you are asked to confirm the purchase.

Add Friends

Friends' Activities

FIGURE 12.11   What have your NOOK Friends been up to?

Tap About Me to see information about you (see Figure 12.12).

This screen shows you the number of your NOOK Friends, NOOK Books owned, and NOOK Books recommended. You also see a list of your recent activity (and what your NOOK Friends see in their Friends' Activities screen). In addition, if you have posted recommendations for books that you have not purchased, you can purchase a copy here. For example, if you read a book in the old-fashioned "print" version but you posted a recommendation for the NOOK Book version, you are offered the opportunity here to purchase that NOOK Book version.

Chapter 6's section, "Lending and Borrowing Using the NOOK Friends App," covers the LendMe features.

If you tap All Friends, a new screen appears (see Figure 12.13). This screen lists all your friends and how you were matched (for example, through Facebook). Tap Pending if you want to see any pending NOOK Friends requests. Tap the X next to

the LendMe button to remove that person as a NOOK Friend. Tap Yes, Remove This
Friend on the screen that follows or Cancel.

FIGURE 12.12   The NOOK Friends About Me
screen.

FIGURE 12.13   The NOOK Friends All Friends
screen.

If you tap the friend's name, you see a screen of the friend's recent activity. This is a good way to just see what kinds of books the friend has been reading and recommending lately.

If you tap LendMe, you see a list of books you can request to borrow from that friend.

To send a request to new NOOK Friends, tap the Add Friend button. The Add NOOK Friends screen appears (see Figure 12.14).

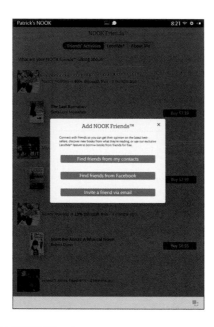

FIGURE 12.14   The Add NOOK Friends screen.

Tap Find Friends from My Contacts to display a screen with a list of your contacts (see Figure 12.15). Tap Add to send an invitation. The invitation is sent immediately. Keep tapping Add until you've sent requests to all the contacts you want to add. Tapping Find Friends from Facebook works the same.

Tap Invite a Friend via Email to enter a person's first and last names and email address. Tap Save and the request is sent immediately. Tap Find Friends from Facebook to see a list of Facebook friends that B&N also has records of them being B&N NOOK users.

FIGURE 12.15   Add NOOK Friends from Your Contacts.

CHAPTER 13

Shopping and Visiting B&N on Your NOOK HDs

One of the greatest features of your NOOK is the capability to sample and buy content from B&N directly from the device. As long as you have a Wi-Fi connection, you can get new content for your NOOK no matter where you are. However, you can also use the B&N website to sample and purchase content for your NOOK.

> NOTE: Only customers with billing addresses in the United States, Canada, a U.S. territory, or UK can order content from the B&N eBookstore. Citizens of U.S. territories are unable to preorder items.

Shopping on Your NOOK

To shop on your NOOK, from the Home screen, tap Shop. Your NOOK displays the NOOK Store Home screen (see Figure 13.1).

Navigating the NOOK Store

The NOOK Store is divided into three parts. The top right features several categories of items: Books, Magazines, Movies & TV, Kids, Apps, Newspapers, and Catalogs. To browse that category, tap category.

The top left highlights features such as bestselling magazines, new NOOK videos, best reading lists, and so on.

The bottom two-thirds contains Channels, which are lists of titles related to your interests (remember selecting those in creating your profile) and purchasing habits. Channels are descriptive and—I have found—useful ways of categorizing titles. Instead of just a big collection of history books, you have History by Plot, Notorious American History, and History Buff. The Channels descriptions are themselves evocative of the types of content you will find. Additionally, Channels allow for titles from multiple genres to appear (Science-Fiction Science-Fact is a good example).

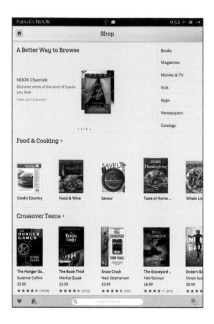

FIGURE 13.1   The opening of the NOOK Store.

The bottom status bar has three options: Wishlist, Recently Viewed, and Search.

The Wishlist option shows your wishlist of items added from your specific NOOK device. While your NOOK HD and NOOK HD+ share a wishlist, it is not the same as your BN.com wishlist or any other NOOK Simple Touch. At this time, each is a separate wishlist.

> TIP: Myself? I dislike managing multiple wishlists, so I use the NOOK's browser to add to my B&N wishlist via the BN.com website. I use the Shop feature on my NOOK for its ease of use.

The Recently Viewed list shows you a list of titles that you have viewed recently in the shop.

Type into the search box keywords, authors, titles—what have you. Tap the search button. A set of results appears. You can tap the cover to see the Details screen and tap the price to purchase the ebook (followed by a Confirm button). You can sort the list by a variety of options by tapping the Refine button (see Figure 13.2).

FIGURE 13.2   Sort your search results.

Browsing the NOOK Store

Tap any of the categories from the NOOK Store to stroll through the available content in that category (see Figure 13.3). From here, you can narrow down even further on the category you want to browse, see all the books, or select a title or list from the options at the bottom of the screen.

As you work your way through the lists, the items are listed in Channels. You can scroll through the Channel's list of titles. In addition, tap the cover to see the Details screen, or tap the price to buy.

Sampling and Buying Content

After you locate and select an item you're interested in, if you tap the cover to get to the Details screen (see Figure 13.4), you see an overview page that describes the item and shows the rating of the item from other B&N readers. In addition, you see the following options:

FIGURE 13.3   Browsing the NOOK Store.

FIGURE 13.4   The Details screen in the NOOK Store.

▶ **Trailer**: For some movies, you'll see a play button on the cover. Tap it to watch the trailer.

▶ **Add to Wishlist**: Adds the item to your NOOK's wishlist. Tap it and the heart turns white, and the plus sign turns to a minus sign. Tap it again to remove it from your wishlist.

▶ **Share**: Gives you the opportunity to recommend the title, like it on Facebook, or rate and review it. **See** Chapter 12, "Using the Social Features of Your NOOK HDs," for more information.

▶ **Profiles**: Tap this and a menu appears that tells you a bit about profiles and provides a link to create new profiles on your NOOK.

▶ **Price**: Tap this button to purchase the book. You are asked to confirm your purchase. For movies and TV shows, you have an option to buy or rent the HD or SD version. Tap the arrow next to the price, and tap the one you want (if it is different than the default HD pricing).

▶ **Free Sample**: Tap this to download a free sample from the book.

▶ **Overview**: The default view displays when you select an item. This includes screenshots for apps. Scroll down to see the full listing.

▶ **Reviews**: Displays reviews from other B&N customers. The number of reviews presented is likely to be smaller than the number of ratings. In addition, you can access the rate and review and like on Facebook social features from this screen. Tap Most Helpful to sort the customer reviews. If a number of reviews are available, you might need to scroll down to see more.

> **NOTE:** On the Reviews screen, you also can provide feedback to the reviewers. Tap Yes or No depending on how helpful you felt the review is. In addition, if you find a review is problematic (for example, it spoils the plot or uses abusive language), tap Report This Review. You are asked to cite a reason, after which you can tap Send. The review is reported to B&N, which may take steps to correct the review.

▶ **More Like This**: Displays similar titles that you might be interested in. Usually these are sorted by what other B&N customers who purchased the book you are looking at have purchased, more titles by the author, and other titles in the series. Tap the cover to jump to that ebook's Details screen.

If you like what you see, you can download a sample to your NOOK by tapping Free Sample. (Sampling is valid only with NOOK Books.) Samples typically consist of the first chapter of an ebook. However, it's up to the publisher to decide what to provide as a sample. In some cases, samples might contain just a few pages. In other cases, samples consist primarily of front matter, such as the title page, table of contents, dedication, and so on.

> NOTE: Samples never expire. You can keep a sample for as long as you'd like. If you send a sample to the NOOK Cloud, you will have an opportunity to redownload it.

If you decide to buy a book after reading the sample, simply go to the Details screen by tapping the cover (you can do this in the NOOK Store, on your Home screen, or in the Library) or tapping Buy Now in the reading screen of the sample. Because samples and full NOOK Books are completely separate products, a purchased book will not open at the point where the sample ended. You need to manually navigate to the point where you stopped reading the sample.

> NOTE: If a B&N gift card is associated with your account, the cost for items purchased from the B&N NOOK Store are applied against that gift card. If there is not enough credit left on the card, B&N charges the remaining balance to your credit card on file.

If you want to remove a sample from your NOOK, press and hold the cover, and tap Delete from the pop-up menu if you want to remove it from your library entirely. Or tap Move to NOOK Cloud if you just want to remove the sample from the NOOK. If you delete a sample unintentionally, you can download it again.

For more information on using My NOOK Library, **see** Chapter 25, "Using My NOOK Library."

Is It Possible to Accidentally Purchase a Book You Have Already Purchased from B&N's eBookstore?

Your NOOK will not present the option to purchase a book you already own. If you select a book in the NOOK Store that you already own, you are shown an option to download or read the book, depending upon whether the book is already on your NOOK. However, you will not be shown an option to buy the book. It will read Purchased.

Some classic titles are released by multiple publishers. Two books of the same title from two different publishers are not considered the same title, so in these cases, you can purchase the same book twice.

Subscription content also enables sampling prior to purchasing, but it works a bit differently than it does with NOOK Books. When you subscribe to a newspaper or magazine, you are given a 14-day free trial (see Figure 13.5). If you cancel your subscription within that 14-day period, you will not be charged. If you cancel after the 14-day trial period, you will be refunded a prorated amount based on when you cancel.

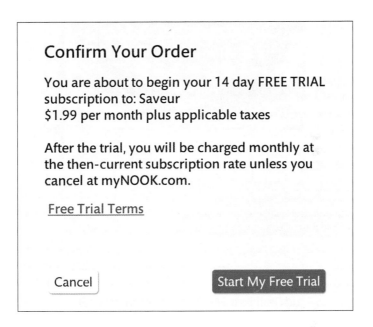

FIGURE 13.5   The trial period for a magazine.

NOTE: You can buy the current issue by tapping Buy Current Issue without subscribing.

You can use a trial subscription only once for any particular item. For example, if you subscribe to *The New York Review of Books,* cancel your subscription within the 14-day trial period, and then later resubscribe again, you will be charged beginning immediately because you have already taken advantage of a trial subscription.

NOTE: Subscriptions can be canceled only using My NOOK Library at bn.com. You cannot cancel a subscription using your NOOK.

Your NOOK automatically downloads subscription content when it's available. In addition to seeing the new content in your library and Active Shelf, you'll also receive notifications in status bar for any new subscription content your NOOK downloads.

> NOTE: You cannot sample NOOK Books for Kids that have Read to Me or Read and Play functionality.

Shopping on Your Computer

Although B&N has made it easy to shop for content directly from the NOOK, sometimes it is easier and more convenient to shop for ebooks from your computer. Any books you purchase on your computer are added to My NOOK Library and are available for reading on your NOOK.

To shop for NOOK Books, magazines, and newspapers on your computer, browse to bn.com/ebooks. You can get samples of ebooks, subscribe to periodicals, and purchase books and apps from the NOOK Store.

When you purchase, subscribe to a periodical, or choose to sample a NOOK Book from the online NOOK Bookstore™, the content is automatically added to your My NOOK Library. You can read the item on your NOOK by connecting to Wi-Fi or Fast and Free Wireless. You can also tap the Sync button in the Library to force your NOOK to connect with B&N and download any new content.

One of the great features of using the B&N website for browsing NOOK Books is that you can see which other formats are available. For example, if an MP3 audiobook is available for a title you're browsing, a link to the audiobook is there, so you can download it if you want.

When shopping for NOOK Books for kids, look for the "NOOK Kids Read to Me" statement in Format section. These NOOK Books have the Read to Me feature enabled. If the format for a NOOK Book for kids is simply NOOK Book, you will not have the Read to Me option for that NOOK Book for kids. You can learn more about this feature in Chapter 5, "Reading and Using NOOK Books for Kids Features."

Whether you choose to shop from your NOOK or your computer, B&N provides plenty of great content for your NOOK at the NOOK Bookstore. However, there are also many other sources for great ebooks for your NOOK and NOOK. Some of those sources you can find in Appendix B, "Sources for ebooks Other than B&N," which you can then sideload to your NOOK or NOOK.

Using Your NOOK in a B&N Store

As mentioned earlier, B&N stores have a Wi-Fi hotspot, so your NOOK can access free Wi-Fi while in the store (see Figure 13.6). B&N uses this hotspot to offer you special promotions called More in Store while in the store. Your NOOK automatically connects to a B&N hotspot when in the store, but you do need to ensure that Wi-Fi is turned on. (It's on by default.)

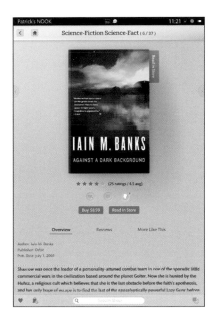

FIGURE 13.6   Tap the Read in Store button to enjoy something to read on your NOOK while drinking a coffee.

After your NOOK connects to the B&N hotspot, from the Home screen, tap Shop.

When you're connected to a B&N hotspot in a B&N store, you have the ability to read nearly any NOOK Book in the B&N store for up to 1 hour. Find a NOOK Book you'd like to read, tap the cover, the Details screen opens (see Figure 13.6). Tap the Read in Store button, which opens a Read In-Store confirmation screen explaining the program and asking you to proceed. Tap Read to continue (see Figure 13.7). At this point, you can read for up to an hour.

> NOTE: Bookmarks, annotations, and highlights are not supported for Read in Store content.

NOTE: You cannot read magazines, newspapers, comics, or NOOK Books for Kids on your NOOK for free in a B&N store.

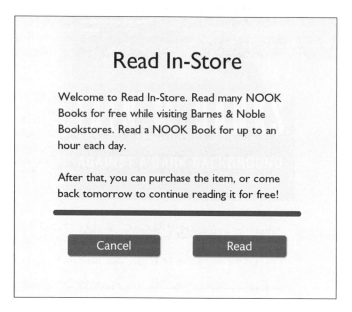

FIGURE 13.7   The details for reading this book in store.

If you read a bit of a book in the store, exit out of the book you were reading, get up for a cup of coffee, and decide you want to keep reading, at the top of the NOOK Store, tap Recently Viewed. Tap the cover to see the Details screen.

If you want to see what is available for reading in the store, go back to the main NOOK Store page, and swipe left in the top half until you get to the Read in Store page. Tap Browse Read in Store eBooks.

There's no doubt that B&N has a unique opportunity because of its brick-and-mortar presence. No other ebook reader has the capability of being paired with a retail outlet, and there's every indication that B&N intends to beef up this feature in the future. It's certainly one of the more unique capabilities of the NOOK, and NOOK owners should be excited about what More in Store might offer in the future.

NOTE: If you had the original NOOK, you know that you could show it to get a free cookie, coffee, smoothie, percentage off something, and more in the store. Currently, you can't get freebies or discounts with the NOOK.

CHAPTER 14

Getting Started with Your NOOK Simple Touch

Congratulations on your new NOOK Simple Touch. The NOOK Simple Touch was released by B&N in June 2011, and the NOOK Simple Touch with GlowLight was released in April 2012. These NOOKs feature a touchscreen interface, remove the dual-screen of the first edition, and are smaller in size; reading on them is comfortable, though, and you won't notice any loss because of the size difference. Actually, the reading experience is significantly improved, especially for the NOOK Simple Touch with GlowLight, which has a built-in light that distributes a soft, even light over the entire screen. Other than the GlowLight, the NOOK Simple Touches are the same as previous Nook readers in all other respects.

> NOTE: Barnes & Noble uses a lowercase *n* when it spells *NOOK* and for the NOOK's logo.

Before getting into the details of using your NOOK Simple Touch, you need to do some things right now.

> NOTE: From here on out, I will simply refer to the NOOK rather than the long-winded NOOK Simple Touch or NOOK Simple Touch with GlowLight.

Understanding NOOK Gestures

You control your NOOK (except the Power button, Home button, and page turn controls) with gestures:

> ▶ **Tap**: This is the most common gesture. Just press your finger to the screen and raise it. Usually, you use this gesture with buttons and covers

▶ **Double Tap**: This is the same as the Tap gesture, but just press twice quickly.

▶ **Swipe Left/Swipe Right**: This gesture is mostly for turning pages. Like a tap, touch your finger on the screen and quickly drag it to the left (or right) and lift your finger up.

▶ **Scroll**: Essentially, this is the vertical version of the Swipe gesture. You can control the speed of the scroll by swiping up or down rapidly. You can slow down or stop the scroll by tapping the screen (to stop) or pressing and holding to slow the scroll.

The NOOK Buttons

The NOOK features six physical buttons:

▶ **Power**: This does what it promises: turns your NOOK on or off. If you press it briefly while your NOOK is on, the NOOK goes to sleep. If the NOOK is asleep and you press it briefly, the NOOK wakes up.

▶ **Home**: The Home button (it's the lowercase n below the screen) shows you the Quick Nav Bar and is your way to change settings, go shopping, and so on. If you want to return to a starting point, just press the Home button and tap Home.

If your NOOK is asleep, press this button to wake it up (and then drag your finger from left to right on the arrows at the bottom of the screen).

▶ **Page Turn**: These four buttons turn the page backward or forward and are alternatives to swiping left or right to turn the page. By default, the top buttons advance you forward one page, and the bottom buttons take you backward in the book.

Registering Your NOOK

When you first turn on your NOOK, it asks you to register it to get started. The first step is to register it with Barnes & Noble (simply B&N from now on). To do that, you need an account on the B&N website. If you don't have one, you can create one in the process of setting up your new NOOK.

NOTE: B&N requires a default credit card with a valid billing address to be associated with your B&N account to register your NOOK.

Tap Next on the screen. You then see a screen with Terms and Conditions. Tap Agree if you agree to the terms. The next screen is the Time Zone screen. Tap the circle corresponding to your time zone, and then tap Next.

The next part is to set up your Wi-Fi connection. (Or you can go into a B&N store where it has a connection you can connect to.) Your NOOK displays the available networks. Tap your network. If it is a secure network, enter the password and tap Done. Tap Continue with Setup.

On the Register Your NOOK screen, enter the email address and password you use to sign in to your account on the B&N website; then tap Sign In on the touchscreen. To move from the email field to the password field on the registration screen, tap in the Password field. If you need to create an account, tap Create Account and enter the required details.

You are then taken to the Get Started screen. You can tap Shop Now to begin shopping, tap Reader Guide to see the preloaded reader guide, or press the Home button to go to the Home screen.

NOTE: If you live outside the United States and have trouble registering your NOOK, make sure you've upgraded to the latest firmware. As of version 1.1, B&N enables registration outside the United States.

For more information on connecting your NOOK to a Wi-Fi hotspot, **see** the next section, "Using Wi-Fi Hotspots."

NOTE: There's a great video walk-through showing how to register your NOOK at http://www.barnesandnoble.com/u/Support-NOOK-Simple-Touch-with-GlowLight/379003533.

Using Wi-Fi Hotspots

Your NOOK can also connect to other active Wi-Fi networks. B&N offers free Wi-Fi access in all B&N stores. If you take your NOOK to a B&N store, it automatically connects to the Wi-Fi hotspot in that store.

For more information on using your NOOK in a B&N store, **see** Chapter 20, "Shopping and Visiting B&N on Your NOOK Simple Touch."

To connect your NOOK to a Wi-Fi hotspot other than one in a B&N store, follow these steps:

1. Tap the Home button.

2. Tap Settings.

3. Tap Wireless. (If Wi-Fi is turned off, tap the Turn On Wi-Fi check box.)

4. Tap the Wi-Fi hotspot you want to use. (Your NOOK displays the SSID for all Wi-Fi hotspots in range.)

5. Tap Connect and enter the password for your Wi-Fi hotspot. (If you want to hide the password while typing, tap the Hide Password check box.) Enter a username or login name as well, if required.

6. Tap Connect.

Your NOOK should now show that you are connected to your Wi-Fi hotspot on the reading screen. You should also see the Wi-Fi signal indicator at the top of the screen next to the battery indicator.

> NOTE: On the Home screen, you can tap the Wireless icon in the top bar. (Or tap just to the left of the battery.) Follow the preceding steps 2 through 6 to complete connecting to a Wi-Fi network.

If your Wi-Fi hotspot isn't listed after you tap Wi-Fi hotspot, but you know you are in range of a specific active Wi-Fi network, tap Other hotspot. You can then enter the service set identifier (SSID), select the type of security (if the Wi-Fi is secured), and enter the password for your Wi-Fi hotspot. If you don't know this information, ask the person who set up the Wi-Fi network.

Your NOOK can connect to a Wi-Fi hotspot that requires you to browse to a web page to authenticate yourself. For example, many hotel Wi-Fi hotspots require you to enter a room number or other information to connect. When you tap this network name to connect to it, you are asked if you want to forget the network or continue to a "redirect" to enter a password or other information. Tap Continue to continue the sign-in procedure. (Your screen basically becomes a web page.)

> **Does My NOOK's Battery Drain Faster with Wi-Fi Connected?**
>
> I tested my NOOK's battery life with both Wi-Fi on and off. In my testing, the battery life was shorter when actively using Wi-Fi than it was when not. However, Wi-Fi affects battery life only when your NOOK is actually connected to a Wi-Fi hotspot. Simply having Wi-Fi turned on does not affect battery life.

Disconnecting from a Wi-Fi Hotspot

If you want to stop using a Wi-Fi hotspot, you need to disconnect your NOOK from the Wi-Fi hotspot. To do that, follow these steps:

1. Tap the Home button.

2. Tap Settings.

3. Tap Wireless.

4. To turn off Wi-Fi access completely, tap the Turn Off Wi-Fi check box. If you want to disconnect from a specific network, tap the name of the Wi-Fi hotspot you use. ("Connected" displays below the name of the Wi-Fi hotspot.)

5. Tap Forget to disconnect from the Wi-Fi hotspot.

Alternatively, you can tap the Wi-Fi icon next to the battery icon on the top status bar. A Quick Setting box appears. Tap the check mark to uncheck. This disconnects you from the Wi-Fi hotspot.

For more information on configuring the settings in your NOOK (including turning off the Wi-Fi card), **see** "Your NOOK's Settings" in Chapter 15, "Customizing and Configuring Your NOOK Simple Touch."

Caring for Your NOOK's Battery

Your NOOK uses a high-tech battery called a lithium polymer battery. Unlike older rechargeable batteries, your NOOK's battery doesn't suffer from a charge "memory." Older batteries (when you recharged them over and over especially without letting them drain all the way) "remembered" the lower charge rather than the real charge capacity. That said, you should still follow some basic rules to maximize the life of your battery:

▶ Try to avoid fully discharging your battery. Recharge it when it gets down to approximately 20%. Although charging it repeatedly is not necessarily a bad thing, the battery seems to function optimally if you charge it only when it drops down toward that 20% area.

▶ To maximize battery life, turn Wi-Fi off and leave it off. Turn on Wi-Fi to download your new books and subscription content and sync your reading across devices.

▶ Avoid high heat. Reading in sunlight is fine, but avoid storing your NOOK near a heat source.

▶ If storing your NOOK for a long period (a week or more), charge the battery to approximately 50% rather than giving it a full charge.

By following these steps, your NOOK's battery should last for years.

Charging Your NOOK's Battery

You can charge your NOOK's battery either by plugging it into your computer's USB port or by plugging it into a wall outlet using the supplied AC adapter. Plugging your NOOK into a wall outlet is preferred because it charges quickly.

Should I Plug My NOOK into a Surge Suppressor?

Just like any electronic device, your NOOK is susceptible to power spikes and other electrical anomalies. If you want to ensure that your NOOK is protected from electrical problems, plug it into a surge suppressor.

When You Are Not Reading

When you finish reading, let your NOOK go to sleep instead of turning it off. You may find it counter-intuitive to leave electronic devices turned on, but because your NOOK uses almost no power unless you do something that requires it to refresh the E Ink display, you can leave it turned on without draining your battery.

By leaving your NOOK on, it occasionally downloads content from B&N such as subscription content (assuming you have Airplane Mode turned off), and any books that you purchase from the B&N website. When you're ready to start reading again, press and release the power switch at the top of your NOOK to wake it up.

How Should I Clean My NOOK's Touchscreen?

Your NOOK's touchscreen is going to get dirty and covered in fingerprints. The best way to clean it is to use a dry, microfiber cloth like the one you would use to clean eyeglasses. If you must use a cleaning fluid, spray it lightly on the cloth and then wipe the touchscreen. Use only cleaning sprays designed for cleaning LCD displays.

CHAPTER 15

Customizing and Configuring Your NOOK Simple Touch

Your NOOK has many features that enable you to easily customize it and make it your own, and many settings control how it operates. In this chapter, you examine how to customize and configure your NOOK.

Using Custom Screensavers

You can customize your NOOK by using custom screensaver images, which it displays on the Reading screen when it is sleeping. Even though your NOOK's Reading screen isn't a color screen, it can display 16 levels of gray, making it ideal for displaying black-and-white versions of your favorite pictures.

Creating Screensaver Images

Before you use a picture as a screensaver on your NOOK, you need to resize it to fit the dimensions of its Reading screen. Screensaver images should be 800 pixels high and 600 pixels wide.

> NOTE: You don't need to resize your images, but by doing so you can display them at their maximum size.

Should I Use a Specific File Format for Images?

Your NOOK supports JPEG (.JPG), GIF, and PNG files. For images, using either JPEG or PNG is your best option. GIF isn't a good option for photographs, but if your image is a line art or text, GIF can work fine. If you're unsure, stick with JPEG. That's what Picasa uses by default.

Copying Screensaver Images to Your NOOK

Screensavers on your NOOK consist of a series of images. Each time your NOOK sleeps, it displays the next image in the series on the reading screen. You select a specific set of images to use as a screensaver by placing them in a folder on your NOOK.

Copy screensaver images to your NOOK by following these steps:

1. Connect your NOOK to your computer with the USB cable. When you do, your device appears in your computer as a new drive called NOOK.

2. If your computer doesn't automatically display the folders on your NOOK, open it via File Explorer on Windows or the Finder on the Mac. You should see the Screensavers folder.

3. Open the Screensavers folder.

4. Create a new folder for your screensaver. The new folder's name is the name of your screensaver on your NOOK. Note that the folder name should not be two words: Vacation-Pictures is correct, but Vacation Pictures is incorrect.

5. Copy the image files for your screensaver into the folder you created in step 4.

For example, if you have a series of images of your summer vacation, you might want to create a new folder in the Screensavers folder called Vacation-Pictures and copy your images into that folder. You can then use the images in that folder as your screensaver by selecting Vacation-Pictures as your screensaver.

Now that you've copied your custom images to your NOOK, you can change its settings to use the new images as your wallpaper or screensaver.

Choosing a Custom Screensaver

Your NOOK's Settings menu enables you to change the screensaver. Here's how:

1. Tap the Home button

2. Tap Settings.

3. Tap Screen on the Settings menu.

4. To change the screensaver, tap Screensaver and select the folder name of your screensaver. The Authors and Nature screensaver folders are on the NOOK by default, and you cannot remove them.

Screensavers from Other Sources

You can use several online sources for NOOK screensavers. One of the best is NOOK-Look (www.NOOK-look.com). NOOK-Look provides a wide assortment of quality screensavers for your NOOK.

Another way you can locate screensavers for your NOOK is by using the image search feature on your favorite search engine. A search for "NOOK Simple Touch screensavers" in Google turns up plenty of images presized for your NOOK. The same search on Bing is less helpful, but by clicking the Images at the top of the screen and selecting Tall on the Layout menu, plenty of correctly sized images are available.

One Step Further—Decals

If you want to take the ultimate step to customize your NOOK, a DecalGirl skin (www.decalgirl.com) is the perfect addition. DecalGirl skins are vinyl skins with adhesive backing that you can easily apply. Many skins also include matching NOOK wallpaper that provides a truly unique look.

Your NOOK's Settings

Your NOOK offers configurable settings for controlling many of its features. Tap the Home button, and then tap Settings to access the Settings menu. Your NOOK displays the following information on the Settings menu.

Device Info

The Device Info section displays a variety of information about your NOOK:

- **Battery**: Displays how charged your battery is and whether it is charging or discharging.

- **Available Storage**: Shows how much free space you have on the internal memory of the NOOK. Your NOOK has 2GB of storage space. Of that, 1GB is available for content, and of that 1GB, B&N reserves 750MB of that for B&N-specific storage. The Available Storage reading shows the percentage available from the remaining 250MB (1GB – 750MB = 250MB).

- **SD Card**: Shows whether you have a microSD card installed. **See** "Adding a microSD Card to Your NOOK" for more about microSD cards.

- **About Your Nook**: Shows the personal information related to your NOOK: Owner name, account to which this NOOK is associated, software (also called firmware) version, and such.

The Software section displays the version of software (called *firmware*) currently installed on your NOOK. B&N releases periodic updates to the NOOK to improve performance and fix known issues. As long as your NOOK has a connection to a Wi-Fi connection, your NOOK automatically downloads any updates that B&N releases.

Not all NOOK owners receive new firmware updates at the same time. B&N rolls out new firmware over a period of about a week. If you would like to update your NOOK manually, you can visit http://www.barnesandnoble. com/u/nook-support-software-updates where B&N typically provides instructions for manually updating your NOOK to the latest firmware.

If I Don't Like Changes Made by a Firmware Update, Can I Go Back to an Older Version?

On some sites, you can download older versions of NOOK firmware (www.NOOKdevs.com), but because it automatically installs firmware updates when B&N makes one available, your NOOK always installs the latest update unless you keep Wi-Fi turned off, or if you root the device and block over the air (OTA) updates.

▶ **Erase & Deregister Device**: Enables you to erase all content from and deregister the device. This action resets the NOOK to factory defaults, which is something you should consider doing if you are going to give it to someone else. B&N technical support also might ask you to reset your NOOK during troubleshooting. However, outside of those reasons, you likely won't ever need to reset it.

CAUTION: Resetting your NOOK to factory defaults removes all content from its internal memory, although content stored on a microSD card is not removed. Before you reset it to factory defaults, make sure you have backups of any personal documents stored in your NOOK's internal memory.

▶ **Legal**: Takes you to a screen where you can choose to read the Terms and Conditions or the Open Source Licenses. Most of the time, you won't need these. (You agreed to the Terms and Conditions already when you got a BN.com account and registered your NOOK.)

Wireless

This setting enables you to turn on or off Wi-Fi access and set up connections to Wi-Fi networks. **See** the section "Using Wi-Fi Hotspots" in Chapter 14, "Getting Started with Your NOOK Simple Touch," for more information about Wi-Fi hotspots.

> TIP: If you travel on a flight that offers Wi-Fi service, and you want to use the hotspot with your NOOK, turn off Wi-Fi access. When aboard and cleared to turn on electronic devices, turn on Wi-Fi access and select the airplane's network. However, check with the flight crew first to avoid any problems.

Screen

Here you can alter the screen timeout length and change screensavers.

The Screen timeout option controls the time interval after which your NOOK puts itself to sleep. This timer is set to 5 minutes by default. To change the interval, tap Screen Timeout, and then tap the wanted time interval.

> TIP: If you set the sleep timer to a time interval shorter than the amount of time it takes you to read a page on the reading screen, your NOOK goes into sleep mode while you are reading. So, be sure you set the interval appropriately for your reading speed.
>
> Because your NOOK uses almost no battery power when you read, 10 minutes is likely a suitable interval for most people.

To change the screensaver, tap Screensaver, and then tap the folder of screensavers you want to use.

Time

These settings enable you to select your current local time zone and select a 12-hour or 24-hour clock format.

Reader

This option enables you to adjust the setup of the physical page control buttons. By default, the top buttons advance you forward in a book. But if you want the bottom buttons to advance you forward in a book, tap the Open button just above Page Forward with Bottom Buttons.

Shop

This option enables you to set up some basic shopping features when shopping from your NOOK:

- ▶ Require Password for Purchases enables you to have the password entered for any purchases.

- ▶ Manage Credit Card enables you to change the default credit card new book purchases are charged against. Tap Change and then enter the necessary information in the Add a Credit Card screen.

- ▶ Clear Wishlist and Clear Recently Viewed Lists do just what they say they do. The wishlist on the NOOK is not connected to any other NOOK Simple Touch, NOOK Simple Touch Tablet, or NOOK Simple Touch Color devices or to your BN.com wishlist, so clearing the wishlist does it for this device only.

Social

This option contains several screens for configuring your NOOK's Social settings, for which you must have an active Wi-Fi connection. Basically, you can link your Facebook and Twitter accounts and Google Contacts lists to this NOOK, which enables you to share quotes and recommendations directly to your and your friends' Facebook walls and your Twitter account.

> TIP: If you have earlier set up your Facebook, Twitter, and Google Contacts info (for example, you have a NOOK Color or NOOK Tablet) for this username, your NOOK automatically sets up your Facebook, Twitter, and Google Contacts information.

- ▶ **Tap Link to Facebook, Twitter, and Google to access these specific settings.** If you have already linked your Facebook account, you can unlink it. To link it, tap Link Your Account. Then enter the required information and tap Log In. You'll be asked to allow Facebook and your NOOK to share information. Tap Allow. For more information about Facebook with your NOOK, **see** Chapter 19, "Using the Social Features of Your NOOK Simple Touch."

  For Twitter, if you have already linked your Twitter account, you can unlink it. To link it, tap Link Your Account. Then enter the required information and tap Sign In. Twitter asks you to allow this linking to occur. Tap Allow to do so. For more information about Twitter with your NOOK, **see** Chapter 19.

► **Google Contacts**: This enables you to link your Google Contacts list to this NOOK. If you have already linked your Google Contacts list, you can unlink it. To link it, tap Link Your Account. Then enter the required information. If you want the NOOK to remember this information should you come back to this screen, tap the Remember Me check box; then tap Go. Google wants to know if you want to grant access to the NOOK to do this linking. Tap Grant Access to do so.

► **Manage My Contacts**: This enables you to add and edit your NOOK contacts list. (For example, if you don't use Google Contacts, you can just use contacts on your NOOK.) When you tap this, you see a list of your contacts. From the drop-down list, you can choose to see only your NOOK Friends or Google Contacts. The default is to see all your contacts. To see the details for your contacts, tap the contact's name. If the contact is not a NOOK Friend, you can tap the check box Invite as a NOOK Simple Touch Friend and tap Send to invite that person. Tap View Emails to see all the email addresses. If the contact is not a Google Contact or NOOK Friend and is one you added directly to the NOOK, you can tap Modify to adjust the contact's information. Those are the only contacts you can delete as well. (Tap Modify and then tap Delete This Contact.) To update Google Contacts, log in to your Google account on your computer and update.

► **Manage My NOOK Friend**: This takes you to a screen to see who your NOOK Friends are, who has requested to be your friend, and who you have invited to be your friend. If you tap the plus button, you are provided a list of contacts. To invite any one of them to be a NOOK Friend, tap Invite. An invitation is immediately sent to that person. **See** Chapter 19 for more information related to NOOK Friends.

► **Manage Visibility of My LendMe Books**: This enables you to control what books your NOOK Friends see as lendable. **See** Chapter 17, "Lending and Borrowing Books with LendMe on Your NOOK Simple Touch," for more details about LendMe.

Search

This option enables you to clear recent searches you have made on your NOOK. For example, if you have searched for "poetry" in your library, that appears when you go to do a new search in your library. If you want to clear those historical searches, tap Clear Recent NOOK Simple Touch Searches.

Adding a microSD Card to Your NOOK

Your NOOK has approximately 1GB of built-in usable memory. That's enough memory for an enormous library of books. However, it might not be enough memory if you add pictures and even more books to your NOOK. Therefore, your NOOK's memory is expandable using a microSD card.

> TIP: A microSD card is not the same as an SD memory card like the kind typically used in digital cameras. A microSD card is approximately the size of your pinky's fingernail.

To install a microSD card, you need to open the flap on the top right of your NOOK:

1. The microSD slot is the small opening. With the metal connectors of the microSD card facing the front of the NOOK, slide the microSD card in, and push until it locks into place. The NOOK automatically recognizes the card, and you hear a beep. Close the metal plate.

2. If the microSD card has not yet been formatted, a screen appears letting you know that formatting it will erase everything on the disk. Tap Format Now. Tap Format Now again to confirm.

On the Device Info screen (from the Quick Nav Bar, tap Settings, and then tap Device Info), tap SD Card (only available to tap if a microSD card is installed). This opens the SD Card screen. Here, you can see information related to the amount of free memory available on the microSD card.

Tap Unmount SD Card if you want to remove or format the microSD card. The card unmounts, and you can follow the preceding step 1 to remove it. (Just press the card in farther and it pops out.)

If you tap Format SD Card, you can format the microSD card, which erases everything on the card. (This option is only available after tapping Unmount SD Card.) A confirmation screen to format and erase all data on the micro SD card appears. Tap Format to do so. Tap OK when done.

When you connect your NOOK to your computer, you now see your microSD card in addition to its built-in memory. (It is the drive called NO NAME.)

NOTE: You can add a microSD card that already has items loaded on it, but the NOOK folder structure is necessary, so it is easiest to install a blank microSD card into the NOOK and then plug it into your computer and load files into the appropriate categories (documents, videos, and so on).

Now that you have a microSD card installed, how do you access those files? From the Quick Nav Bar, tap Library and then tap My Files from the type drop-down list (the far-left drop-down list beneath Library).

Can I Use a High-Capacity microSD Card in My NOOK?

Yes. The NOOK supports microSDHC cards up to 32GB.

CHAPTER 16

Reading on Your NOOK Simple Touch and Beyond

Although your NOOK has many unique features and capabilities, when it comes right down to it, its primary purpose is for reading books and other content. One of the benefits of owning a NOOK is that you can carry a complete library with you everywhere you go. If you don't have your NOOK with you, you can also read your ebooks on your PC, Mac, iPhone, iPad, iPod touch, Android phone, and Blackberry.

Various forms of content are available to read on your NOOK, such as NOOK Books, PDFs, and other EPUB ebooks. Appendix A, "Understanding ebook Formats," explains more about the details of ebook formats.

Can I Read Word Documents or TXT Files on My NOOK?

If you want to read Word documents or TXT files on your NOOK, you need to first convert them into a compatible format.

Calibre can convert TXT files to the EPUB format for your NOOK. If you want to read a Word document, you should save the file as a PDF file. (Recent versions of Word provide this functionality.) If you cannot save the Word document as a PDF, first save it as an HTML file, and then use Calibre to convert it for your NOOK.

For more information on using Calibre to convert ebooks, **see** Chapter 24, "Managing Your ebooks with Calibre."

Browsing Your Library

There are two main places for content on your NOOK: The Home screen and My Library.

The Home Screen

The Home screen includes information automatically delivered to your NOOK in the New Reads section, which includes new subscription content, new samples, and new ebooks. Tap See Library at the bottom of the New Reads section to go to your full library.

> TIP: Some notifications, such as new subscription content and LendMe offers, show up as balloon tips in the top information bar on your NOOK's Home screen. You can access more details on these notifications by tapping the balloon.

The Reading Now section shows the last item you were reading along with which page you are on. Tap the cover to continue reading that content.

On the Home screen, B&N also provides recommendations for what to read next at the bottom of the screen. These picks are based on what your NOOK Friends have been reading. Tap a cover to see more details about that NOOK Book, including an option to purchase it. Tap See All Friends' Activity to launch the NOOK Friends Activities screen to see what others have been reading and rating. **See** Chapter 20, "Shopping and Visiting B&N on Your NOOK Simple Touch," to learn more about shopping on your NOOK.

The Library

The Library contains all the content you purchase from B&N. This includes not only books you purchase, but also magazine and newspaper subscriptions, sample books, free books downloaded from B&N, documents you place on the NOOK, and everything else.

First, consider the basic controls in the Library:

- ▶ **Sync (button is two arrows forming a circle)**: The Sync button forces your Library to update, which means that it downloads any new content that has not yet downloaded and syncs reading location, annotations, highlights, and bookmarks on NOOK Books across NOOK reading devices (NOOK HD+, NOOK HD, NOOK Simple Touch, NOOK for iPad™, and so on).

- ▶ **Search (button is a magnifying glass)**: Tap this to search your Library. When the search screen appears, type your search criteria, and tap the Search key. You can scroll through the results (if more than a few). Tap the item to open it. Tap Close to close the search screen and return to the Library. This feature doesn't search inside your content. It searches only the *metadata* for your content. Metadata includes the title, author, publisher, contributors, and subject.

▶ **Type**: The default is All, but you can narrow what you see in your Library by choosing what type of content you want to see: All, Books, Newsstand, LendMe, Shelves, My Files, Archived, or Everything Else.

> NOTE: Here "All" doesn't actually mean "all content." If you choose All, you are viewing all content *except* for Archived and Everything Else items. However, while searching, archived content that matches your search criteria appears.

To change what you want to see, tap the drop-down list, and then tap your choice. A few of them offer additional actions beyond seeing what's available. Newsstand items show the overall subscription with the number of issues available. Tap the cover to see the individual issues. Tap the individual issue's cover to open it.

LendMe shows your NOOK Books available to Lend.

Shelves enables you to see any shelves you created and enables you to add more. **See** the section "Shelves" later in this chapter for more information about using them.

My Documents enables you to navigate the NOOK internal memory and the microSD card for non-NOOK Books content. Tap the folder to navigate to the location you want, and then double-tap the file to open it.

In Archived, tap the Unarchive button on the cover (or to the right of the title's name) to unarchive the title.

▶ **Sort**: Enables you to sort what you are viewing by the Most Recent items (that is, added to the NOOK), by title, or by author.

▶ **Grid/List View**: These two options determine how you view the content in the Library. (Grid view is a set of nine boxes in a grid format, whereas List view is a set of five stacked lines.) Grid shows the covers. List shows the title without the cover.

▶ **Library**: This is, of course, the main reason for this screen. You can scroll through the Library. Double-tap the cover (or the title if in List view) to see the Title Details screen. **See** "View Item Details & Options" for more information about that screen. Tap the cover (or the title if in List view) to open that ebook.

Items in the Library are in one of three categories:

▶ **Items on your NOOK**: Items on your NOOK are available for reading immediately by selecting the item. They are stored in your NOOK's memory or on a microSD card if one is installed.

▶ **Archived items**: These are items in My NOOK Library on bn.com and that have been downloaded to your NOOK device or app at one point but that have since been removed from your archive (not necessarily from the same device or app on which it was downloaded).

▶ **Everything else**: These are items in My NOOK Library that are not compatible with the NOOK. For example, the NOOK HD+ and NOOK HD support apps, but the NOOK Simple Touch does not. So, the Library shows any apps you have purchased. Other examples include NOOK Books for Kids, some magazines (for example, *National Geographic*), and textbooks, among others.

For more information on using My NOOK Library on bn.com, **see** Chapter 25, "Using My NOOK Library."

When you purchase a NOOK Book, that book is added to My NOOK Library on bn.com and is downloaded to your NOOK.

CAUTION: If you plan to be away from Wi-Fi hotspots, you should make sure that the items that appear in the Library have actually been downloaded to your NOOK.

Some items in the Library might have an indicator banner on the top-right corner of the cover or to the right of the title. This icon indicates special properties of the item (such as the ability to lend the item to a friend using the LendMe feature), or it might indicate that an item has been lent to someone or is borrowed from someone.

For more information on the LendMe feature, **see** Chapter 17, "Lending and Borrowing Books with LendMe on Your NOOK Simple Touch."

The following icons might be displayed for an item:

▶ **LendMe**: Indicates that the item can be lent to a friend using the LendMe feature.

▶ **On Loan**: Indicates that the item has been lent to a friend. You cannot read this item for a period of 14 days from the lend date.

► **Borrowed**: Indicates that the item has been borrowed from a friend. The item will be available to you for 14 days.

► **Lent to You**: Indicates that the item is one that a friend has offered to lend to you. After you accept the offer, the item shows a Borrowed banner.

► **Sample**: Indicates that the item is a sample ebook from B&N.

► **Returned**: Indicates that a NOOK Book you borrowed has been returned.

You can also see the buttons Download and Unarchive on the cover in Grid view (or the right of the title in List view). Tap Download to download the NOOK Book from B&N. Tap Unarchive to unarchive the book.

View Item Details and Options

When you double-tap a cover in the Library, you see the Title Details screen. The available options differ depending on the content you select:

► **Download**: Displayed only when the content has not already been downloaded to your NOOK. Tapping Download transfers it using Wi-Fi.

► **Read**: Displayed only when the content has been downloaded to your NOOK. Tapping Read opens the content on the reading screen.

► **LendMe**: Displayed only when the publisher has enabled the LendMe feature. This menu item enables you to lend the content to a friend.

► **Rating**: A series of stars is available so that you can rate your content. Tap the stars, and five large stars display. Touch the star that corresponds to your rating.

> TIP: If you want to remove your rating, tap the leftmost star, and drag your finger toward the left away from the stars.

► **Overview**: This displays a description of the item (if available) and other details.

► **Reviews**: For B&N content, you can see customer and editorial reviews of that NOOK Book. You can also add a review. **See** Chapter 20 for more information.

► **Related Titles**: This displays similar titles divided by either Those Who Bought This Book Also Bought These Others or Other Books by the Author.

▶ **Share**: For more information about this feature, **see** Chapter 20.

▶ **Archive**: Removes the selected content from your NOOK's storage. The item is still visible in the Library, but if you want to read the content, you need to unarchive it first.

NOTE: There isn't a way to delete content from your library from the NOOK. To delete content (including sample books), you need to use My NOOK Library at the B&N website.

For more information on using My NOOK Library, **see** Chapter 25.

Shelves

You can organize your ebooks into shelves, aligning them into whatever categories you want for easier access to similar ebooks. You can go directly to a shelf of books by pressing the Home button, tapping Library, and tapping Shelves in the Type list. If you have more than four titles on the shelf, tap See All to see all the titles on that shelf.

If you have shelves you created and you want to place ebooks onto those shelves, tap Edit. A list of title appears. Scroll to the title or titles you want, tapping the check box along the way. Tap Save to add those titles to the shelf. If you want to remove titles from the shelf, simply tap the check box to clear out the check mark, and tap Save. You can add and remove titles at the same time.

The Sort options for shelves changes to Most Recent and Shelf name. Just tap the Sort drop-down list, and tap the sort order you want.

To create a new shelf, from the Shelf screen, tap Add Shelf. Type the name of the shelf and tap Save. Add titles (although this is not required). Tap Save.

To remove a shelf, tap Edit for the shelf you want to delete, tap Delete Shelf, and tap OK.

To rename a shelf, tap Edit for the shelf you want to delete, tap Rename, update the name, and tap Save.

Archiving Library Items

As mentioned earlier, you can archive an item by double-tapping the cover and then tapping Archive on the Overview tab. Archiving is a means to remove an item you purchased from B&N from your NOOK. Archived items still appear in the Library but with the Unarchive banner appearing instead of the Download banner on the cover.

When an item is archived, you can still view details on the item, rate the item, and lend the item to a friend using the LendMe feature. However, to read the item, you must unarchive it.

To unarchive an item, tap Unarchive on the cover. The item begins downloading and disappears out of the Archived view.

> TIP: You can manage your ebook library (including archiving and unarchiving items) using My NOOK Library at bn.com. My NOOK Library is covered in detail in Chapter 25.

My Files

My Files contains content you manually copy to your NOOK from other sources. B&N calls the process of manually copying books and other content to your NOOK *sideloading*, and any reading content you sideload onto your NOOK appears in the My Files portion of the Library (and also when you view All content).

You can put files on the NOOK's built-in memory or on a microSD card. When you connect your NOOK to a computer, the folder structure is the same regardless of which memory it is (see Figure 16.1).

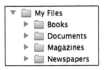

FIGURE 16.1   The folder structure for placing your files.

Any content you place in Books appears whenever you sort your library by Books. If you put files in Magazines and Newspapers, when you filter on Newsstand in the Library, those items appear there.

Regardless, you can get to any of your files by filtering to My Files. Tap either NOOK Files (those stored on the built-in memory) or Memory Card (those stored on the microSD card). Tap My Files—and so on until you get to the files.

> TIP: If you view the Library, you can switch to My Files by tapping My Files from the Type drop-down list.

View Item Details and Options

When you double-tap a My Files cover, you see the details for the selected item. Details include the publisher, publication date, and so on if available. You also see the file path for the selected item.

> TIP: The file path begins with my media if the selected item is stored in your NOOK's internal memory. If the item is stored in a microSD card, it begins with sdcard.

You have only one option from this Details screen: Open.

> **How Can I Delete Sideloaded Content Because There Isn't a Menu Option to Remove It?**
>
> Sideloaded content must be deleted by connecting your NOOK to your computer and removing the content. The easiest way to manage your sideloaded content is to use Calibre, a free ebook management application. **See** Chapter 24.

Reading Books on Your NOOK

If you open a NOOK Book or sideloaded EPUB file for the first time, after you select it, you go to the starting point that the publisher chose for that item. This might or might not be the first page. For example, this ebook opens on the first page of Chapter 1, "Getting Started with Your NOOK HDs." Other ebooks open on the cover or title page. The publisher of the book decides which page is visible when you first open an ebook.

If you open a NOOK Book that you have read on the NOOK before in any of the NOOK Apps, NOOK Study, NOOK HD+, or NOOK HD, you are taken to the last location you were reading. If you open a sideloaded EPUB file you have read on the NOOK before, it opens to the last page you were on. In other words, non-B&N content does not sync across applications.

As you're reading, swipe right across the page to go to the previous page, swipe left across the page to go to the next page, or use the buttons to the left and right.

Of course, there's more to reading books than just reading, right? To see the Reading Tools, quickly tap the reading screen. (B&N recommends tapping the middle of the screen.)

The following are the Reading Tools options:

- **Content**: This opens up a screen to navigate the table of contents, notes and highlights, and bookmarks. To go to a specific table of contents, note, highlight, or bookmark, simply tap the appropriate tab, and tap the table of content location you want to go to. **See** Chapter 18, "Using Highlights, Bookmarks, and Annotations," for more details about using these features.

- **Find**: Tap this option to search the text within this book. Type the text and tap Search. The NOOK searches through the book and displays the results, providing the page number and some context for the search word. If you want to go to the location of that search, tap the row and you are taken there. Otherwise, tap Close. When you are taken back to the page after selecting a search location to go to, the bottom of the screen shows a bar where you can change the search term and move back and forth between the results (using the arrow keys). At the far left, you see button with four horizontal lines. Tap that to return to the search results screen.

TIP: Typing lots of uppercase letters? Tap the Shift key twice. (It has a white highlight around the key.) This enables you to enter only uppercase letters. Tap the Shift key again to release the Caps Lock.

- **Go To**: Tapping this displays a scrollbar, your location within the book, and two options: Go Back and Go to Page. To scroll to a specific page, tap the vertical bar, and drag it to the location you want to go to. As you scroll the page number and location information change to reflect that location. To go to a specific page, tap Go to Page, type the number of the page, and tap Go. In either case of scrolling or going to a specific page, if you want to go back to the position in the book you were at immediately prior, tap Go Back.

- **Text**: Tap this to access the font and size options. **See** the "Changing the Text Font and Text Size" section for more details.

- **More**: This opens up the Details screen.

To exit the Reading Tools, tap anywhere on the reading screen without those tools appearing.

Finally, while reading, you can press and hold on a word. The Text Selection Toolbar appears. If you want to select more than that single word, drag the selection highlight to the end of the block of text you want to select. For the Highlight, Add Note, and Look Up buttons, **see** Chapter 18. For the Share button, **see** Chapter 19, "Using the Social Features of Your NOOK Simple Touch." The "Looking Up Words" section of this chapter discusses looking up words.

Changing the Text Font and Text Size

Your NOOK enables you to easily change the text font and text size while you read.

The text options are available from the Text option on the Reading Tools screen. An array of options display: Size, Font, Line Spacing, Margins, and Publisher Defaults. (If the options are locked down by the publisher, you may have only an option to adjust the text size.)

Your NOOK supports seven text sizes, represented by the A. The current text size A is black, whereas the sizes not used are gray. (In addition, a small arrow appears above the size in use.) Tap the A for the size you want. You can see the text size adjust behind the text menu. Adjust the text size to whichever size you want.

The current font used has an arrow next to it. To change the font, tap from the six available fonts:

▶ You cannot change the text font if the publisher created the content with a specific font embedded in it.

▶ You cannot change the text font for PDF files. If the creator of the PDF file embedded a particular font, your NOOK uses that font. Otherwise, it uses the default font.

▶ Some ebooks consist of pages scanned as images, usually as PDF files. You cannot change the text font for these ebooks.

NOTE: Tapping Publisher Defaults to On changes all settings on this screen to the options chosen by the Publisher for all content that you read. You can toggle that back to Off at any time.

The Line Spacing options are similar to using single space or double space. The current selection is the darker option and has an arrow above it. You have three options. Tap the option you want. The reading screen adjusts.

The Margin options determine the amount of white space on the right and left sides of the text. The current selection is the darker option and has an arrow above it. You have three options. Tap the option you want. The reading screen adjusts.

Looking Up Words

One of the most convenient features of your NOOK is to quickly look up the definitions of words you don't know. If you're reading a book and encounter a word you don't know or are curious about, press and hold on that word until the Text Selection toolbar appears. Tap Look Up. A window appears with a dictionary entry.

> NOTE: Looking up words is not supported for certain types of ebooks—for example, ADE PDFs and PDFs.

Reading Magazines and Newspapers on Your NOOK

In addition to books, B&N provides magazine and newspaper subscriptions for your NOOK that it can deliver if a Wi-Fi connection is available.

For more information on subscribing to content on your NOOK, **see** Chapter 20. Some magazines are not supported for reading on your NOOK (for example, *National Geographic*), so be sure to check the supported NOOK devices and apps on the B&N website.

Unlike books, magazine and newspaper content isn't presented in a linear format. Content is often presented as article headlines followed by a small synopsis of each article. To read the specific article, tap the headline for that article. After an article is open, use swipe left and right gestures to navigate between pages just as you do when reading a book.

Tapping the screen displays the Reading Tools, which are the same as the ebook Read Tools.

Newspaper content often contains links that make navigating the content easier. For example, when reading *The New York Times*, you can move to the next or previous articles (as available) by tapping Previous Article or Next Article.

For more information on subscription content, including when your NOOK automatically deletes subscription content, **see** Chapter 20.

This chapter covered a lot of information on reading content on your NOOK. However, your NOOK is only one device of many that provides access to your My NOOK Library. You can also read content on your computer, your iPhone, and your other devices.

CHAPTER 17

Lending and Borrowing Books with LendMe on Your NOOK Simple Touch

To keep readers from sharing ebooks with all their friends, publishers usually protect ebooks with digital rights management (DRM), which ties an ebook to an individual. Unless that individual can prove that he is an authorized reader, the ebook does not open.

DRM is one of the reasons some people don't like ebooks. After all, when readers find a good read, they like to pass it on to friends and family. The number of people with whom you can share a physical book is fairly limited, but because ebooks are digital copies of a book, they can literally be shared with millions of people quite easily via email, Facebook, and any number of other methods.

One of the unique features that B&N added to your NOOK is the ability to lend some ebooks to other readers using the LendMe feature. Although there are some serious restrictions when lending and borrowing books, the LendMe feature is a step in the right direction.

Lending Books with LendMe

To lend a book to someone, the book must support LendMe. Not all books do. If a book does support lending, you will see the LendMe logo on the book's page on bn.com, as shown in Figure 17.1. You also see the LendMe banner on the book's cover in the Library on your NOOK and in the NOOK App.

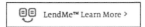

FIGURE 17.1   The LendMe logo appears on a book's page at bn.com if the book is lendable.

> **TIP:**   To see a list of LendMe books on your NOOK, go to the Library and choose LendMe from the Type drop-down. You are presented with only LendMe NOOK Books.

To lend a book to someone using LendMe, follow these steps:

1. Browse to the book on your NOOK, and double-tap the cover to see the Details screen.

> **TIP:**   If you view only LendMe NOOK Books in the Library, you can tap the cover to immediately open the LendMe screen.

2. Tap LendMe. The LendMe screen appears.

3. Tap Contacts to select someone from your contacts, or tap Facebook to send the offer via Facebook.

4. Tap Next.

5. Tap Select a Contact to add a contact to receive this LendMe offer; select the contact and tap Done. Type a message to send with the lend invitation. (The message is optional.) The same goes for Facebook LendMe offers, but Select a Contact is instead Select Friend.

6. Tap Send or Post.

Your NOOK then displays a message that it's taking care of your LendMe request. When that message disappears, you're taken back to your Library.

What Happens If I Lend My Friend a Book She Already Owns?

If you attempt to lend a book to a friend who already owns the book you're lending, a lending error occurs. On your NOOK, you simply see a message that says, "Sorry, Your LendMe Request Was Not Possible." On the NOOK for PC™ app, you see an error that says, "Lending Error." Unfortunately, B&N doesn't provide any useful information about why the failure occurred, so you're left to wonder if it's because your friend already owns the book or if something else went wrong.

If you see a lending error when attempting to lend a friend a book, check with your friend to see whether she owns the book already. If she does not yet own the book, contact B&N for information on why the LendMe attempt failed.

Choose carefully when lending a book because after you lend a book, you can never lend that particular book to anyone again. However, a book is considered to be on loan only if your friend accepts the LendMe offer. If your friend rejects the offer or if she allows the offer to expire without accepting it, you can lend the book again after it's returned to My Library.

I Want to Lend a Book to One of My Friends. Does My Friend Need to Own a NOOK for Me to Lend Her a Book?

No. Your friend can read an ebook you've lent to her using a NOOK desktop or mobile app. However, your friend cannot read the book unless the email address you used to send the LendMe offer is associated with her B&N account.

The person to whom you've loaned the ebook has 7 days to accept the loan offer. If she doesn't accept within 7 days, the book is returned to your library. The loan offer can also be rejected, in which case the book is returned to your library immediately.

You see notifications in the status bar about your loaned ebook if your friend accepts the loan offer or rejects the loan offer and when the loaned book has been automatically returned to your library. Loan offers and notifications are visible on the status bar and on your NOOK.

While an ebook is loaned, On Loan appears next to the title in the Library, and you cannot read the book. When you loan a book, you also loan your DRM rights to the book. Only one person can possess the DRM rights to a book at one time, so you need to wait until the book is returned to your library before you can read the book again.

If My Friend Finishes a Loaned Book Before 14 Days Have Elapsed, Can She Return the Book to Me Immediately?

Yes. Your friend can click the Return It link that appears in the book's listing in the NOOK App. However, you cannot manually return a book using your NOOK.

If your email goes awry and the offer doesn't arrive to the lendee, you cannot force a re-send of the offer email, and there's no way to cancel the offer. Just wait the seven days for the offer to expire and then send the offer again.

Borrowing Books

When a friend lends you a book, you can see the loan offer in the status bar (or in your NOOK App, on the NOOK HD+ or NOOK HD, via email, and so on). You have 7 days to either accept the offer or reject it. Tap the talk bubble in the top status bar to see the available LendMe offer. If you have only one offer, the offer appears. Tap No Thanks or Accept depending on what you want to do. If you have multiple offers pending, when you tap the talk bubble, you are presented with a list of offers. Tap View Offer to go to the specific item. Tap No Thanks or Accept.

If you accept a loan offer from your NOOK, that book is also available for the loan period in the NOOK Apps, NOOK HD+, NOOK HD, and vice versa. However, if you accept the offer from the NOOK App and then try to read the book on your NOOK, it might not realize that you've accepted the offer and might ask you to accept the offer again. When you do, the LendMe request will fail, and you'll see a message telling you that the LendMe request was not successful. When this happens, tap the Sync button from the Library, and your NOOK synchronizes with the loan offer you accepted in the NOOK App. You can then read the book you were loaned without any problems.

You can determine how much time is left on your loan period by tapping Library from the Quick Nav Bar and tapping LendMe from the Type drop-down list. The banner on the cover shows the time left. If you don't finish the book within the loan period, you can buy the book (or go into a B&N store and read in the store). When you buy a book that was lent to you, the lent copy is immediately returned to your friend.

CHAPTER 18

Using Highlights, Bookmarks, and Annotations

Take a look at one of your favorite books, and you can likely find notes in the margins and perhaps dog-eared pages. Jotting down notes about passages that impact you or marking pages you want to come back to visit later is how you make books personalized possessions. Fortunately, you don't need to forgo these things when using ebooks because your NOOK enables you to highlight passages and add bookmarks and notes to pages.

Using Highlights, Notes, and Bookmarks on Your NOOK

When you think of highlighting something in a book, you typically think of using a yellow highlighter marker to draw attention to portions of the text. Highlighting on your NOOK is similar to that.

A note in an ebook is simply a highlighted area with a message attached. Therefore, the steps necessary to add, view, edit, and delete notes are the same as the steps for using highlights.

Adding a Highlight or a Note

To highlight text or add a note in an ebook, follow these steps:

1. Press and hold a word. The word appears in a bubble, and that is your signal to raise your finger. The word is highlighted, and the Text Selection toolbar appears.

2. If you want to highlight only that word, move to step 3. If you want to highlight a block of text, notice the highlighted word is bounded by two black bars. Press, hold, and drag one of the bars to the location you want to end the highlight.

> NOTE: The initial word highlighted must always be the first or last word in the highlight.

3. Tap Highlight to just add a highlight. Tap Add Note if you want to add a note. If you chose the former, the text is highlighted. If you chose the latter, the Add Note screen appears.

4. Type your note and tap Done.

5. The highlight is added, and a Note icon appears next in the margin.

Viewing, Editing, and Deleting Highlights and Notes

The simplest way to edit a note is to tap the highlighted text. A menu appears, giving you several options:

▶ **View Note**: Tap this to view the note. This appears only if a note is attached to that highlight. After you are in the note, you can tap Edit to edit the note.

▶ **Edit Note**: Tap this to edit the text of the note. This appears only if a note is attached to that highlight.

▶ **Add Note**: Tap this to add a note to highlighted text. An Add Note screen appears. Type in your note and tap Done. This appears only if no note is attached to that highlight.

▶ **Remove Note**: Tap this to remove the note. The highlight remains. This appears only if a note is attached to that highlight.

▶ **Remove Highlight**: Tap this to delete both the note and highlight.

> TIP: You can view the note text by tapping the Note icon on the page. From there, you can then tap Edit to edit the text of the note.

To navigate or jump to notes throughout an ebook, from the Reading Tools toolbar (tap the screen), tap Content. Then tap Notes & Highlights. You see a listing of the notes in the ebook. (Scroll if you need to see more.) You see the text that was highlighted, the page number of the note, and the date and time it was last edited. Tap the particular note you want to jump to. The contents screen disappears, and you go to the page with the highlight or note you tapped.

Here are a couple other notes about this screen's contents. Two other options exist: Clear All and Show Notes & Highlights. If you tap Clear All, you delete all notes and highlights in the ebook. If you turn off Show Notes & Highlights (removing the check mark), you turn off the visibility of the highlights and notes. You can turn them back on by turning on Show Notes & Highlights.

Using Bookmarks

Bookmarks enable you to easily return to a particular page. Unlike notes, bookmarks do not have any text associated with them. Bookmarks work in all your ebooks, magazines, and newspapers.

For ebooks, magazines, and newspapers, to add a bookmark on the page you're reading, tap the reading screen, and then tap the icon that looks like a bookmark in the top-right corner. It drops down a bit and changes to black. Tap it again to remove the bookmark. Alternatively, you can tap the upper-right corner of the screen to place a bookmark or tap the bookmark to remove it.

To return to a bookmark, from the Reading Tools toolbar, tap Content and then tap Bookmarks. A list of pages containing bookmarks appears. Tap the bookmark you want to go to; your NOOK immediately takes you to that page.

Tap Clear All to remove all bookmarks in that ebook, magazine, or newspaper.

CHAPTER 19

Using the Social Features of Your NOOK Simple Touch

As I'm sure you know, Facebook and Twitter are big deals these days—everyone is sharing everything. The NOOK makes this sharing even easier. You can share your reading status and quotes and rate and recommend books. You can share to specific contacts on BN.com, Facebook, and Twitter. Because many of these options overlap and at the same time are scattered across the interface, this chapter focuses on Facebook sharing and the NOOK Friends app.

> NOTE: Although the locations for the sharing features are scattered, they make sense in their location. Basically, B&N provides many locations for the sharing features to make it easy to share.

> NOTE: For LendMe coverage, **see** Chapter 17, "Lending and Borrowing Books with LendMe on Your NOOK Simple Touch."
>
> Using Facebook and Twitter features requires that you link your Facebook and Twitter accounts to your NOOK. **See** "Social" in Chapter 15, "Customizing and Configuring Your NOOK Simple Touch," for linking your accounts.

> NOTE: The social features work only for NOOK Books, magazines, and newspapers purchased from B&N.

You can access the social features in several ways:

- ▶ From the Details screen (remember, you get there by double-tapping the cover image), tap Share.

- ▶ From the Reading Tools toolbar, tap More, and then tap Share.

- ▶ From the Text Selection toolbar, tap Share.

Now consider each of these contexts.

Using Share from the Details Screen or Reading Tools Toolbar

Double-tapping a cover either from the Library or from the Reading Tools toolbar displays the View Details Screen. Tap Share and then tap Recommend to see your recommend options: Contacts, Facebook, and Twitter. Tap Facebook and then tap Next to see the Facebook Recommendation screen—if you are not currently connected to a Wi-Fi hotspot, your NOOK asks you to connect to one.

To post to your Facebook wall:

1. Tap Post to My Wall.

2. Type your message that will appear. As you type, you see the number of available characters (max of 420) go down, giving you an indication of how much space you have left.

3. Tap Post. Your NOOK sends the recommendation to your wall.

If you want to post to a friend's wall, tap Post to a Friend's Wall, and then tap Select Friend. You can search for a name. To select a friend, tap the button on the right of the name. Tap Done. Type your message and then tap Post. Your NOOK sends the recommendation to your friend's wall.

After tapping Share from the Details screen, you have some other options: Post Reading Status, Rate and Review, and Like on Facebook.

▶ **Post Reading Status**: This option enables you to post how far along you are in reading this NOOK Book to Facebook or Twitter. A brief headline indicating how far you are into the NOOK Book and its title is followed by the synopsis of the NOOK Book as found on BN.com.

  After tapping Share and tapping Post Reading Status, tap the check box for Facebook or Twitter (or both), and then tap Post. The update is sent.

▶ **Rate and Review**. Tapping this allows you to rate and review the book on BN.com, which appears on the B&N book's specific web page. You must provide both a rating and either a headline or review before you can post. After you tap Post, the information is sent to BN.com.

▶ **Like on Facebook**: This option enables you to post to your Facebook wall that you like this book. Tap this link, and your NOOK makes the connection that you like that NOOK Book.

Using Share from the Text Selection Toolbar

Use this share function when you have a quote you want others to see. You can share on Facebook, with a contact, or via Twitter:

1. Press and hold the word you want to start the quote.

2. When the Text Selection toolbar appears, finish highlighting the quote by dragging to the end of the text you want.

3. Tap Share.

4. Tap Facebook, and then tap Next.

5. Tap either Post to My Wall or Post to a Friend's Wall.

   For Post to My Wall, type a message and tap Post.

   For Post to a Friend's Wall, tap Select Friend. Select your friend and tap Done. Type your message. Tap Post.

The appropriate wall or walls are updated.

What About Twitter and Contacts?

NOOK's support for Twitter and Contacts functions identically to Facebook, except that you share with specific contacts via email or your Twitter feed. Twitter has a more limited character count, however.

Using NOOK Friends

NOOK Friends is, to quote B&N, "the place for people who love to share their love for reading!" Here, you can connect with friends to lend and borrow books, see what your friends have been doing, and other things.

You access NOOK Friends by double-tapping a cover in the library and tapping Share. Then tap View Friends' Activity. You are already set up with an account. NOOK Friends shows what your friends have been reading, what they are recommending, how far along they are in a book, and more. If you tap Details, you are shown the details for that title.

Adding Friends

If you want to add a friend or accept a request, tap Settings from the Quick Nav Bar, tap Social, and tap Manage My NOOK Friends. A screen appears with your existing friends. If you tap one of your friend's name, you see a screen that shows which of her books are available to borrow. Tap Requests when someone requests to be your NOOK Friend, which you can accept or decline. Tap Sent to see which NOOK Friends requests you have sent.

To send a request to become a NOOK Friend, tap the plus button. The Add NOOK Friends screen appears.

All Contacts displays to see all your contacts. Tap Invite to invite that contact, and they are sent an email as well as see the request on their NOOK. Tap Suggested to see a filtered list of your contact that B&N knows already has a B&N account. You can also add a new contact by tapping Add New. Enter his first and last names and the email address. Leave the Invite as NOOK Friend check box marked to send that contact a request to become a NOOK Friend. Tap Save to send the request and save the contact.

Controlling What LendMe Books Your NOOK Friends Can See

Ever had a friend see a book of yours and request to borrow it, and you felt that you had to loan it even though it was the next book you wanted to read? Well, on your NOOK, you can hide any of your NOOK Books that have LendMe capability so that your friends cannot see it to request to borrow it.

First, make sure you have an active Wi-Fi connection. Then from the Quick Nav Bar, tap Settings, and then tap Social. Tap Manage Visibility of My LendMe Books. On the screen that appears, you see a list of any LendMe books you own that your friends could request. To turn off a specific book from being seen, scroll to that title, and tap Show so that the slider changes to Hide. Tap Hide to switch it back to Show.

If you don't want to show any of your LendMe books to your friends, tap the check box with the long label Show All My Lendable Books to My NOOK Friends so that the check mark is removed.

CHAPTER 20

Shopping and Visiting B&N on Your NOOK Simple Touch

One of the greatest features of your NOOK is the capability to sample and buy content from B&N directly from the device. As long as you have a Wi-Fi connection, you can get new content for your NOOK no matter where you are. However, you can also use the B&N website to sample and purchase content for your NOOK.

> NOTE: Only customers with billing addresses in the United States, Canada, or a U.S. territory can order content from the B&N NOOK Store. Citizens of U.S. territories cannot preorder items. U.K. citizens can purchase NOOK content from http://uk.nook.com/.

Shopping on Your NOOK

To shop on your NOOK, from the Quick Nav Bar, tap the Shop button. Your NOOK establishes a network connection using Wi-Fi (assuming it has one) and displays the NOOK Store Home screen, what B&N calls the *shopfront*.

Browsing the NOOK Store

The shopfront is divided up a lot like the Home screen. You have Browse Shop, Popular Lists, and a scrolling list of recommendations and B&N bookseller picks. To start browsing, tap Browse. The Browse Shop and Popular Lists are existing options within the overall Browse list, so tap one of those if you want to jump right to browsing books or new releases. In addition to collections such as NOOK Books, Magazines, and Newspapers, you also see special collections such as NOOK Books Under $5 and LendMe NOOK Books.

At the bottom of the shopfront is a section displaying picks (B&N Recommends, Jules' Picks, and so on). These are often based on your past purchase or browsing history. Also some deals are tossed in there as well. This section cycles through a series of six screens. You can watch them cycle or swipe through them by either swiping across the screen or tapping the small arrows on either the bottom right or bottom left.

> TIP: You've been browsing and searching for awhile, and you want to get back to the shopfront quickly and easily. Tap the Home button at the top of the screen to return to the front page of the NOOK Store.

Searching for Content

If you want to find a particular item in the NOOK Store, tap Search and enter your search terms. Your NOOK displays the results of your search after several seconds. The results show all the items in which your search terms appear in one or more of the following:

- ▶ Title

- ▶ Author

- ▶ Publisher

- ▶ Subject

- ▶ Contributors

When your search results appear, you can view the results by covers in Grid view or by list view. In addition, you can sort by choosing Top Matches, Best Selling, Title, Price, or Release Date by tapping the drop-down list.

Sampling and Buying Content

After you locate and select an item you're interested in, tap the cover to see an overview page that describes the item and shows the rating of the item from other B&N readers. In addition, you see the following options:

- ▶ **Overview**: Displays the default view when you select an item. You can tap the stars to give the NOOK Book a rating, tap Share to access the social options, or tap My Wishlist to add this title to your wishlist.

> NOTE: This wishlist is *not* the same wishlist as on BN.com or on your NOOK HD+ or NOOK HD. Treat all three wishlists as separate lists. Perhaps some day, B&N will have one synchronized wishlist.

> ▶ **Reviews**: Displays editorial and customer reviews for the item. Editorial reviews often show details from the publisher along with critic reviews of the item. It can span multiple pages. Customer reviews are comments from other B&N customers.

> ▶ **Related Titles**: Displays either more titles by this author or more titles that other people purchased along with the book you are looking at. Tap the cover to see information about that title.

If you like what you see, you can download a sample to your NOOK by tapping Free Sample. (Sampling is only valid with NOOK Books.) Samples typically consist of the first chapter of an ebook. However, it's up to the publisher to decide what to provide as a sample. In some cases, samples might contain just a few pages. In other cases, samples consist primarily of front matter, such as the title page, table of contents, dedication, and so on. One sample I downloaded contained nine pages of front matter and two pages of actual manuscript—hardly enough to actually get a feel for the book.

> NOTE: Samples never expire. You can keep a sample for as long as you want.

If you decide to buy a book after reading the sample, tap Buy; the book is then added to your library. Because samples and full ebooks are completely separate products, a purchased book does not open at the point where the sample ended. You must manually navigate to the point where you stopped reading the sample.

> NOTE: If a B&N gift card is associated with your account, the cost for items purchased from the B&N NOOK Store are applied against that gift card. If there is not enough credit left on the card, B&N charges the remaining balance to your credit card on file.

If you'd like to remove a sample from your NOOK, you must visit My NOOK Library at bn.com from your computer or archive the sample in the Library. If you delete a sample unintentionally, you can download it again.

For more information on using My NOOK Library, **see** Chapter 25, "Using My NOOK Library."

Is It Possible to Accidentally Purchase a Book I Previously Purchased from B&N's NOOK Store?

Your NOOK does not even present the option to purchase a book you already own. If you select a book in the NOOK Store that you already own, you are shown an option to download or read the book, depending upon whether the book is already on your NOOK. However, you will not be shown an option to buy the book.

Some classic titles are released by multiple publishers. Two books of the same title from two different publishers are not the same title, so in these cases, you can purchase the same book twice.

Subscription content also enables you to sample prior to purchasing, but it works a bit differently than it does with ebooks. When you subscribe to a newspaper or magazine, you receive a 14-day free trial. If you cancel your subscription within that 14-day period, you will not be charged. If you cancel after the 14-day trial period, you will be refunded a prorated amount based on when you cancel.

You can use a trial subscription only once for any particular item. For example, if you subscribe to *The Wall Street Journal* and cancel your subscription within the 14-day trial period, and you then resubscribe to *The Wall Street Journal,* you are immediately charged the normal subscription fee because you have already taken advantage of a trial subscription. To help you keep track of when you've used up a trial offer, when you revisit the Details screen for that magazine or newspaper, the Free Trial button is replaced with a Subscribe Now button.

NOTE: Subscriptions can be canceled only using My NOOK Library at bn.com. You cannot cancel a subscription using your NOOK.

Your NOOK automatically downloads subscription content when it's available. In addition to seeing the new content in the Library, you'll also receive notifications in The Daily for any new subscription content your NOOK downloads.

Using Your NOOK in a B&N Store

As mentioned earlier, B&N stores have a Wi-Fi hotspot, so your NOOK can access free Wi-Fi while in the store. B&N uses this hotspot to offer you special promotions called More in Store while in the store. Your NOOK can automatically connect to a B&N hotspot when in the store, but you do need to ensure that Wi-Fi is turned on. (It's on by default.)

After your NOOK connects to the B&N hotspot, tap Shop (which now displays an In-Store banner) from the Quick Nav Bar. One of the banners in the store has links for Read in Store, More in Store, Browse Read in Store Books, and Read Free Content.

Tap Read in Store to see the available Read in Store books (with an In Store banner). To read in store, tap the cover, and tap Read In Store. The book downloads. Tap Read. You can read it in store for 1 hour a day.

More in Store contains free content. If you tap More in Store, you are shown a list of the available content. Tap the cover and tap Free. Tap Confirm. The item downloads. Tap Read to read it.

The typical More in Store offerings consist of several articles B&N feels might be interesting. You are likely to find some interesting and others that don't interest you at all. If you'd like to get a sneak preview of what's available before you drive down to your local B&N, you can browse to http://www.barnesandnoble.com/NOOK/moreinstore/, which shows the current list of free content you can download at B&N.

> **NOTE:** You need to connect to the B&N hotspot to download and read the More in Store offerings.

When you connect to a B&N hotspot in a B&N store, you can read nearly any ebook in the B&N store for up to 1 hour. There's no doubt that B&N has a unique opportunity because of its brick-and-mortar presence. No other ebook reader has the capability of being paired with a retail outlet, certainly one of the more unique capabilities of the NOOK, and these owners should be excited about what More in Store might offer in the future.

CHAPTER 21

Rooting Your NOOK Simple Touch

The beginning of this book mentions that B&N used Google's Android operating system in your NOOK. Choosing Android makes business sense because it's an open-source operating system, and B&N didn't pay a small fortune to use it. However, the most exciting thing about Android for you is that it enables you to easily root the NOOK and add new and exciting features.

The idea of rooting your NOOK may seem daunting or too technical. However rooting the NOOK to get basic Android Market apps installed is easy, only requiring a bit of prep work and a few steps. This minimal effort (can be done inside a one-half hour) is well worth the benefits, for you can turn your NOOK into more than just an E Ink reader (albeit without a microphone or camera), with access to the Android market among other benefits.

> NOTE: To complete the steps in this chapter, you must have at least a 2GB microSD card.

> NOTE: Rooting is another term for hacking, though without the illicit connotation of hacking.

An Introduction to Rooting Your NOOK

B&N locked down Android on your NOOK to prevent you from accessing some of Android's capabilities. However, by following a process called rooting your NOOK, you can open up these capabilities to make your NOOK more powerful and useful.

> NOTE: In the Android OS, *root* is the superuser who has access to everything in the OS. By rooting your NOOK, you can become the superuser on your NOOK.

Following are just a few of the things you can do after you root your NOOK:

▶ Add music players and PDF readers.

▶ Add a browser and cruise the web.

▶ Add calculator and note-taking apps.

▶ Access the Android Market.

These are just a few examples of the power unleashed by rooting your NOOK.

Is It Risky to Root My NOOK, and Does It Void My Warranty?

If you decide to root your NOOK using a process called *softrooting*, which involves installing a special software update for your NOOK, rooting is no more risky than installing a software update, and it's a completely reversible process.

With that said, rooting your NOOK is not sanctioned by B&N. Rooting is one of those things you must do at your own risk. *Rooting does void your warranty.*

How to Root Your NOOK

The experts on rooting your NOOK all hang out at nookdevs.com and XDA-developers.com. Everything you need to know about rooting your NOOK, installing applications, and hacking the NOOK in general is available on these sites. All the files required to root your NOOK are freely downloadable from nookdevs.com or XDA-developers.com. The following steps provide the links to retrieve the files and provide instructions that are, well, less technical than what you can find on the forums.

Prerequisites

Consider a few prerequisites before venturing down the path to root your NOOK. First and foremost, you obviously need to have a registered NOOK.

CAUTION: If you do not register your NOOK with B&N prior to rooting, you cannot buy books from the NOOK Bookstore.

Second, you need a 2GB or higher microSD card. (I recommend using a 4 or 8GB card.) Any existing data on this card will be completely erased, so make sure you have it backed up. Third, you need a computer that can read that microSD card. Fourth, you need a working Wi-Fi connection for your NOOK. Finally, you need to have a Google account. You can get one from http://mail.google.com/mail/signup. You do not need to use it ever again, although you do need it for this process.

After you decide to experience the new functionality of your NOOK by rooting it, the steps required are easy:

1. Download the necessary files.

2. Create a disk image on a microSD card.

3. Install the microSD card disk image on your NOOK.

4. Enter some information into a couple of applications.

5. Install Android Market.

6. Install any additional applications you want on your NOOK.

Now look at each of these steps in detail.

> TIP: The steps are documented at http://forum.xda-developers.com/showthread.php?t=1351719. However, there are a few points of possible confusion on that page. So although you can use it as a reference, follow these steps for a successful rooting experience.

Download the Necessary Files

The first activity is to download the necessary files:

1. Go to http://tinyurl.com/7nt6nm2 and click Direct Download. This downloads the SalsichaNooter04.img.zip file. Unzip the file and place the contents someplace easily accessible.

2. Go to http://tinyurl.com/lhq2nz. This downloads the win32diskimager-RELEASE-0.1-r15-win32.zip file. Unzip the file, and place the contents someplace easily accessible.

3. Go to http://www.megaupload.com/?d=HSBVN3ZK and wait for the Regular Download button to become active. Click it. The Minimal Touch.rar file downloads. Unzip the file. (You can download a free RAR extractor from CNET at http://tinyurl.com/d8ba3d.) Place the files in an easy-to-access location.

Create a Disk Image

In this step, you create a bootable "disk" on the microSD card. To do this, use the win32diskimager-RELEASE-0.1-r15-win32 files download earlier. This is a small piece of software (WinImager) that takes a file and creates the bootable disk.

For Linux and Mac instructions to create a disk image, see http://nookdevs.com/ NookColor_Rooting.

If you are on a PC:

1. Plug in a microSD card to your PC.

> CAUTION: Following these steps completely erases the microSD card, so make sure you back it up to another drive.

2. Find the win32DiskImage.exe file you downloaded in the previous section. Double-click the file, which starts the program.

3. Browse to the SalsichaNooter04.img file, and select it.

4. For Device, choose the drive letter of the microSD card. If you're not sure of the drive letter, open the My Computer window from the Windows Start menu and locate it there.

5. Click Write. The disk image is created. When it finishes, click Exit. The microSD card is now ready to install in your NOOK.

Rooting Your NOOK

Now you can actually do the rooting process, which is strikingly easy. Follow these steps:

1. Unplug your NOOK from your computer and power it off.

> CAUTION: Before you proceed any further, make sure that your NOOK has at least a 50% battery charge.

2. Insert the microSD card on which you created a disk image in the previous section into your NOOK.

3. Power on your NOOK.

4. You see Rooted Forever. Let it run. Then you see the regular NOOK logo and the booting up screen.

5. After a while it seems to freeze. That's okay. You have two options: Keep waiting (give it 2 to 3 minutes) and it may reboot or remove the microSD card. Either way, remove the microSD card go to the next step.

6. Press and hold the Power button. Hold it for some time (20 seconds). Press and hold the Power button again briefly.

7. The NOOK then boots normally.

But, you say, did I root it? When you slide to unlock, you are presented a choice: ADW.launcher and Home. ADW.launcher is the rooted version of the Home screen. Home is the Home screen you are used to. Tap ADW.launcher.

NOTE: You may need to tap the far right, middle of the screen, which opens a set of transparent icons. Tap the button that looks like a Home icon, and then tap ADW.launcher.

Now remember those files you unzipped from the Minimal Touch.rar file in step 5 in the previous section? Take the microSD card used in the previous steps, and place it into your computer. Copy the System and Data folders from the Minimal Touch.rar files to the microSD card. It is okay to overwrite them.

Place the microSD card into the NOOK. Power it off and then back on again. You see the Rooted Forever screen. Let this ride for 2 to 3 minutes. Again, it appears to freeze, which is normal. Eject the microSD card; hold the Power button down until it powers off. Power on.

After the NOOK has powered on, slide to unlock and tap ADW.launcher. Then follow these steps:

1. Tap the middle icon at the bottom of the screen (four squares and a light gray)—the Apps button. Tap Nook Color Tools. The Nook Color tools screen appears.

2. Tap the Allow Non-Market Apps check box so that it is cleared. Tap it again to refill in the check box.

3. Tap the Return arrow at the top, middle part of the screen. This takes you back to the Home screen.

4. Tap the Apps button.

5. Tap YouTube. YouTube opens and gives you a dialog box about terms of service.

6. Tap Accept. The dialog box disappears, and you see the main YouTube screen.

7. Tap the Settings button at the top of the screen (three horizontal lines in a circle). A set of menus appears at the bottom.

8. Tap My Channel, which displays a Sign In or Create Account dialog box.

9. Tap Sign In to see the screen to enter your Google account information.

10. Enter your Google account username and password. Tap Sign In. You see a screen about terms of service.

11. Tap Allow. Your Google account is synced to the NOOK. When it completes, the screen indicates success.

12. On the right side of the screen, you see a set of transparent icons or buttons: an x in a circle, an ellipsis, a left-pointing arrow, a set of four squares, and a house button. Tap the house button, which is called the Home button. (If you don't see these four buttons, you will see a small left-pointing icon. Tap it to show those four buttons.) After you have tapped the Home button, you are presented with two options: Home and ADW.launcher.

13. Tap ADW.launcher. This takes you back to the Home screen.

14. Tap the Apps button at the bottom of the screen. Tap Market. You are presented with a terms of service message.

15. Tap Accept.

That's it! You have successfully rooted your NOOK!

If you do run into problems, sometimes the easiest way to deal with it is to unroot your NOOK and start over (**see** the "Unrooting Your NOOK" section).

Installing Applications on Your Rooted NOOK

Now that you have your NOOK rooted, you want to install applications, right? Well, it is super easy:

1. Tap the Apps button. (It's in between the Phone and Internet buttons.)

2. Tap the Market button. The Market page opens.

3. Tap the Search button. Type NOOK and tap Go.

4. Tap the NOOK for Android™ by B&N app line. Tap Free and then tap OK. You will be informed that it is downloading. Tap the Back button and then My Apps to watch the progress.

5. When it finishes downloading and installing, tap the Home button from the transparent buttons on the right side, and tap ADW.launcher.

6. Tap the Apps button.

7. Tap the NOOK button.

> TIP: To add an app to the Home screen, after tapping Apps, press and hold the app icon. You will be taken to the Home screen with the app there.

8. Enter your B&N account information. Your app is synced up with your B&N account. (If you have a large library, the syncing can take some time.) You can now read your NOOK Books on the rooted portion of your NOOK.

Simple, right? And that's how installing other apps works. Check out what the Android Market has out there!

A Few Things to Note

Now that your have rooted your NOOK, keep a few things in mind:

▶ The NOOK does not have a GPS, camera, or microphone, so apps that use those features will not work. (For example, you cannot make calls with the Skype app—although you can IM.)

▶ Many of the references in the apps and market refer to your phone. This is quite natural because Android is widely deployed on phones. This terminology will change over time as more Android tablets (for example, the Samsung Galaxy) reach the market.

▶ You can always easily return to the regular NOOK interface, press the Home button, and tap Home.

▶ When you use the rooted ADW.launcher as home, you see on the right side of the screen some transparent buttons. These are the ways to interact with the rooted portion of the NOOK. You can access them by tapping the left-pointing arrow to show them. The x in a circle closes the buttons in case they get in your way during typing.

You can always choose the open ADW.launcher whenever you tap the Home button. If you do that, you can always get to the regular NOOK Home screen by pressing the Home button.

▶ The Return and Menu options change from app to app. The menu options in particular provide access to settings, viewing options, and so on.

Unrooting Your NOOK

Want to go back to stock NOOK software? Turn off your NOOK and remove the microSD card. Press the Home button, tap Settings, tap Device Info, and tap Deregister and Erase Your Device. Your NOOK goes through the process to restore to factory settings.

Your NOOK is no longer rooted and just as you received it brand new.

CHAPTER 22

Reading Beyond Your NOOK: Mobile Apps

If you don't have your NOOK handy, you can read items from your ebook library using the B&N NOOK mobile apps. B&N provides a version of the NOOK application iPhone, iPad, iPod Touch, Android phone, and Android tablet—even a NOOK Kids for iPad app. All the apps are free.

The experience the NOOK App provides varies depending on which device you use. On a tablet, the experience is similar to reading on your NOOK HD+. On other devices, the experience is a bit more scaled-down.

To obtain the app for your device, you can do either of the following:

▶ Go to http://www.barnesandnoble.com/u/nook-mobile-apps/379003593, click the appropriate link for your device, and then click Download Now. This opens up a web page at either Apple or Google Play. For Apple, click the View in iTunes, and then click Install after iTunes opens. For Google, click Install when the web page opens.

▶ From your device, go to the App Store (Apple) or Google Play (Google). Search for NOOK and then click Install. After the app installs and opens, enter your B&N username and password.

"Wait a second," you say, "I have a NOOK HD+, an iPhone, and a PC. How does that work with my library?" First and foremost, your reading location in a book or magazine is, assuming you have an active Wi-Fi connection, synchronized to B&N, stored there, and then pushed out to other apps or devices you may have. So if you are reading the latest thriller on your iPhone while waiting for your take-out order, jump to read a chapter on your PC while working in the evening, and then settle down later that night with your NOOK HD+ to continue reading, your NOOK HD+ version of the thriller will open up to that page.

Using NOOK Apps on Your iPad, iPhone, or iPod Touch

When you launch the NOOK App from your device, it syncs with your NOOK library and opens your library home page. You have quite a few options on this screen (see Figure 22.1):

▶ **Sync**: Tapping this synchronizes page location, notes, and so on with your NOOK Library.

▶ **Sort**: Tapping these options sorts your list by the designated category.

▶ **Type**: Tapping this lets you see either your All Items, Books, Magazines, Newspapers, My Files, Archived, or Everything Else. By default, your All Items are sorted by most recent.

> TIP: Everything Else is all the content that you *cannot* read in that app.

▶ **Search Library**: Tapping this allows you to search your library for a specific book.

FIGURE 22.1   The NOOK App interface has a lot of options.

NOTE: As of this writing, B&N has disabled reading some subscription content on the NOOK App (particularly newspapers). If you want to read content other than ebooks, you need to use either NOOK for PC app, NOOK Study app, or NOOK.

NOTE: The focus of this section is on the iPad app, but the iPhone and iPod Touch apps are identical—just on a smaller screen.

Browsing My NOOK Library

Browsing your library is easy; just swipe up and down with your finger to scroll.

CAUTION: On the iPhone of iPod Touch, don't be surprised if while you scroll through your library, you accidentally tap the Download icon and download the book to your device.

To read an ebook, you first need to download it to your device. It's easy to tell whether a book has been downloaded. If a Download button appears, you have not downloaded it to your device. Just tap the button to do so. After the ebook has been downloaded to your device, tap the cover to open the book.

If you press and hold a cover, a details screen appears (see Figure 22.2). Here you can download a book if it is not yet downloaded, open it (tap Read), and archive or unarchive a book. You can even delete the book permanently.

CAUTION: Deleting a book, newspaper, or whatnot *deletes* it from your NOOK library. To *remove* it from your iPad only, tap Archive.

Reading Books in the NOOK App

To read an ebook in the NOOK App, just tap the cover image to open it in reading mode. When there, to move to the next page, swipe your finger from right to left. To move to the previous page, swipe your finger from left to right. The reading screen, however, offers more options than just reading (see Figure 22.3).

FIGURE 22.2   The Details screen for a NOOK book.

FIGURE 22.3   The NOOK App reading interface.

If you do not see the surrounding bars in the reading screen, just tap the page, and they will appear. Before discussing some of these options, take a quick tour:

▶ **Back to Library**: Tapping this returns you to your NOOK library.

▶ **Back**: This icon appears when you have tapped a footnote link (refer to the "204 Sailing to Byzantium" in Figure 22.3), going to the footnote. Tapping the Return button takes you back to the page you were originally on.

▶ **Contents**: Tapping this opens the table of contents with tabs to see your annotations and bookmarks. You can scroll through any of these items and click the appropriate link to go quickly to that spot in the ebook.

▶ **Text Options**: Tapping this allows you to adjust the specific font, theme, margins, line spacing, font size, justification, rotation, and defaults.

▶ **Brightness**: Tapping this lets you adjust the brightness.

▶ **Search**: Tapping this lets you search for specific text in this ebook.

▶ **Bookmark**: Tapping this adds a bookmark.

▶ **Book Details**: Tapping this brings up a page with details related to the book.

Two of these screens deserve more attention: Contents and Text Options. Now take a closer look at these.

Using the Contents Screen

After tapping Go To, you see a screen like Figure 22.4. The screen has three tabs: Contents, Bookmarks, and Annotations. Tap the tab you want to navigate to.

You can scroll through any of the tabs. If you have made bookmarks or annotations, they appear in the tab; otherwise, only blank screens appear. To quickly navigate to the chapter, bookmark, or annotation, tap the corresponding item you want to go to. The Contents screen disappears, and the Reading screen reappears at the location you tapped to go to.

Adjusting Text Options

After tapping Text Options, you see a screen like Figure 22.5. The general purpose of this screen is to provide settings related to the reading experience in the NOOK App. To close the screen, tap anywhere outside of the Text Options screen.

In an ebook, the publisher often provides a series of defaults (font size, type of font, and so on). Changing the Publisher Defaults option to On sets the settings to use those publisher default settings instead of your own. You can change it to Off any time you want and then customize the screen layout as you see fit.

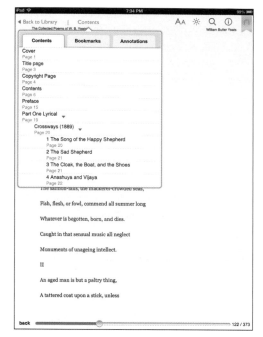

FIGURE 22.4   The NOOK App's Contents screen.

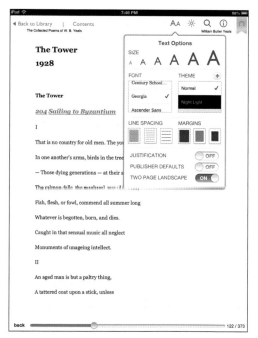

FIGURE 22.5   The NOOK App's Text Options screen.

Clicking the A icon adjusts the font size. The current font size is a teal color. As you tap different sizes, the Reading screen adjusts. Depending on what the publisher of the ebook allows, you can further adjust the font. You can scroll through the available list. (A check mark appears to the right of the currently selected one.) You have options between serif and sans serif fonts. Serif is a technical term that refers to the "hanging structure" on a letter. In Figure 22.5, if you look at the word "Georgia," notice the little hanging things off the top of the G? That's a serif. Sans (French for "without") serif fonts lack these structures. In general, most people find reading serif fonts easier on the eyes. But go with whatever appeals to you.

> NOTE: Of the available font options, Century Schoolbook, Georgia, and Dutch are serif fonts. Ascender Sans, Gill Sans, and Trebuchet are sans serif fonts.

The set of icons beneath the font size determines line spacing. Think of this like single space, double space, and so on. The current setting is colored teal.

Margins determine how close to the edge of the screen the text goes. The more "dark" space in the center, the more the text appears on the screen. The currently selected Margin setting is colored teal.

The Justification setting is either On or Off (and is Off by default)—whether the text has margin on the right side always end in the same place on the edge or wherever the line ends (also called a ragged margin). You won't see any difference in the reading screen with this option On or Off.

Two Page Landscape is either On or Off. Figure 22.6 shows what both look like.

Back toward the top, to the right of Font, you see Themes. You can choose from the predefined themes. (A check mark is next to the currently selected option.) You can also create your own. Tap the plus button next to Theme to see the Create and Edit a Theme screen (see Figure 22.7). If you have already created a theme, the plus button is Edit instead. The bottom part of this screen gives you options for color related to the text, highlights, page, and links. Tap it and you end up in the reading screen color options screen.

FIGURE 22.6 On the top, Two Page Landscape is Off. On the bottom, Two Page Landscape is On.

The first thing to do is to give your theme a name. Tap in the Theme Name box and type the name. Next, select the particular part of the reading screen you want to change the color on: Text, Links, Page, or Highlights. You have a few color options. In the rainbow area, you can select any color you want. Below that is a gradient that goes from white to black, so if you want to operate only with making items some variant of black and white, you can use this instead of the rainbow area. Beneath that, you can see how your choices will appear on the reading screen. When you adjust the text color, the "Preview Text" item adjusts—ditto for Link Color and Highlight Color. Tap Save to save your theme.

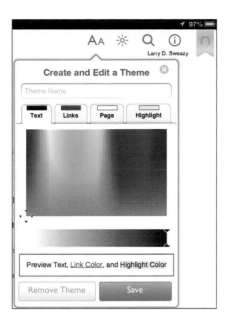

FIGURE 22.7 Create your own theme.

To edit, tap the Edit button next to Theme, and tap the theme name you want to modify or delete. The Create and Edit a Theme screen appears. Make any changes and tap Save or tap Remove Theme to delete it.

Adding Notes and Highlights in the NOOK App

Adding Notes, Highlights, and Bookmarks in the NOOK App is as easy as using your finger to select the part of the ebook to which you want to add a note or highlight. Here's how to do it:

1. Using your finger, select the word you want to add a Note or Highlight to. If you want to highlight more than one word, tap a single word first, and then use the teal lines to drag left or right to highlight more text. The text will be highlighted according to the Font settings' Highlight color. As soon as you lift your finger from the selection, you get a few options (see Figure 22.8).

2. Tap Highlight to add the highlight and nothing else. The text is highlighted.

3. Tap Add Note to go to the Add Notes screen, where you can type in a note and tap Save. A small Post-It-like note appears in the margin.

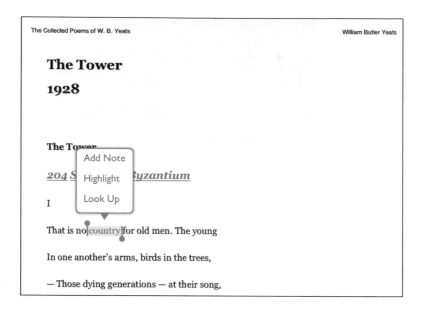

FIGURE 22.8   Adding a note or highlight.

4. Tap Look Up to get a definition or search the phrase (see Figure 22.9). If you select a single word, the definition appears (if one is available). You can also use Google or Wikipedia to launch the Safari browser with the text you selected entered as the search criteria and found (if results are available).

> NOTE: To get definitions, you must have a dictionary installed (*Merriam-Webster's Collegiate Dictionary*, 11th Edition, is available for free). If you have not installed it (you can do this in the Settings menu), and you highlight a single word or tap Look Up, you are offered an opportunity to download and install the dictionary. If you do have the dictionary installed, when you highlight a single word, the definition appears at the bottom of the reading screen. You don't need to tap Look Up.

The note and highlights are available for easy access using the Contents menu from the reading screen.

To view an existing note, simply tap the Post-It Note that appears whenever a Note is already in place, and then tap View Note (see Figure 22.10). This same menu enables you to edit the note, delete it, or delete the note and the highlight.

FIGURE 22.9   The Look Up screen.

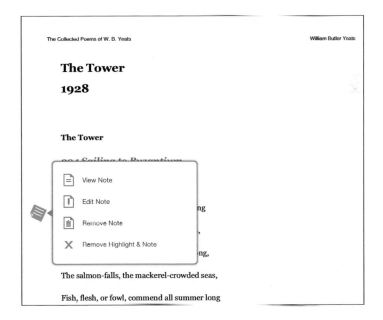

FIGURE 22.10   Changing Notes or Highlights.

If you have text that is highlighted only, tap quickly on the highlight, and then tap Remove Highlight from the menu that appears.

If you want to add a note to a highlight, tap quickly on the highlight, and then tap Add Note from the menu that appears. Enter your note and tap Save. The Post-It Note appears in the margin.

Reading Magazines and Newspapers in the NOOK App

In general, reading newspapers is a lot like reading books. However, because the Publisher Defaults are always on and you cannot turn them off, you usually can't alter text options for them.

Magazines, however, function a bit differently. Although you cannot read enhanced magazines on the iPad (for example, *Time*), many magazines are available without video, and so on. Magazines offer thumbnails that you can scroll through. To see that, just tap the screen to get the reading options (see Figure 22.11).

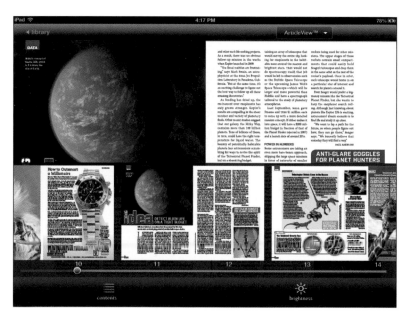

FIGURE 22.11   Reading a magazine.

You can scroll through the thumbnails to see what is covered on those pages. Just tap the thumbnail to go to that page. Tap Contents to see a vertical scrolling list of the magazine's contents or your bookmarks. Tap the article or bookmark you want to navigate to. Tap Brightness to adjust the brightness of the screen.

When reading an article, you can pinch and zoom in or out to get closer into the text. However, you may find this tedious, which is why the app offers ArticleView. Tap it to start reading the article in a "bubble" area (see Figure 22.12). If you are on a page with more than one article, ArticleView gives you the option of which article you want to read.

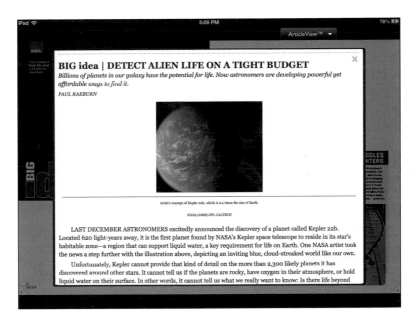

FIGURE 22.12   Reading an article.

When in ArticleView, you have a couple of options. Tap the reading screen to see the Contents, Text, and Brightness options. The Contents and Brightness function just like the regular magazine reading screen. Text, however, gives you options very similar to reading a book (see Figure 22.13). You can also move back and forth between articles by swiping right or left.

The general purpose of the Text screen is to provide settings related to the reading experience in the NOOK App. To close the screen, tap anywhere outside of the Text Options screen.

Clicking the A icon adjusts the font size. The current font size is a teal color. As you tap different sizes, the Reading screen adjusts. Depending on what the publisher of this ebook allows, you can adjust the font. You can scroll through the available list.

The bottom-left set of three icons determines line spacing. Think of this like single space, double space, and so on. The currently selected setting is colored teal.

FIGURE 22.13   A magazine's Text options.

The bottom-right set of three icons determine how close to the edge of the screen the text goes. The more "dark" space in the center, the more the text appears on the screen. The currently selected Margin setting is colored teal.

Adding a bookmark to a magazine is a bit different than a book. Instead of the bookmark icon appearing in the top right, you need to look at the bottom left, where you see a small triangle with a plus sign. Tap it to fold the page over. That's a bookmark. Tap it again to remove the bookmark.

Reading PagePerfect Books in NOOK App

Much like your NOOK HD+, you can now read PagePerfect books with your NOOK App (see Figure 22.14).

In many ways, reading a PagePerfect book is like reading a magazine, though you have slightly different options. The thumbnail scroll is like a magazine's. Just swipe left or right to see the contents. Tap the thumbnail for the page that you want to go to. Tap Contents to see a vertical list of the book's contents, your notes and annotations, or bookmarks.

Tap Go to Page if you want to go to a specific page number. Type the number and tap Go. The screen jumps to that page.

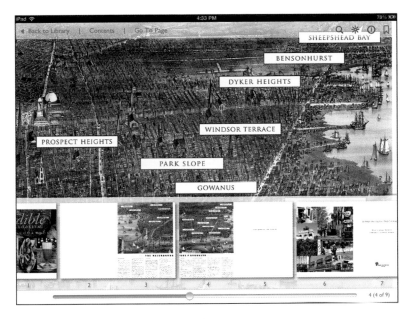

FIGURE 22.14   Reading a PagePerfect book.

The Search button offers similar search functions as reading a regular book.

You can add notes and highlights to PagePerfect books, but only to those areas that are *not* images.

Finally, you can pinch and zoom in or out like a magazine to read the text or get a better view of the picture.

Adding Content to Your NOOK App

You may have noticed in the NOOK Library a filter option titled My Files. The NOOK App now enables you to upload your own content to this area. You can upload ePub (those without DRM) or PDFs to your NOOK Library.

> CAUTION: Any content you sideload into the NOOK app is not synched across devices.

You have two ways to do this: from the iPad or from your laptop.

From Your iPad

Many apps you on your iPad enable you to add an ePub or PDF file directly to the NOOK app. For example, I am a big fan of Dropbox. I store a lot of my files there because I can easily access them. When you open a PDF or ePub in Dropbox, you see the Open In/Print button. Tap it, and then tap Open In. A list of apps appears that are applicable to that type of file (see Figure 22.15). Tap Open in nook to launch the NOOK app and open the file. Doing so also adds the file to your library.

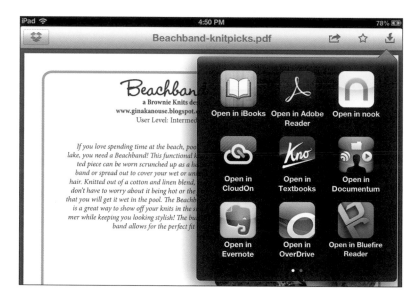

FIGURE 22.15   Opening in the NOOK from Dropbox.

Another method to open this content from on the iPad is from Safari. If you like Project Gutenberg (tons of free books), you can browse their offerings on Safari and open an ePub file directly into the NOOK app. First, find your book (see Figure 22.16). Tap EPUB, which opens up the screen in Figure 22.17. Tap Open In and choose Open in Nook to launch the NOOK app and open the file. Doing so also adds the file to your library.

From Your Laptop

You can also use iTunes on your Laptop to add files. First, connect your device to a power source and start iTunes. From devices, choose the iPad and then select Apps. In this screen, scroll down until you see File Sharing (see Figure 22.18). Scroll through the Apps list and choose Nook. Click Add, browse to the file you want, and click Open. The file is added to the list, and when you synch, it is added to the list of files available in the NOOK app. To delete it, just highlight, and press Delete.

FIGURE 22.16   Found an ePub file to open.

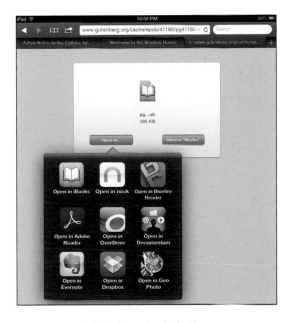

FIGURE 22.17   Opening in the NOOK from the Safari browser.

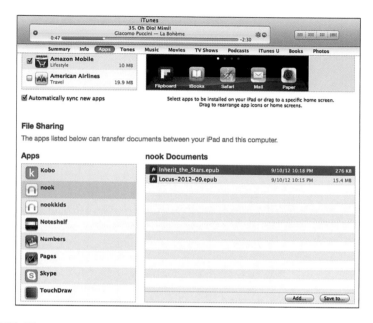

FIGURE 22.18   Adding content from within iTunes.

Also, if you have added a file from the iPad, you can see it here, highlight it, and click Save To to save it to your laptop for safekeeping.

Using NOOK Apps on Your Android Device

When you launch the NOOK App on your Android device, it immediately syncs with your NOOK library. You have quite a few options on this small screen (see Figure 22.19):

▶ **Shop**: Tapping this synchronizes page location, notes, and so on with your NOOK Library.

▶ **Help**: Tapping this launches Chrome to the NOOK Reading Apps FAQ page.

▶ **Settings**: Tapping this opens a number of options you explore later.

▶ **Sync**: Tapping this synchronizes page location, notes, and so on with your NOOK Library.

▶ **Sort**: Tapping these options sorts your list by the designated category.

FIGURE 22.19   The NOOK App interface has a lot of options.

▶ **Type**: Tapping this lets you see either your All Items, Books, Magazines, Newspapers, My Files, Archived, or Everything Else. By default, your All Items are sorted by most recent.

TIP: Everything Else is all the content that you *cannot* read in that app.

▶ **Search Library**: Tapping this allows you to search your library for a specific book.

NOTE: As of this writing, B&N has disabled reading some subscription content on the NOOK App (particularly newspapers). If you want to read content other than ebooks, you need to use either NOOK for PC app, NOOK Study app, or NOOK.

NOTE: The focus of this section is on the Android phone app, although the tablet app is identical—just on a bigger screen.

NOOK App Settings

Tap Settings from the main screen to show a variety of options (see Figure 22.20).

FIGURE 22.20   The NOOK App's settings.

At the top, it shows you which account you are logged in under. Tap Logout to log out if you want to log in as someone else.

The credit card information is the same as the one tied to your BN.com account. Tap Edit if you want to update or enter new credit card information for making purchases.

In the Page Settings area, you have a few options:

▶ **Animated Page Turns**: This option simply turns on or off the appearance of a page turn when reading a book. If it is on, you see the page curl and lift before showing the next page. With it off, one page of text simply slides off and is replaced with another. The animated page turns take a bit more processing power, so on older devices, page turning may take longer with those on. Mostly, though, it's a matter of aesthetics.

▶ **Lock Page Orientation**: Tapping this shows you three options: Automatic (default), Portrait, and Landscape. If you leave it in Automatic, how you hold the phone determines the orientation. Choosing Portrait or Landscape *locks* the NOOK app on the phone from switching when you alter the position of the phone.

▶ **Hide Status Bar**: Tapping this lets either display or not display the time and battery life. When reading a book, if you hide the time and battery life, you get a larger screen to read on, for the bottom bar where that information disappears. Leave the box unchecked to keep the battery life and time bar visible.

▶ **Two Page Mode**: Tapping this lets you determine how the reading screen appears when in landscape mode. If this is off, the reading screen is one column. If on, the reading screen splits into two columns.

▶ **Zoom View Letterboxing**: Tapping this controls how the screen appears when using Zoom View in comic books. Without Zoom View letterboxing off, the surrounding panels are still visible, but with this setting on, when you zoom from panel to panel, the panels not part of the focus are hidden.

In the Other Settings area, you have two options:

▶ **Download over WiFi Only**: This setting enables you to control when to download large files. Some comic books and magazines can exceed 20MB, and you may not want to use up valuable data over the cellular network. In that case, turn this setting on, and any files larger than 20MB must wait until a Wi-Fi connection is established.

▶ **Dictionary Options**: Use this setting to control which dictionary (if more than one exists) to use. If you have a dictionary installed, it shows here. Just tap to see what your available dictionaries are or download another free one (currently, only the *Merriam-Webster's Collegiate Dictionary*, 11th Edition, is available—to use that, you must download it).

Browsing My NOOK Library

Browsing your library is easy; just swipe up and down with your finger to scroll.

To read an ebook, you first must download it to your device. You can easily tell whether a book has been downloaded. If a Download button appears, you have not downloaded it to your device. Just tap the button to do so. After the ebook has been downloaded to your device, tap the cover to open the book.

For subscription content (magazines and newspapers), the items are "put together." You can see this when multiple covers appear behind the front cover. Tapping the screen opens up a detail screen that shows more of the available content (see Figure 22.21). Tap the cover again to close it.

FIGURE 22.21   Seeing available subscription items.

If you press and hold a cover, a details screen appears (see Figure 22.22). Here you can download a book if it is not yet downloaded, open it (tap Read), buy it if it is a sample, and archive or unarchive it. You can even delete the book permanently.

FIGURE 22.22   The Details screen for a NOOK book.

You can also see what other customers have said about the book by tapping Customer Reviews.

If you have added notes, highlights, or bookmarks, you can also see them from the details screen by tapping the Notes, Highlights, Bookmarks tab. You can then tap the note, highlight, or bookmark to open the book to that location.

> CAUTION: Deleting a book, newspaper, or whatnot *deletes* the book from your NOOK library. If you want to *remove* the book from your iPad but keep the book, tap Archive.

Reading Books in the NOOK App

To read an ebook in the NOOK App, just tap the cover image to open it in reading mode. When there, to move to the next page, swipe your finger from right to left. To move to the previous page, swipe your finger from left to right. The reading screen, however, offers more options than just reading (see Figure 22.23).

FIGURE 22.23   The NOOK App reading interface.

If you do not see the surrounding bars in the reading screen, just tap the page, and they appear. Before discussing some of these options, take a quick tour:

- ▶ **Home**: Tapping this returns you to your NOOK library.

- ▶ **Back**: This icon appears when you tap a footnote link. Tapping the Return button takes you back to the page you were originally on.

- ▶ **Contents**: Tapping this opens the table of contents with tabs to see your annotations and bookmarks. You can scroll through any of these items and click the appropriate link to go quickly to that spot in the ebook. Also, if you know the page you want to go to, type it into the top text box and tap Go To.

- ▶ **Search**: Tapping this lets you search for specific text in this ebook. **See** the section "Looking Up Words."

- ▶ **Text**: Tapping this allows you to adjust the specific font, theme, margins, line spacing, font size, justification, rotation, and defaults. **See** the section "Adjusting Fonts."

- ▶ **Brightness**: Tapping this lets you adjust the brightness.

- ▶ **Details**: Tapping this brings up a page with details related to the book.

Two of these screens deserve more attention: Contents and Text.

Using the Contents Screen

After tapping Go To, you see a screen like Figure 22.24. The screen has three tabs: Contents, Notes & Highlights, and Bookmarks. Tap the tab you want to navigate to.

You can scroll through any of the tabs. If you have made bookmarks or annotations, they appear in the tab; otherwise, only blank screens appear. To quickly navigate to the chapter, bookmark, or annotation, tap the corresponding item you want to go to. The Contents screen disappears, and the Reading screen reappears at the location you tapped to go to.

Looking Up Words

If you're reading a book and encounter a word you don't know or are curious about, press and hold on that word until the Text Selection toolbar appears. Tap Look Up. A window appears with a dictionary entry (see Figure 22.25). You can also tap Wikipedia or Google. Tapping either takes you to the browser, opens up the corresponding website, and enters that word as the search criteria. If you want, you can look up another word by tapping in the Edit Your Search box and editing the word and tapping return.

FIGURE 22.24 The NOOK App's Contents screen.

FIGURE 22.25 Your dictionary goes wherever your NOOK App goes.

To search your ebook for a specific word or phrase, tap the Search button, and then type the text you want to search. A keyboard and text entry box appears. Type your search words and tap Search. If it finds your word, your NOOK Tablet displays the locations of that word in a scrollable window (see Figure 22.26). The scrollable window provides a bit of context. Tap the location of the word you want to go to. You are taken to that location, the word is highlighted, the scrollable window disappears, but you still see the search text box. You can tap the bottom-left button to redisplay the scrollable window, or you can tap the left or right keys next to the search word to go to and highlight the next appearance of that word. Tap the X, or tap the reading screen to exit search mode. If you want to search for a different word or phrase, tap in the box that contains your original search term.

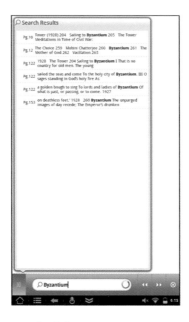

FIGURE 22.26   Searching your ebook is easy.

Finally, if you select a word while reading, from the Text Selection toolbar, you can tap Find. Your NOOK Tablet performs a search for that word or phrase in that ebook, displaying the results like any other search.

Adjusting Fonts

After tapping Text, you see a screen like Figure 22.27. The general purpose of this screen is to provide settings related to the reading experience in the NOOK App. To close the screen, tap anywhere outside of the Text screen.

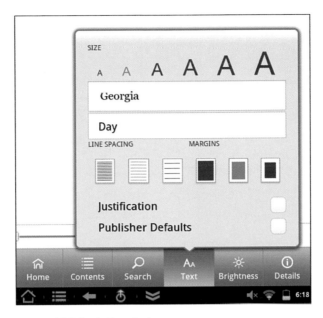

FIGURE 22.27 The NOOK App's Text Options screen.

Clicking the A icon adjusts the font size. The currently selected font size is a teal color. As you tap different sizes, the Reading screen adjusts.

Depending on what the publisher of this ebook allows, you can adjust the font. You can scroll through the available list. (A check mark appears to the right of the currently selected one.) You have options between serif and sans serif fonts. Serif is a technical term that refers to the "hanging structure" on a letter. In Figure 22.27, if you look at the word "Georgia," notice the little hanging things off the top of the G? That's a serif. Sans (French for "without") serif fonts lack these structures. In general, most people find reading serif fonts easier on the eyes. But go with whatever you want.

> **NOTE:** Of the available font options, Century Schoolbook, Georgia, and Dutch are serif fonts. Ascender Sans, Gill Sans, and Trebuchet MS are sans serif fonts.

Beneath the type of font, you can choose from a number of themes, which determine the font and page colors. The current selection has a check mark next to it. Scroll to the one you like and tap it to switch.

The three icons below the theme for line spacing determine how much space is between the lines. Think of this like single space, double space, and so on. The current setting is colored teal.

To the right of line spacing, margins determine how close to the edge of the screen the text goes. The more "dark" space in the center, the more the text appears on the screen. The currently selected Margin setting is colored teal.

The Justification setting is either On or Off (and is Off by default)—whether the text has the margin on the right side always ends in the same place on the edge or where ever the line ends (also called a ragged margin). I have yet to see any difference in the reading screen with this option On or Off.

If you'd like, you can turn on Publisher Defaults, which set the font, size, spacing, and so on to what the Publisher feels is optimal.

Adding Notes and Highlights in the NOOK App

Adding Notes, Highlights, and Bookmarks in the NOOK App is as easy as using your finger to select the part of the ebook to which you want to add a note or highlight. Here's how you do it:

1. Using your finger, select the word you want to add a Note or Highlight to. If you want to highlight more than one word, you can either drag your finger to the end point or tap a single word first and then use the teal lines to drag left or right to highlight more text. As soon as you lift your finger from the selection, you get a few options.

2. Tap Add Highlight to add the highlight and nothing else. The text is highlighted.

3. Tap Add Note to get a text box. Type your note and tap Save. A small Post-It-like note appears in the margin.

4. Tap Look Up to get a definition or search the book (**see** the earlier section "Looking Up Words"),

The note and highlights are available for easy access using the Contents menu from the reading screen.

To remove or edit an existing note, simply tap highlighted text; tap either Remove Note or Edit Note. If you choose the latter, the text box appears with your existing note, which you can change. Tap Save to update it.

If you have text that is highlighted only, tap quickly on the highlight, and then tap Remove Highlight from the menu that appears. You can also choose to add a note. Enter your note and tap Save. The Post-It Note appears in the margin.

Reading Magazines and Newspapers in the NOOK App

In general, reading newspapers is a lot like reading books. Generally, however, you cannot alter the text options because the Publisher Defaults are always on, and you cannot turn them off.

Magazines, however, function a bit differently. Although you cannot read enhanced magazines on an Android device (for example, *Time*), many magazines are available without video, and so on. Magazines offer thumbnails that you can scroll through. To see that, just tap the screen to get the reading options (see Figure 22.28).

FIGURE 22.28 Reading a magazine.

You can scroll through the thumbnails to see what is covered on those pages. Just tap the thumbnail for the page you want to go to. Tap Contents to see a vertical scrolling list of the magazine's contents or your bookmarks. Tap the article or bookmark you want to navigate to. Tap Brightness to adjust the brightness of the screen.

When just reading an article, you can pinch and zoom in or out to get closer into the text. However, you may find this tedious, which is why the app offers ArticleView. Tap it to start reading the article in a "bubble" area (see Figure 22.29). If you are on a page with more than one article, ArticleView gives you the option of which article you want to read.

When in ArticleView, you have a couple options. Tap the reading screen to see the Contents, Text, and Brightness options. The Contents and Brightness function just like the regular magazine reading screen. Text, however, gives you options similar to reading a book (see Figure 22.30). You can also move back and forth between articles by swiping right or left.

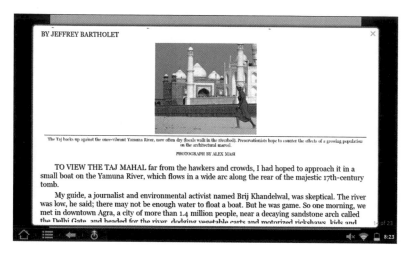

FIGURE 22.29   Reading an article.

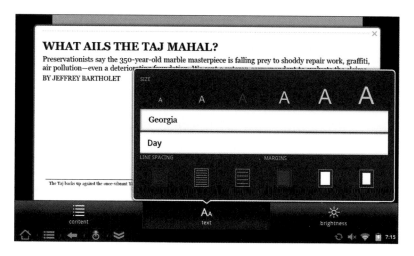

FIGURE 22.30   A magazine's Text options.

You can adjust the font size. The general purpose of this screen is to provide settings related to the reading experience in the NOOK App. To close the screen, tap anywhere outside of the Text Options screen.

Clicking the A icon adjusts the font size. The current font size is colored red. As you tap different sizes, the Reading screen adjusts. Depending on what the publisher of this ebook allows, you can adjust the font. You can scroll through the available list.

The bottom-left set of three icons determines line spacing. Think of this like single space, double space, and so on. The current setting is colored red.

The bottom-right set of three icons determines how close to the edge of the screen the text goes. The more "dark" space in the center, the more the text appears on the screen. The currently selected Margin setting is colored red.

Adding a bookmark to a magazine is a bit different than a book. Instead of the book-mark icon appearing in the top right, you need to look at the bottom left, where you can see a small triangle with a plus sign. Tap it to fold the page over. That's a book-mark. Tap it again to remove the bookmark.

Reading NOOK Comics

Reading comics in your NOOK app is straightforward. Mostly, you have fewer options. The thumbnail view is available that allows you to scroll through the pages (see Figure 22.31). The Content screen provides the vertical view while also letting you see your bookmarks.

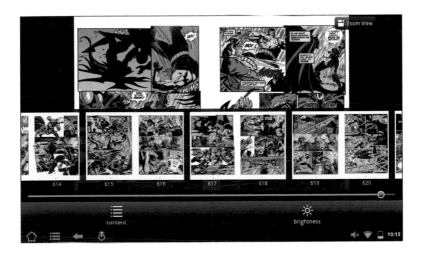

FIGURE 22.31 Reading comics.

You can use pinch and zoom gestures to zoom in on the page. However, the NOOK app also offers Zoom View, which appears at the top of the screen. When you use this, the screen zooms in on a specific panel (see Figure 22.32). When you swipe left or right, instead of advancing to the next page, you are advanced (or taken back) to the next panel. To turn on Zoom View, simply tap the button. When you use the thumbnails to advance to a different page, you are automatically taken out of Zoom View. You can also tap Zoom View again to leave that particular way of reading the comic.

FIGURE 22.32   Using Zoom View in comics.

Adding Content to Your NOOK App

You can add non-DRM ePub files to your NOOK app. The procedure is simple:

1. Connect your Android device to your laptop.

2. When its drive appears in Finder (Mac) or File Explorer (Windows), open the NOOK folder.

3. Open the My Documents folder.

4. Drag or copy and paste any ePub files you want into that folder.

5. Disconnect your device.

When you open the NOOK app, you will have access to them. You can narrow down into them by filtering to just My Files.

Shopping from the NOOK App

You can shop for new books, magazines, and newspapers directly in the NOOK app. Tap the Shop button to open the NOOK Shop (see Figure 22.33). This screen is divided into two parts. At the top, the tag Customers Who Bought This Also Bought gives an indication of what those covers mean. The leftmost cover is something that you have purchased in the past. Based on what others have purchased, you see a list of those items. You can scroll through them to see the full list. If one of the titles interests you, tap the cover to see a detailed info screen about that title.

FIGURE 22.33   The NOOK Shop.

The bottom part of the screen defaults to the B&N Top 100 sellers list. You have several options here. First, you can change the list of what you're viewing by tapping the drop-down list and selecting from the available options (see Figure 22.34).

If you tap one of the Browse categories (Books, Magazines, and Newspapers), a screen pops up with additional categories. You can continue to drill down to a list of titles to browse. If you tap My Wishlist, you see items that you have added to your wishlist. Note that this wishlist is separate from your BN.com or NOOK device wishlists.

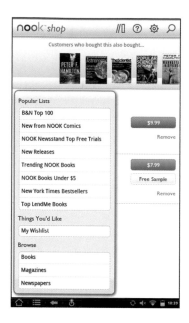

FIGURE 22.34   A multitude of ways to browse the NOOK Shop.

In the listing of titles, you can tap the price button to purchase the book. The button changes to Confirm. Tap it again to complete the purchase. If you tap Free Sample, it is downloaded immediately to your library. Samples typically consist of the first chapter of an ebook. However, it's up to the publisher to decide what to provide as a sample. In some cases, samples might contain just a few pages. In other cases, samples consist primarily of front matter, such as the title page, table of contents, dedication, and so on. One sample I downloaded contained nine pages of front matter and two pages of actual manuscript—hardly enough to actually get a feel for the book.

> NOTE: Samples never expire. You can keep a sample for as long as you want.

Also, you can tap Add to Wishlist, which adds the title to your wishlist. When you view the wishlist, you can purchase books from that list by tapping the Purchase button and then tapping Confirm. This removes the item from your wishlist and adds it to your library. Also, you can tap Remove to remove that title from your wishlist.

While browsing titles, if you tap the cover, you are taken to a details screen (see Figure 22.35).

FIGURE 22.35   Details screen.

From this screen, if you tap the Purchase button and then Confirm, you'll buy the book and add it to your library. You can choose to get a free sample from here and add it to your wishlist. The Overview tab provides a description. You can tap Customer Reviews and Editorial Reviews to see what others have to say. On the Customer Reviews tab, you can add your own review, which will be posted to BN.com. Tap Write a Review. The Rate and Review screen appears. Provide a star rating, a headline, and your review. (You must provide all three.) Tap Post when you finish.

To exit the Details screen, tap the X in the upper-right corner.

The Details screen for magazines and newspapers are a bit different (see Figure 22.36).

If you want to buy the current issue, tap the Current Issue button, and then tap Confirm. This adds that issue to your library. You do not automatically receive the next issue. For that, you must subscribe. If you have never subscribed to the newspaper or magazine, you can tap Free Trial, which opens a Confirm Your Order screen (see Figure 22.37).

FIGURE 22.36   A magazine's Details screen.

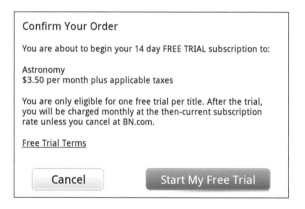

FIGURE 22.37   Confirming if I want to start a trial.

When you subscribe to a newspaper or magazine, you receive a 14-day free trial. If you cancel your subscription within that 14-day period, you will not be charged. If you cancel after the 14-day trial period, you will be refunded a prorated amount based on when you cancel.

You can use a trial subscription only once for any particular item. For example, if you subscribe to *The Wall Street Journal* and cancel your subscription within the 14-day trial period, and you later resubscribe to it, you will be charged immediately because you have already taken advantage of a trial subscription. When you revisit the Details screen for that magazine or newspaper, the Free Trial button is replaced with a Subscribe Now button.

> NOTE: Subscriptions can be canceled only using My NOOK Library at bn.com. You cannot cancel a subscription using your NOOK app.

Finally, if you want to search the NOOK Shop for a title, an author, or whatnot, tap the Search button (the magnifying glass), enter your search term(s), and tap Go on the keyboard. You see results displayed onscreen just like the B&N Top 100 list.

To get back to your library, tap the Library button.

Using the NOOK for Kids App for Your iPad

When the Barnes and Noble NOOK Color was released on November 19, 2010, one of its signature features was NOOK Kids Read to Me ebooks. These books featured a narrator (and not a fake, mechanical-sounding one) if you wanted it. Moving from page to page, a child could hear the words read to them. Tapping the text reread that particular segment. Thumbnail views of each page mimicked the visual magazine representation. The downside of these books is that they were only available for the NOOK Color. (This was all prior to the NOOK Tablet's, NOOK HD+'s, and NOOK HD's releases.)

Fortunately, Barnes and Noble released the NOOK for Kids app for iPad, which enables the same experience with NOOK Kids Read to Me ebooks whether you have a NOOK Color or an iPad.

Installing and Setting Up NOOK Kids for Your iPad

Find the NOOK Kids app in iTunes, whether on your computer or on the iPad (see Figure 22.38). (In that case, use the App Store.)

After you find the app, install it. If you downloaded it via iTunes, sync your iPad to load the app. With your iPad on, tap the NOOK Kids app icon.

FIGURE 22.38   The NOOK Kids app in the iTunes store.

The first time you start the app, you will be asked to enter your Barnes & Noble account information and name the library (for example, Raleigh's Library)—see Figure 22.39.

You are ready to start browsing and reading NOOK Books.

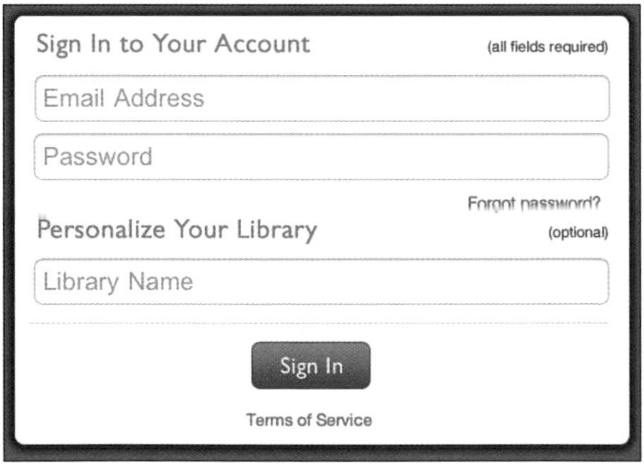

FIGURE 22.39   Enter your account information to start.

Browsing Your B&N Library

After you have installed the NOOK for Kids app and so long as you are connected via Wi-Fi or 3G/4G, your B&N NOOK Books library will appear on the shelves (see Figure 22.40). Anything that is a NOOK Kids Read to Me ebook or NOOK Book for kids (that is, ones without the Read to Me feature but are "traditional" children's books, like *Curious George Goes to the Ice Cream Shop*). You may also notice NOOK Books that don't fit these categories directly: *The Adventures of Tom Sawyer* or *Grimm's Fairy Tales*. I have been unable to discern why those appear but others do not, although I assume that Barnes and Noble considers them appropriate children's books. No matter, you can control which titles you want to appear in the NOOK Kids app (**see** "Using the Parents Button," later).

FIGURE 22.40   Browsing the library.

NOTE: Double-check BN.com when you purchase kids books that says Read to Me if you want the Read to Me feature.

To download the book to your iPad so that you can read it, tap the Download button. You can tap the red x button to stop the download (see Figure 22.41).

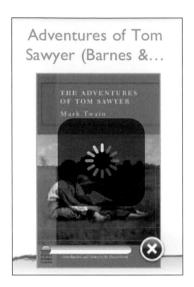

FIGURE 22.41   Downloading a NOOK Book.

To scroll up and down in your library, press the screen, and while holding your finger to the screen, drag your finger up or down.

If you tap the Refresh button, any new purchases appear or archived items disappear.

You have one other option here: Parents. The "Using the Parents Button" section covers this.

Reading a NOOK Kids ebook

To open a book, tap the book's cover in the library. Essentially, there are two types of books that you can read in the NOOK for Kids app: your traditional young children's book with a focus on images and text, and more straightforward texts, like *The Adventures of Tom Sawyer*. Both are covered here, but focus first on the former.

> NOTE: NOOK Kids Read and Play NOOK Books are not compatible with the NOOK for Kids app.

Reading NOOK Books for Kids

These books, such as *The Elephant's Child: How the Elephant Got His Trunk*, always open and are read in landscape view (that is, wider rather than taller). Many of these books have the Read to Me feature available. (These books are labeled as NOOK Kids Read to Me on BN.com.)

When you open these types of books, you are presented with two options: Read by Myself and Read to Me (see Figure 22.42). If the book is not a NOOK Kids Read to Me book, you have only the option Read by Myself, which means just that—no audio reading of the book occurs.

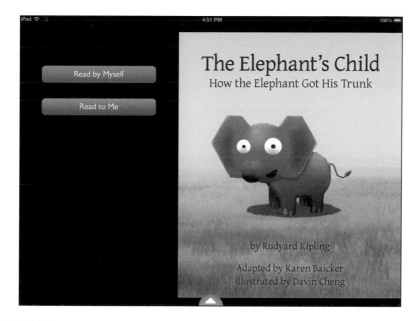

FIGURE 22.42   The opening page for a NOOK Kids Read to Me ebook.

If you choose Read to Me, as you advance from page to page, you hear a person reading the text to you. You can pause the text, and you can replay the text. If you do not make a choice and flip to the first page of the book, the default is Read to Me.

The basics are this: To advance a page, swipe the screen from right to left. To go back to a previous page, swipe the screen from left to right. Double-tapping the text places the text in a balloon, and you have a play button at the corner of the text (see Figure 22.43). Tapping this play button reads that portion of the text. If the button has a square in it, tapping that pauses the reading. If you chose Read to Myself, you can double-tap the text and press the play button to have it read the recording to you.

If the book is not a Read to Me book, if you double-tap the text, it is shown in a balloon without the play or pause button.

FIGURE 22.43   You can replay specific portions of the text.

As you read these books, you notice an upward arrow button at the bottom of the page. If you tap this, a variety of reading options appears at the bottom of the page, and thumbnails of the pages appear (see Figure 22.44):

- ▶ **Library**: Tap Library to return to your B&N library.

- ▶ **Play/Pause**: Plays or pauses the reading for that page. If you choose Read to Myself, this option does not appear here, but you can double-tap the text and choose the play button to play the recording.

- ▶ **Pages**: Tap this to hide the thumbnails if they are visible or show them if they are hidden.

- ▶ **Brightness**: Adjust the brightness of the screen.

- ▶ **Thumbnails**: The current page you are on is marked with a blue outline. Press, hold, and drag the thumbnails back and forth to scroll through them. Tap a thumbnail to advance to that page. As you scroll, you see a small light gray bar increase or decrease as you advance or retreat through the thumbnails. This is an indication of your overall location in the book.

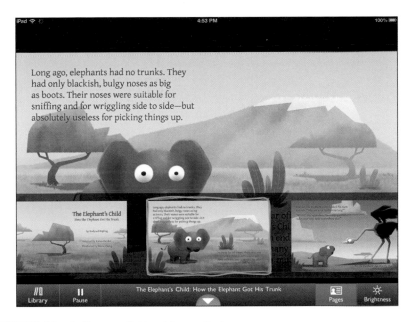

FIGURE 22.44   Options available while reading.

Reading NOOK Books

These books, such as *The Adventures of Tom Sawyer*, open in either landscape or portrait mode. When there, to move to the next page, swipe your finger from right to left. To move to the previous page, swipe your finger from left to right. The reading screen, however, offers more options than just reading (see Figure 22.45).

If you do not see top light teal bar and the bottom scroll bar in the reading screen, just tap the page and they appear. Before exploring some of these options, take a quick tour:

- ▶ **Library**: Tapping this returns you to your NOOK library.

- ▶ **Go To**: Tapping this opens the table of contents with links to see your notes and annotations and bookmarks. You can scroll through any of these items and click the appropriate link to go quickly to that spot in the ebook.

- ▶ **Bookmark**: Tapping this adds a bookmark to this page.

- ▶ **Search**: Tapping this lets you search for specific text in this ebook.

- ▶ **Brightness**. Tapping this lets you adjust the brightness.

▶ **Font**: Tapping this allows you to adjust the specific font, justification, colors, and font size.

▶ **Scroll Bar**: Tapping and holding this lets you move quickly from page to page.

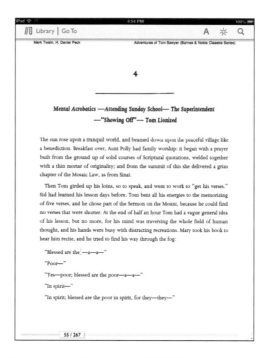

FIGURE 22.45   Options when reading regular NOOK Books.

Adjusting Fonts

After tapping Fonts, you see a screen like Figure 22.46. The general purpose of this screen is to provide settings related to the reading experience in the NOOK App for regular NOOK Books. Tapping outside the Fonts screen closes it, returns you to the reading screen, and makes any changes that you have indicated.

Tapping Change Themes changes the screen, which actually means text color, background color, and highlight color. You have five themes you can choose from. Tap the theme, and either tap Back to adjust more font items or touch the reading screen.

Back at the Fonts screen, you can choose Use Publisher Settings. In an ebook, the publisher often provides a series of defaults (font size, type of font, and so on). Changing this option to On sets the settings to those publisher default settings. You can change it to Off at any time you want.

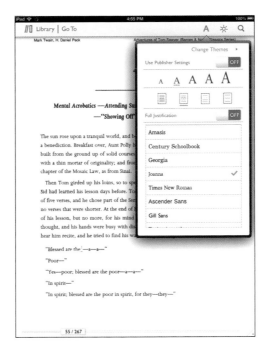

FIGURE 22.46   The font options when reading regular NOOK Books.

Tapping the A icon adjusts the font size. The current font size has an underline beneath it.

The set of icons beneath the font size determines line spacing. Think of this like single space, double space, and so on. The current setting has a line beneath that icon.

The Full Justification setting is either On or Off (and is Off by default). I have yet to see any difference in the reading screen with this option On or Off.

Depending on what the publisher of this ebook allows, you can adjust the font. You can scroll through the available list. (A check mark appears to the right of the currently selected one.) You have options between serif and sans serif fonts. What is this? Serif is a technical term that refers to the "hanging structure" on a letter. In Figure 22.46, if you look at the A icons, notice the little base at the bottom of each leg of the A? That's a serif. Sans (French for "without") serif fonts lack these structures. In general, most people find reading serif fonts easier on the eyes.

> NOTE: Of the available font options, Amasis, Century Schoolbook, Georgia, Joanna, and Times New Roman are serif fonts. Ascender Sans, Gill Sans, and Trebuchet MS are sans serif fonts.

Adding Notes, Highlights, and Bookmarks in the NOOK for iPad App

Adding notes, highlights, and bookmarks in the NOOK for iPad app is as easy as using your finger to select the part of the ebook where you want to add a note or whatever to. Here's how you do it:

1. Using your finger, press and hold until you see the word your finger is on become highlighted; then select the text you want to add a Note or Highlight to. (If you just want that word, you can lift your finger.) The text will be highlighted according to the Font settings' Highlight color. As soon as you lift your finger from the selection, the Note & Highlights screen opens (see Figure 22.47).

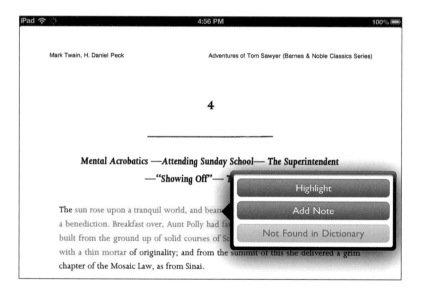

FIGURE 22.47   Adding a note or highlight.

2. Tap Highlight to add the highlight and nothing else.

   Tap Add Note to go to the Add Notes screen where you can type in a note and tap Save Note.

   If you select a single word, the Search Dictionary is an available option. Tapping it brings up a dictionary entry for the word. Tapping outside the definition screen takes you back to the reading screen.

3. The note and highlights are available for easy access using the Go To menu from the reading screen.

Using the Go To Menu

Speaking of the Go To menu, you use this menu to access the NOOK Book's table of contents or any note and highlights you have added.

While reading a NOOK Book, tap Go To to access the table of contents (see Figure 22.48). Tap any location in the table of contents to go to that spot in the NOOK Book.

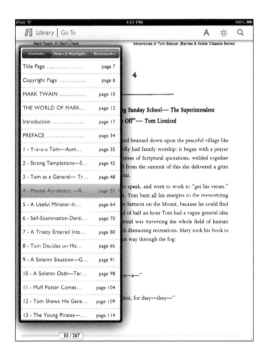

FIGURE 22.48   Accessing the table of contents.

Tap Notes & Highlights or Bookmarks to access any of these that you have added to the NOOK Book. Tap the specific one you want to go to.

Using the Parents Button

You need to explore the final areas of the NOOK for Kids iPad app: Parents. The Parents options provide a way to limit which books appear in the library and control password access. Tapping Parents first asks you to enter your password. After you do that, you see a new screen that defaults to the Manage Kids' Library section (see Figure 22.49).

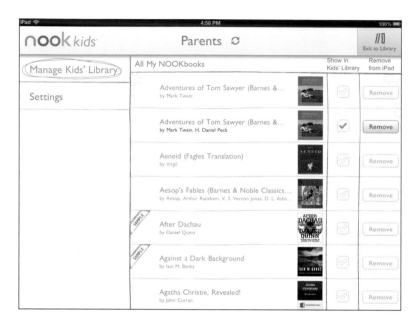

FIGURE 22.49   The Manage Kids' Library screen.

On this screen, you can control which books appear in the library and are stored on the iPad. For example, if you want to allow *The Aeneid* to be read in the NOOK for Kids iPad app, you can tap the check box in the Show in Kids' Library column.

If you want to remove a book from the library in the NOOK for Kids app, you can tap the check box so that the check mark no longer appears. In addition, you can tap Remove to remove the file from the app. (You can always re-add it by downloading it again.)

When you tap Settings, you get the Settings screen (see Figure 22.50).

If you choose Save Parent Password, anyone accessing the Shop or Parents button does not need to enter a password. If you choose to not save the password (by removing the check mark), any time users tap the Shop or Parents button, they are required to enter the password. In other words, if you don't want your kids to control what ebooks appear in the Library, do not save the password.

Also, here you can change the Library Name.

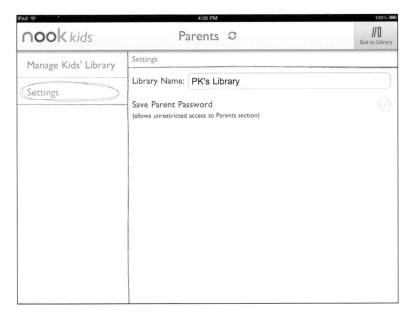

FIGURE 22.50   The Settings screen.

As you can tell, the NOOK for Kids app for iPad is an easy-to-use app, but its primary distinction is that it enables you to use the Read to Me features for kids books whether you have a NOOK HD/HD+ or not.

CHAPTER 23

Reading Beyond Your NOOK: Desktop Apps

In this chapter, you look at the NOOK apps B&N provides for reading NOOK Books, Newspapers, and such on your desktop or laptop: NOOK for PC/Mac, NOOK Study, and NOOK for Web. If you don't have your NOOK handy, you can read items from your ebook library using these apps.

You can download the NOOK App for your PC or another device by going to http://www.barnesandnoble.com/u/nook-mobile-apps/379003593, clicking the appropriate NOOK App device link, and clicking the Download Now button.

If you have multiple NOOKs and NOOK apps, B&N keeps them all synchronized (assuming you have active Wi-Fi connections for each device) so that when you jump from device to device, you can pick up right where you left off.

Using the NOOK for PC App

After you install the NOOK for PC app, when you first launch the app, you'll be asked to sign in to your B&N account. Enter your username and password, and click Sign In if you already have an account on bn.com. If you don't have an account, you can click Create an Account to create one.

Browsing Your B&N Online Library with the NOOK for PC App

After you sign in to your account, the NOOK for PC app checks in with My NOOK Library and synchronizes samples, last pages read, and so on. You then see a series of buttons along the left side (see Figure 23.1).

By default, the NOOK for PC app displays all items. However, you can filter the view to show only ebooks, emagazines, enewspapers, archived items, and manually added content (what B&N calls "my stuff") by clicking the appropriate option in the My Library menu.

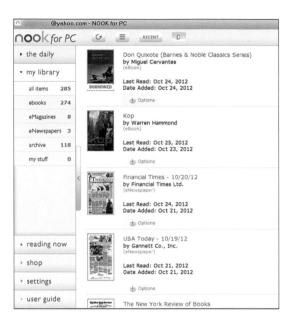

FIGURE 23.1   The menu buttons in the NOOK for PC app mirror several of those on your NOOK.

Along the top of the NOOK for PC app are buttons to manually refresh your library, control the views of your library, sort your library, and search your library, as shown in Figure 23.2.

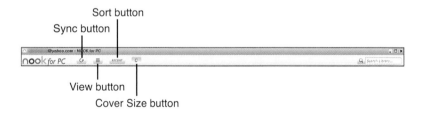

FIGURE 23.2   Function buttons at the top of the NOOK for PC app enable you to control how you view your library.

Clicking the Sync button synchronizes your B&N NOOK Library with the NOOK for PC app. Use this to synchronize your notes and page location.

The View button controls how your ebook library appears in the NOOK for PC app and shows what view you are currently in (three lines for list view and six boxes for grid view). By default, the NOOK for PC app shows your library in list view. In this view, a small image of the cover of each item displays along with items such as the author, the last read date, and so on. You can switch to a grid view that shows only large images of each item's cover by clicking View button, as shown in Figure 23.3.

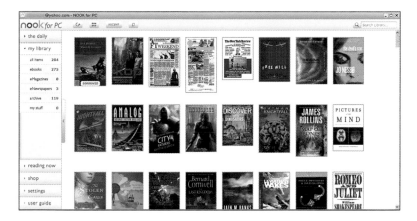

FIGURE 23.3   Viewing My Library in grid view.

When you select to show your items in grid view, the Cover Size button enables you to control the size of the cover image that displays. (The button shows a small rectangle.) The smallest size is slightly smaller than the size displayed when in grid view, and the largest size is approximately twice the size of the covers shown in grid view.

> NOTE: Most covers provided with ebooks and other content look terrible when you select the largest available size in list view because they're not intended for display at such a large size.

You can sort your online library in the NOOK for PC app by clicking the Sort button, which defaults to Recent but changes to Title and Author as you continue to click it.

As you accumulate a library of digital content, the NOOK for PC app enables you to easily find content by searching for it. When you click inside the Search Library box, you're given a choice to search for a title, an author, a publisher, or all three. Select an option, enter your search text, and either click the magnifying glass or press Enter to search your library.

> TIP: Searches are filtered based on how your library is filtered. For example, if you select eMagazines from the My Library menu, searches show only magazines that match your search terms, so if you actually want to search your entire library, make sure you click All Items in My Library.

If you want to view all the items in your NOOK library instead of just those that match your search terms, click the X inside the Search Library box. Doing so clears your search term and shows all the items in your online library.

Shelves on the NOOK for Mac App

On the NOOK for Mac app, you can also create shelves. Just click Create Shelf. The Create a Shelf dialog box appears. Enter a name for the shelf and select an icon. You can add a title to the shelf by clicking and dragging a title from the My Library screen.

At the bottom of the screen, you see the My Archive, Settings, Info, Sync, and Notification buttons. Click My Archive to see your archived items. **See** the "Configuring the NOOK for PC App Settings" section to learn about these settings. The Info option enables you to check your system, review the privacy policy, and so on. Clicking the Sync button forces the NOOK app to sync with your other NOOK devices and apps. If you receive LendMe offers, you see it appear in the Notification button. Click it to see the offer. You can choose to Accept or Reject.

Viewing the Daily in the NOOK for PC App

Clicking the Daily menu button displays the Daily. Assuming you are connected to the Internet, it updates with the latest articles and loan offers. Click Read Now to read the particular article, which appears in a small box. Clicking Close hides the article from view.

NOTE: On the NOOK for Mac app, the Daily does not exist. Instead, you have just My Library.

For a loan offer, you can click Accept or Decline. Or you can click Details, which refreshes the screen to show just that book, some additional details, and buttons to Buy Now and More by Author. Clicking either of these last two options opens your browser to the book page (where you can purchase it) or to a listing of that author's titles.

Shopping for ebooks in the NOOK for PC App

Clicking the Shop button opens up your web browser at BN.com. For more information about shopping for ebooks, **see** "Shopping on Your Computer" in Chapter 13, "Shopping and Visiting B&N on Your NOOK HDs."

Item Options in the NOOK for PC App

Click the More Options button (see Figure 23.4) or hover your mouse pointer over an item (see Figure 23.5) in My Library to see several options:

▶ **Read Now**: Opens the item in the NOOK for PC app. If the item hasn't been downloaded to your computer, the NOOK for PC app downloads it first and then opens it.

▶ **LendMe**: Displayed only for items you can lend to friends. When clicked, it opens a dialog box for entering the email address of a friend to whom you'd like to lend the item. **See** the section "Using LendMe in the NOOK for PC App," for more details about the LendMe feature.

▶ **Download**: Displayed when the item hasn't been downloaded to your computer. When clicked, the item is downloaded to your local computer, and Download changes to Remove Local Copy.

▶ **Remove Local Copy**: Displayed when the item has been downloaded to your local computer. When clicked, the item is removed from your local computer. If you want to read it at a later time, you need to download it again. Note that this does not remove the items from your NOOK library; it removes it only from the particular computer you use.

▶ **Move to Archive**: Moves the item to your archive. Archived items appear in the Archive category in My Library.

▶ **Unarchive**: Displayed only for archived items. When clicked, the item is moved from the archive to your main digital library.

FIGURE 23.4 Available options for when in list view.

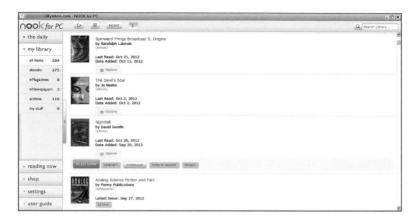

FIGURE 23.5   Available options for when you hover over a cover.

▶ **Details**: Opens a screen that provides a bit more information, including buttons for Remove Local Copy, Move to Archive, Read Now, and More by Author.

> TIP: Archiving or unarchiving an item in the NOOK for PC app on your PC also archives or unarchives the item for all your NOOK devices and apps.

For subscription content for which you have more than one copy available to read, when you click Details, a new screen appears (see Figure 23.6). From here, you can pick the specific issue you want to read, download, or archive.

FIGURE 23.6   Subscription content details.

Reading Books in the NOOK for PC App

To read a book, click the cover or click Read Now from the available options described previously. Your book opens, hiding the My Library, My Daily, and so on bar (see Figure 23.7). You can always see My Library again by clicking the large gray box with the right pointing arrows. This slides the My Library bar over (see Figure 23.8). While you're reading content, the NOOK for PC app displays the Reading Now menu, as shown in Figure 23.8. Using the Reading Now menu, you can easily navigate to the last page read, access the table of contents, and access bookmarks, annotations, and highlights for the item you're reading.

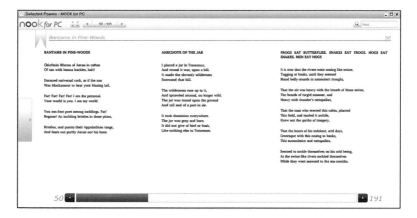

FIGURE 23.7   How a book opens in NOOK for PC.

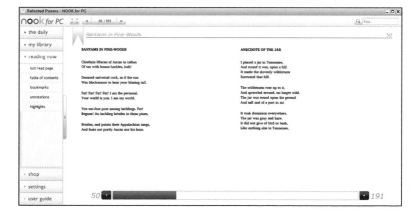

FIGURE 23.8   Reading a book with My Library visible.

While reading, you navigate the pages by pressing the arrow keys (right and down advance a page; left and up retreat a page) or clicking the arrows in the scrollbars at the top or bottom of the screen. In the top scrollbar, you can click the page number and enter a new page number to be taken directly to that page.

At the top of the screen, the Full Screen button adjusts the screen by removing the clutter (see Figure 23.9). Press Esc or click the button again (its arrows now point toward each other) to return to the default reading screen.

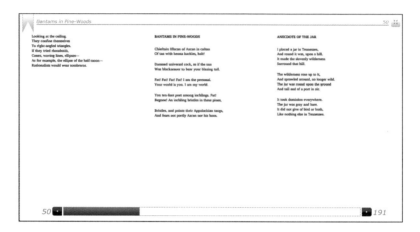

FIGURE 23.9 Reading in Full Screen mode.

In the Search box, you can type a word or phrase to search the book on. Type the text you want to search on, and press Enter. If a result is found, you are taken to that page with the word highlighted. Click the magnifying glass to advance to the next instance of that word found in the book. When no more instances of that word are found, a small dialog box appears that states, No Matches Found. If you type a word that does not appear in the book, a dialog box appears that states, No Matches Found.

If you want to navigate to a particular chapter or location in the book, you can use the Table of Contents option. Just click that, and the table of contents appears next to the reading screen (see Figure 23.10). You can scroll through this table of contents using the scrollbar. Just click the entry you want to navigate to, and the reading screen jumps to that location. Click the X button to close the table of contents.

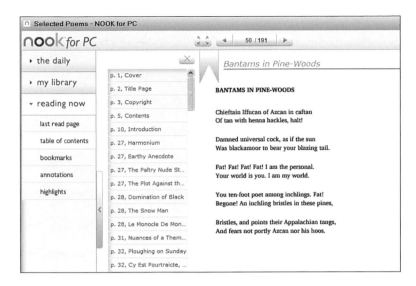

FIGURE 23.10 Using the table of contents to navigate the book.

Before moving to notes, highlights, and bookmarks, a couple features are available to you while reading: definitions and Wikipedia lookups. To access either of these features, highlight the text in question in the reading screen by clicking your mouse at the starting point, dragging to the end point, and releasing the mouse button. A pop-up menu appears (see Figure 23.11). At the bottom of that menu, you have two options: Look Up with Dictionary.com and Look Up with Wikipedia. Selecting either option opens up your browser with the highlighted term or phrase automatically entered as the search criteria and found (if applicable) at the respective site. Of course, your selection determines what is found—for example, selecting a phrase does not produce any definition results.

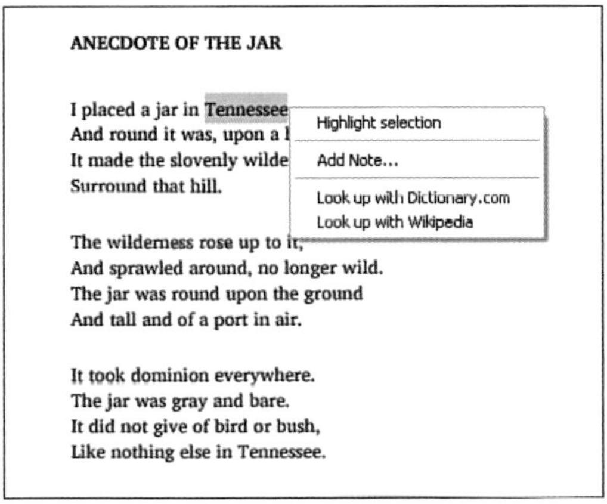

ANECDOTE OF THE JAR

I placed a jar in Tennessee
And round it was, upon a l
It made the slovenly wilde
Surround that hill.

Highlight selection

Add Note...

Look up with Dictionary.com
Look up with Wikipedia

The wilderness rose up to it,
And sprawled around, no longer wild.
The jar was round upon the ground
And tall and of a port in air.

It took dominion everywhere.
The jar was gray and bare.
It did not give of bird or bush,
Like nothing else in Tennessee.

FIGURE 23.11 Selecting text gives you options.

When reading magazines and newspapers, reading functions is essentially the same. One difference is that newspapers and magazines are typically set up with a linkable front page or list of contents (see Figure 23.12). In this image, each of those items is an article. You can click Spanish Premier Suffers Setback to jump to that article (see Figure 23.13).

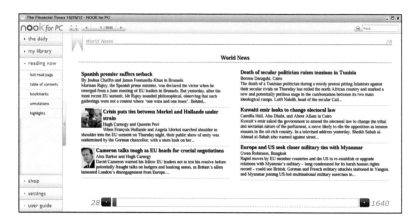

FIGURE 23.12   Reading a newspaper.

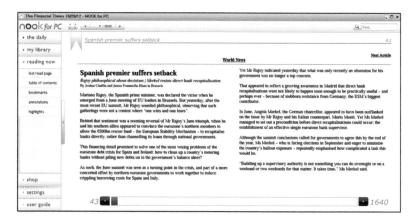

FIGURE 23.13   Reading an article.

In Figure 23.13, you can quickly navigate to the list of contents by clicking the World News link. You can also advance quickly to the next article by clicking Next Article. (If you were in the second article of this section, you would see a Previous Article link on the top-left portion of the screen.) In addition, you can use the arrow keys and scrollbars to navigate from article to article in a page-by-page method.

NOTE: Want to adjust the font size you are reading? **See** the section "Configuring the NOOK for PC App Settings."

Using Highlights, Notes, and Bookmarks in the NOOK for PC App

You can also use highlights in the NOOK for PC app. However, you cannot add highlights or notes to subscription content.

Adding Highlights and Notes

To add a highlight to an ebook in the NOOK for PC app, click your mouse on the starting point where you want your highlight. While holding the mouse button, drag your mouse to the ending point for the highlight. When you do this, the NOOK for PC app highlights the text and displays a pop-up menu (see Figure 23.14). To make the highlighted text an actual highlight, click Highlight Selection.

If you want to add a note, click Add Note from the pop-up menu. Type your note, and then click OK. If you want to add a note to text that is already defined as a highlight, highlight a portion of that text again. The pop-up menu offers a couple extra options (see Figure 23.14). Click Add Note to add a new note to the existing highlight. Add the text for your note, and then click OK.

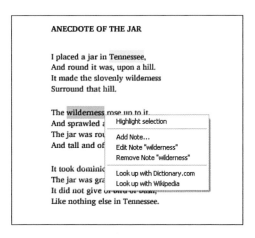

FIGURE 23.14   Editing an existing note or highlight

Viewing Highlights and Notes

To view highlights, click Highlights under the Reading Now menu. Highlights that don't have notes associated with them can be found by clicking Highlights. If a note is associated with the highlight, click Annotations in the Reading Now menu to see the note. You can quickly jump to any note or highlight by clicking the specific note or highlight.

> **Can I Change the Green Color the NOOK or PC App Uses for Highlights?**
> You can't change the color of highlights on the PC.

Editing and Deleting Highlights and Notes

To edit a note associated with a highlight, highlight a portion of that text that composes the note, and click Edit Note. Enter the new text for the note, and click OK. To delete the note, select Remove Note; then click Yes when asked to confirm that you want to delete the note. Follow the same steps to remove a highlight that doesn't have a note associated with it.

Using Bookmarks

To add a bookmark to a page in the NOOK for PC app, click the ribbon with pointed ends in the corner of the page. When you do, the ribbon drops down onto the page, and your bookmark appears in the bookmark pane when you select Bookmarks from the Reading Now menu. To remove the bookmark, click the ribbon again.

You can easily navigate to a particular bookmark by clicking the bookmark in the bookmark pane.

Importing Books into the NOOK for PC App

All books in your B&N online library are automatically added to the NOOK for PC app. If you want to read a book you purchased from another source or your own content, you can add it to the NOOK for PC app by clicking the My Library, the My Stuff menu, and then the Add New Item button (see Figure 23.15).

> NOTE: You can import only eReader format (PDB files) and EPUB format ebooks along with PDFs into the NOOK for PC app.

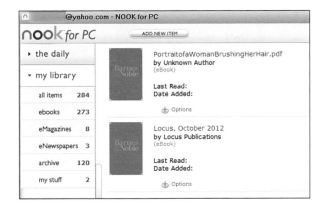

FIGURE 23.15   Click this button to add non-B&N ebooks and content.

If the book you import contains DRM, you will be asked for your name and credit card information when you attempt to read the book in the NOOK for PC app. You need to supply this information only the first time you read the book.

Can I Read Books in Formats Other Than eReader and EPUB in the NOOK for PC App?

Kind of. To read a book in the NOOK for PC app, you must first convert the book to either eReader format or EPUB format. You can use Calibre to convert books into a format compatible with the NOOK for PC app, provided the book is not protected with DRM. To learn how to use Calibre, **see** Chapter 24, "Managing Your ebooks with Calibre."

Configuring the NOOK for PC App Settings

Clicking the Settings menu lets you change the appearance of content in the NOOK for PC app and change your account settings.

To change the appearance of content, click Settings and then click Reader Settings. From this screen, you can change the font size and margin spacing used in the NOOK for PC app. Clicking the font size adjusts the sample text size to give you an idea of how it will appear when reading an actual ebook. The Margins option is controlled by clicking and dragging the Indicator icon or clicking anywhere along the bar. Toward the right increases the amount of white space on either side of the text. Toward the left decreases the amount.

> NOTE: Account Settings appears by default when you click Settings.

To change account settings, click Account Settings. You can sign in or sign out of your B&N account from this screen. You can also choose whether recent purchases are downloaded automatically. The other option you have is Autohide Navigation When Opening Reading Now. By default, this is selected, and what it means is that when you are reading an ebook, the Daily, My Library, and such options on the left disappear. (You can get it back by clicking the left-facing arrow bar.) Otherwise, the menu is always available.

Using LendMe in the NOOK for PC App

On the NOOK for PC app, you can not only read books that you have borrowed using the LendMe program but also offer books to friends and family who have a NOOK device or app.

Any offers you receive (that is, books offered to you to borrow), appear in the Daily initially (see Figure 23.16). You can accept or decline the offer by clicking the appropriate button. If you accept, the book is added to your library with the banner Borrowed on the cover.

FIGURE 23.16   Offers available to you.

If you would like to lend a book, the book must first be in the LendMe program. If it is, you see a LendMe button in the Details (see Figure 23.17). To lend the book, click the LendMe button, which opens up a screen like Figure 23.18.

FIGURE 23.17 The LendMe button.

NOOK for PC Lend to a Friend

Lend to a Friend

Lend your eBook to a friend for up to 14 days - they'll have up to 7 days to accept your offer. Please note that during this period, you won't have access to your copy.

Nightfall
David Goodis
eBook

To

Personal Message (optional)

Your Email Address   pkanouse@yahoo.com

SEND   CANCEL

FIGURE 23.18 Sending a LendMe offer.

Here, enter the recipient's email address and an optional message. Your email address is filled out automatically from your account information. Click Send. The offer is then sent to your friend to accept or decline.

Using the NOOK Study App on PC

NOOK Study is an app for the laptop or desktop developed by Barnes & Noble for reading and marking textbooks while at the same time prepping for tests, papers, and so on. Although intended for students, the NOOK Study app is a useful, feature-rich program. For PC users, you do not need both apps, though having both doesn't cause any problems.

Following are the feature highlights. (The NOOK Study app for both the PC and Mac are essentially identical, so the focus is on the PC version for the rest of this section.)

▶ Syncing with your online library.

▶ Viewing multiple books at once and dual-book view.

▶ Customizable courses, which is a fancy way to say, "You can organize your books into categories."

▶ Enhanced note and lookup features.

These are covered while looking at the program.

Downloading, Installing, and Setting Up the NOOK Study App

To use this software, you need an Adobe Digital Editions (ADE) account. Go to adobe.com/products/digitaleditions/ to create one if you do not already have one. It's free!

You can find the NOOK Study app at barnesandnoble.com/nookstudy/download/index.asp. Download the appropriate version for your operating system. After the file has downloaded to your computer, double-click the file, and follow the instructions.

> NOTE: On the Mac, you first need to unzip the file. Then double-click the setup file.

After NOOK Study has installed, start the program. When you first start it, you are asked to agree to the License Agreement. Click Agree. You are then asked to enter your B&N account information. (This is the same account you use to purchase books on BN.com.) You can also create an account by clicking Create Account. If you have an account, click I Have an Account, and enter the account information. Next, enter your Adobe ID and password. Finally, enter your school. That's it! You are now ready to use NOOK Study.

> NOTE: If you are not a student and just want to use NOOK Study, enter a school near you. I, so far, have not gauged any effect on how the school matters.

Navigating NOOK Study

When you open NOOK Study (see Figure 23.19), it syncs with your My NOOK Library, so if you were on page 400 of *Moby-Dick* on your NOOK for iPhone® app, when you open *Moby-Dick* on NOOK Study, it opens at page 400.

FIGURE 23.19   The My Library screen.

Unlike the NOOK App for PC, there is no My Library, Shop, and such buttons. Instead, your library (called My Library) is shown. At the top of the screen, you have four buttons:

- ▶ **Reading Now**: Clicking this takes you to the reading pane, where all ebooks you have open appear in tabs (much like the omnipresent browser tabs).

- ▶ **Shop**: Clicking this opens a dialog box. Enter a title, author, or ISBN, and click Search Now. Your browser opens, goes to BN.com, and performs a search based on what you entered.

- ▶ **Notifications**: If you receive a LendMe offer, you see it appear in the Notification button. Click it to see the offer. You can choose to Accept or Reject.

- ▶ **Settings**: Clicking this enables you to modify your account settings, check for updates, and such.

These four buttons are always present and available.

Navigating NOOK Study's My Library View

While at the My Library screen, choose to see all your books and documents. You can also choose a particular course, which filters your viewing list to just books in that course. If you haven't yet done so, you can create a course. To create a course:

1. Click Add Course.

2. Give the course a name.

3. To change the icon of the course, click the Folder icon next to the course name, and select the one you want (see Figure 23.20). (You'll notice these are thematic according to probable types of courses: Law, Science, Economics, Classics, and so on.)

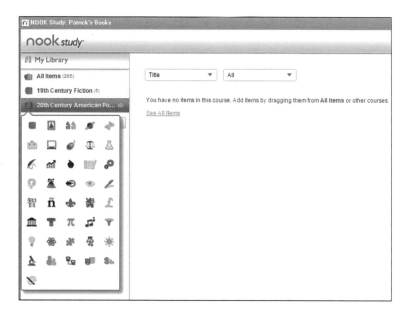

FIGURE 23.20   Changing the folder icon.

4. You can now select books from your library and drag them to the course to add books to that course. Note, doing this does not remove them from the All Books & Docs view.

After you finish with the course or if you need to make changes at any point in time, this is easy to do:

1. Click the course name, and click the right-pointing arrow that appears. When you do this, you see two options: Edit and Remove This Course.

2. Click Remove This Course to delete the course. NOOK Study asks you to confirm that you want to delete the course. You are not deleting the books from your library, just deleting that particular course.

3. Click Edit to edit the name for the course.

You have a few more options on this screen. You can choose to view My Archive. From here, you can unarchive books or documents.

The Sync button forces a sync with My NOOK Library, which means that the existing page you were reading is sent to your library. When you next open your NOOK for iPad app or NOOK Color, you will be taken to that same page.

In the view of your books, you see some features similar to the NOOK for PC app. You can choose to Sort your books by Title, Author, Last Read, Markup Count, or Recently Added.

You can also choose what type of books and documents you are looking at in this view by choosing the Filter drop-down list. Your options here are All, Books, Textbooks, Newsstand (both magazines and newspapers), and My Files.

You use the Search Library box to search the entire contents of your NOOK Study library. If you type **conscious**, NOOK Study searches for that word in all titles, notes, and text. If you click the down arrow in the Search Library box, you can filter the results (see Figure 23.21). For example, if you turn off the check mark next to Title, Author, and ISBN, NOOK Study does not search those items. Clicking the results found link below the title displays the results in detail where the search term was found in that particular book (see Figure 23.22). Click the specific result to go to that page in the book.

FIGURE 23.21 NOOK Study searches not only the titles but also the notes you've added and the full text.

FIGURE 23.22   Specific results for a search.

You can also choose to see your books in either grid or list view. In grid view, clicking the book cover opens the books for reading. If you have not downloaded the book yet, it will download first. If you hover your mouse over the cover, you can see an "i" button in the bottom-right corner of the cover. Clicking it gives you a variety of options depending on if you have downloaded the ebook or issue, added notes, and so on. If you haven't downloaded the book yet, you are also given an option to download the book.

Book Info is straightforward (see Figure 23.23): It takes you to a page with some information about the book along with options to Read Now, Download, Remove the Local Copy, and Archive it (or unarchive it if you have archived it).

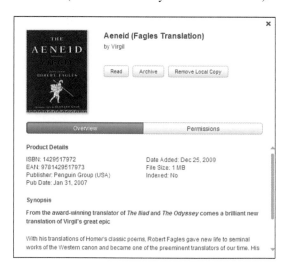

FIGURE 23.23   The Book Info screen.

In list view, clicking the cover image opens the book for reading. The Book Info link takes you to the Book Info page that is the same as what you get from the grid view. If you have added notes to the ebook, to the far right, you see a list of links for the type of notes you have made. Clicking one of the types of notes opens the ebook with the Notes view open, which is discussed in the section "Using the Highlights, Notes, and Look Up Features of NOOK Study."

If the content is subscription content, the options are slightly different. First, if you have multiple copies of a magazine or newspaper, when you click the cover image, a drop-down appears displaying all the issues available to you (see Figure 23.24). Click the one you want to read.

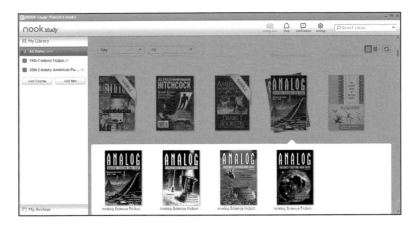

FIGURE 23.24   Click the issue you want to read.

If you click to go to the Subscription Info screen (the equivalent to the Book Info screen), the main Overview screen provides a description just like the Book Info screen. But here, things begin to differ (see Figure 23.25). If you click Manage Subscriptions, your browser opens to BN.com's My Account page. Scroll down and click Manage Subscriptions to cancel or modify a subscription.

If you click Read, the magazine or newspaper opens for reading. Click Previous Editions to see a list of the issues you have. Place your mouse over issue date, and you see options to read, remove the copy from your computer, and archive. If you click Archive, you remove it from this view. However, if you were in My Archive, the Subscription Info's Previous Issues screen would give you the option to Unarchive the issue.

FIGURE 23.25   The Subscription Info screen.

Reading Your Books in NOOK Study

Clicking the Now Reading button or a book cover takes you to the reading view (see Figure 23.26). Although initial impressions may be that this functions the same as the reading view in the NOOK App for PC, that impression quickly disappears when you see the variety of options you have available.

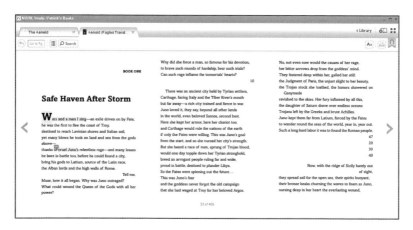

FIGURE 23.26   The Reading Screen in NOOK Study.

First and foremost, you can have multiple books open at once and navigate between them by clicking the tabs. Beyond that you have a host of buttons and options to explore, so dive into those features.

Dual Book View

You can look at books side by side to compare. Say you wanted to compare the Latin and English versions of *The Aeneid*. Easy.

1. Open one of the books, and then click the Dual Book button. The Dual Book View screen appears.

2. Either scroll or search for the book you want to open. (You can open the same book you initially started with in Dual Book View.)

3. The second book opens and you get two reading screens, both with the same options (see Figure 23.27). The book that you are in (that is, the one where if you press the arrow key to turn the page and the page turns) is the one that you click in.

FIGURE 23.27   Reading two books side by side.

4. You can then interact with each book individually just like you do regularly reading.

When you finish looking at the books in Dual Book view, click the Chain icon that connects the two tabs of the books. Each book then appears on its own tab.

Font

Click the Font button to adjust the font and font size for the book (see Figure 23.28). The size you currently have selected is highlighted in gray, as is the font you have currently selected. To change either, just click what you would like. The screen adjusts automatically.

FIGURE 23.28   Adjusting font settings.

Page Turning

Pull your mouse over the reading area of the screen. Two arrows appear on both sides of the screen. You can click the page right or page left buttons to turn the page (or use the arrow keys on your keyboard). Or you can enter the page number in the Go to Pg box.

Contents View

Click this to open a screen on the left side of the reading screen to see a table of contents, notes and highlights, and bookmarks for this ebook (see Figure 23.29).

The table of contents is a scrollable list that you can use to navigate the book. If you want to go to a specific location indicated in the table of contents, click it and the reading screen jumps to there.

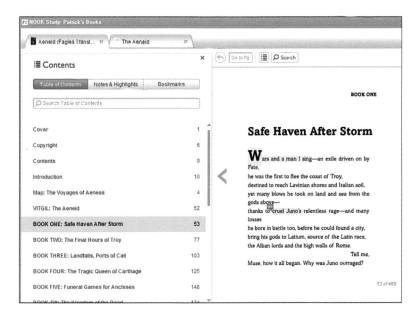

FIGURE 23.29 Viewing notes while in the Reading screen.

The notes and highlights are presented in tabular format. The Type column indicates the type of note (Highlight, Asterisk, or Question). The Page column provides the page number of the note.

> NOTE: For more about entering notes and highlights and the associated options, **see** "Using the Highlights, Notes, and Look Up Features of NOOK Study."

> TIP: For the Type, Page, Added, and Tag columns, if you click the column header, you can sort the table based on that column's information.

The Excerpt column provides a snippet of text where the note is located. The Added column provides the date the note was added. The Tags column lists any associated tags you indicated in the note. Clicking the individual notes displays the note on the page and provides note details.

At the bottom of the Notes and Highlights section, you can see the full note and any links associated with it. In addition, you can Export or Print your notes. If you choose

Export, you can sort them by the page they appear on, type, the color, or date added. You can export to a Word or text file.

You can also search for specific content in the notes by entering search criteria.

When you access the bookmarks, you see a list of all the bookmarks in the book. Click the bookmark link to go to it in the Reading Screen.

Full Screen Mode

Click this to open the book to take up the entire screen. Press Esc to close full screen mode.

Search

Use this button to search for a word or phrase in the ebook.

Using the Highlights, Notes, and Look Up Features of NOOK Study

Adding notes and highlights to ebooks in NOOK Study is easy, and you have a variety of options. To add a highlight, follow these steps:

1. With the ebook open, select the text you want to highlight with the cursor. A pop-up menu appears (see Figure 23.30).

2. Click Apply Markup. You can choose Highlight, Underline, Asterisk, or Question from the menu. Other than using them for three different types of highlighting, the distinction is the icon used:

    Highlight: No icon.

    Asterisk: Asterisk icon.

    Underline: Text is underlined.

    Question: Question mark icon.

To add a note, follow these steps:

1. With the ebook open, select the text you want to highlight with the cursor. A pop-up menu appears.

2. Click Add Note. The Add Note dialog box appears (see Figure 23.31).

3. Set the Markup Style to Highlight, Underline, Asterisk, or Question.

4. Enter the text of your note.

5. Add tags if you want them.

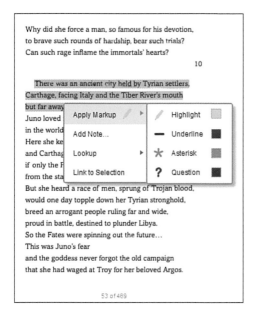

FIGURE 23.30   Text selection tools.

NOTE: Tags can be useful for identifying notes with a similar type or theme. These can then come in handy if searching notes.

FIGURE 23.31   The Add Note dialog box.

6. Add a hyperlink to outside research or articles. Just paste a link here and click Attach.

7. Click Save.

You can always edit the note by clicking the note in the reading screen.

NOOK Study also provides some lookup features. Just like creating a note, select the text on which you want to perform a search at one of seven websites (see Figure 23.32):

▶ Search This Book

▶ Dictionary.com

▶ Google

▶ Google Scholar

▶ YouTube

▶ Wikipedia

▶ Wolfram Alpha

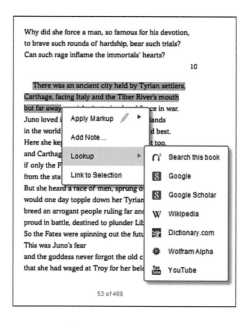

FIGURE 23.32   A multitude of lookup sites.

The final option you have after you select text is Link to Selection. NOOK Study creates a link that you can send to other NOOK Study users, and when they receive it, they can link to it and go directly to that page in their NOOK Study.

Using LendMe in NOOK Study

With NOOK Study, you can use B&N's LendMe feature. You can access the LendMe options, assuming LendMe is available for that NOOK Book, either from the plus sign menu or the Book Info screen. Clicking LendMe in either location opens the LendMe dialog box (see Figure 23.33).

FIGURE 23.33   NOOK Study's LendMe dialog box.

Enter the email address of the person you want to lend the NOOK Book to, enter a personal message if you want, and click Send.

The normal LendMe rules apply.

Using Print to NOOK Study

If you have a PowerPoint or Word document you want to add to your NOOK Study library, you can easily do so. When you installed NOOK Study, it placed a print driver on your computer. So, if you are in PowerPoint or another program and you want to add that file to your NOOK Study library, choose File, Print. In your printer options, choose Print to NOOK Study (see Figure 23.34). (On the Mac, choose PDF in the bottom left, and click Print to NOOK Study from there.) Click Print. The file is automatically placed into your NOOK Study library.

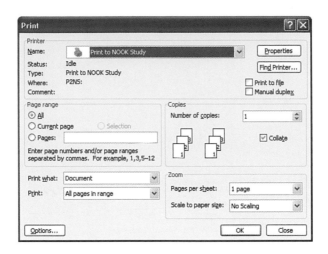

FIGURE 23.34   Printing to NOOK Study in Word.

Adding Your Own Files to NOOK Study

If you have a PDF or ePub file you want to add to NOOK Study, click Add Item, navigate to the file, and click Open. The file is added to your library, and you can manipulate it like any other document.

Using NOOK for Web

On July 18, 2012, Barnes and Noble launched NOOK for Web—a browser-based way to read your NOOK Books. NOOK for Web is connected to your account and lets you read NOOK Books without having any of the iPhone, iPad, or Android apps, the PC or Mac NOOK or NOOK Study applications, or even a NOOK device. You can buy NOOK Books and read them on your computer without downloading them. The good news is, if you own a NOOK or use any of the apps or applications, your NOOK library is synched, so jumping from device to device retains your reading location (but not, currently, bookmarks, notes, or highlights).

To use NOOK for Web, you need a PC or Mac running one of the following browsers:

> Chrome on PC or Mac
> Internet Explorer 9
> Safari on PC or Mac
> Firefox on PC or Mac

Currently, you cannot use NOOK for Web using an iPhone, iPad, or Android tablet browser, though B&N says those will be supported later this year.

You also need a B&N account if you do not already have one here: https://mynook.barnesandnoble.com/index.html. Just click the Create an Account now link. When you have an account, you can start reading with NOOK for Web.

Opening NOOK Books in NOOK for Web

You have a few ways to read content in NOOK for Web. If you are on a product page (see Figure 23.35), you can hover your mouse over the cover until Open This Book appears. Click Open This Book, and NOOK for Web starts. If you own the NOOK Book, you have access to the entire book. If you do not own it, the sample (the first 10–20 pages) appears in NOOK for Web.

FIGURE 23.35   Click Open This Book to start NOOK for Web.

> NOTE: Now the bad news. Not *all* NOOK Books can be read in NOOK for Web, though the vast majority can be. Also, magazines, newspapers, textbooks, NOOK Books for kids, enhanced NOOK Books, PagePerfect NOOK Books, and comics cannot be read in NOOK for Web.

However, probably the most common way you will access your NOOK Books in NOOK for Web is through your library at BN.com. From BN.com, click My NOOK.

When the My NOOK page loads (see Figure 23.36), click Library.

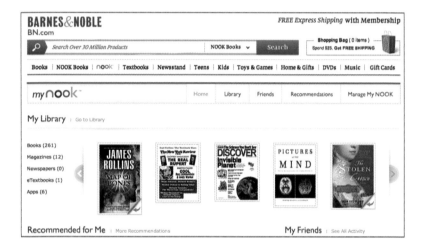

FIGURE 23.36   Click Library to go to a listing of your NOOK Books.

Scroll and click until you reach the NOOK Book you want to open. You can use the features at the top to help make finding the book you want faster. You can sort the content differently or filter the content. By default, All Items is selected, but clicking any of the other check boxes shows *only* that set of content.

When you see the NOOK Book you want to read, click the Read Instantly button (see Figure 23.37) to open that book in NOOK for Web. You can also click the cover to start NOOK for Web.

FIGURE 23.37   Click Read Instantly to open the NOOK Book in NOOK for Web.

Reading in NOOK for Web

When you start NOOK for Web, the NOOK Book opens either to the publisher's default starting position (if this is the first time you are opening this on *any* device) or to the last location you were reading whether that was in NOOK for Web or on any NOOK app, application, or device. Now let's get oriented to this screen (see Figure 23.38).

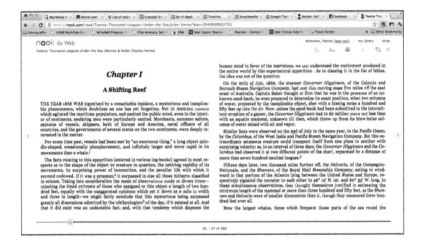

FIGURE 23.38   NOOK for Web's reading screen.

Contents

The Contents menu displays that book's table of contents (see Figure 23.39). Simply click the table of contents entry you want to advance to. The browser screen refreshes to that location.

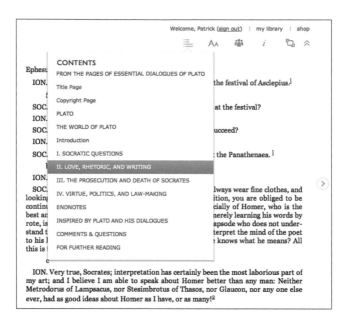

FIGURE 23.39   The Contents menu for a NOOK Book.

Text

The Text menu shows text display options (see Figure 23.40). To adjust the size of the text, click the A you want. The current size displays in a turquoise color. When you click the size, the text changes in the background. To change the font (the current font displays in a turquoise color), click the font you want. It changes in the background. Choose the font you want first; then adjust the size.

If you want to use the Publisher's Defaults to display text size and particular font, click the Publisher's Defaults check box. You can always click it again to turn it off.

By default, NOOK for Web displays books in a two-column format. If, however, you prefer to see only one column, click Single Page Layout, which shifts the view from two columns to one column.

Share

The Share menu displays the different options you have to share your reading experience.

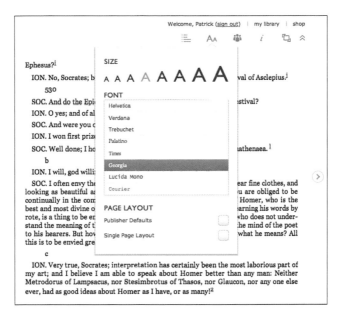

FIGURE 23.40 The Text menu for a NOOK Book.

> NOTE: The share features assume you have linked at least your Facebook, Twitter, or Gmail accounts. If you have a NOOK device or app, you may have already linked accounts, but if you have not or want to link more (or unlink), go to https://mynook.barnesandnoble.com/friends.html. Click the Link Accounts button and enter the required information.

If you click Rate and Review, a dialog box appears (see Figure 23.41). Indicate a number of stars for the review, type in a headline for your review (for example, Fantastic trip through philosophy!), and enter your review. The review will be shared on BN.com, where other B&N shoppers can see what you have said. In addition, if you click the Facebook or Twitter buttons, the review will be shared on those respective sites as well with the accounts linked to your BN.com account. Click Submit Review when you are ready to share with BN.com.

If you click Recommend, the Recommend dialog box appears. You can recommend this book via Facebook, Twitter, or email. Click the Facebook tab to recommend on Facebook. It defaults to displaying the recommendation as a post on your timeline. If you want to recommend to one of your Facebook friend's timeline, click the people button, and select the friend from the drop-down menu. Type your message and click Recommend.

FIGURE 23.41   Rate and Review a NOOK Book.

Click the Twitter tab to recommend on Twitter. Enter your recommendation and click Recommend.

Click the Email tab to recommend via email. Select from the drop-down list the email you want, type your message, and click Recommend.

Click Like on Facebook if you want to post on your Facebook timeline that you like that book. If you have liked it already, the menu option here is Unlike on Facebook. Click it to unlike it.

About

The About menu displays two options: Book Details and More Books Like This. If you click Book Details, a dialog box appears (see Figure 23.42). The information here is standard stuff: author, title, format, and cover. You can read the Overview, which is a short description of the book. You can also click Customer Reviews to see what others have said. If you click Find Other Formats, the B&N product page for this book appears so that you can buy the hardcover, trade paperback, audio, or whatever format it is available in. If you click Learn About NOOK, your browser switches to the NOOK device product page.

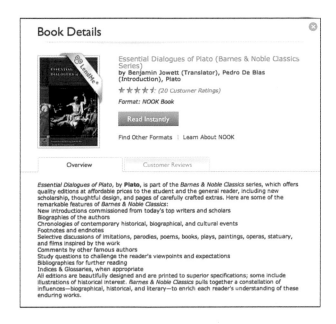

FIGURE 23.42   The Book Details dialog.

If you click More Books Like This, a dialog appears. This dialog has two options: More Like This and More by This Author. More Like This shows book that B&N thinks are similar. If you click one of the covers, NOOK for Web opens a sample of that book, with a Buy Now button should you want to purchase it. If you click More by This Author, you see more titles by that author. Click the cover to open a sample in NOOK for Web.

Full Screen

If you click Full Screen, the window around the reading screen (that is, the browser's menus and Open and Close buttons) and anything outside that window disappear (see Figure 23.43). All the functionality is the same, but it provides a more pristine reading experience. (When you first start, switch to full screen; you may see a message that tells you if your browser is in full screen; this disappears in a few minutes). To exit full screen, either press Esc on your computer or click Full Screen again.

Simple View

If you click Simple View, the Contents, Font, Share, About, Full Screen, My Library, and Shop links disappear, and Simple View changes to a nondescript two downward arrows in gray. Click those to leave Simple View.

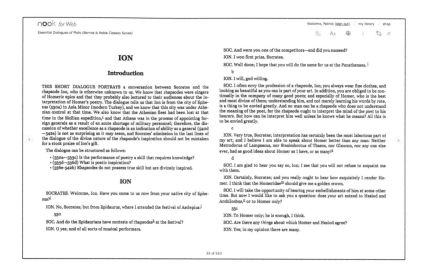

FIGURE 23.43   Reading a NOOK Book in Full Screen.

To advance forward or backward in the book, you have a few options. First, you could use the Contents menu and click the location. Second, you can click either the previous page or next page buttons either side of the text to advance or retreat a single page. Press the left or right arrow buttons on your computer to do the same. Third, you can use the Page Scroll feature at the bottom of the page. With this, you can either click directly some place on the scrollbar and your screen jumps immediately to that page, or you can click and hold the turquoise circle and drag to the location you want and release the mouse button.

If your book contains footnotes, those will look like hyperlinks (colored blue). You can click the footnote, and it takes you to the location. Click the corresponding link in the footnotes to go back. For example, if you click footnote B in the main body, when you go to the footnotes, you see B next to the actual footnote. Click that B to go back to the main text.

The last few options at the top of the screen are a welcome note, My Library, and Shop. You can click Sign Out to sign out. Doing so, takes you back to BN.com. You can click Sign In to sign in under a different account or just re-sign in. If you started reading a sample without being signed in, Sign Out is, instead, Sign In. Click that to sign in. If you click My Library, you are taken to My NOOK Library at BN.com. Click Shop takes you to BN.com's NOOK Book Store where you can browse and shop for more NOOK Books.

That's all there is to NOOK for Web. You can access your NOOK Books without having a NOOK device or app.

CHAPTER 24

Managing Your ebooks with Calibre

I have a huge library of ebooks. Because I get my ebooks from many different sources, they are spread out all over my hard drive. My ADE books are in one folder, books I've bought from Fictionwise are in another folder, my Project Gutenberg books in yet another, and so on. All my files on my computer are backed up, so I'm not concerned about losing them, but it sure is easier to manage them when they are all in one location.

Awhile back I discovered Calibre, a free application for managing an ebook library. Calibre is incredibly powerful, but it's also easy to use. In this chapter, you learn to use Calibre to manage your library; edit the metadata for your ebooks so that they show up correctly on your NOOK HD+, NOOK HD, and NOOK Simple Touch; get cover art when covers are missing; and sideload books to your NOOK HD+, NOOK HD, and NOOK Simple Touch.

Configuring Calibre

You can download Calibre from calibre-ebook.com. There's a version for practically every type of computer on the market today. After you install Calibre, you need to specify a location for your Calibre library. When you add books to Calibre, it copies the ebook to your Calibre library. That way, all your ebooks are kept in one location.

To set up your Calibre library, simply launch Calibre, and it starts the Welcome Wizard. In the first step of the wizard, specify where you want Calibre to store your ebooks. You can choose any disk location you want, or you can leave it at the default setting.

> **Is There Any Advantage to Using a Custom Location for My Calibre Library?**
> In some situations, yes. Let's put it this way: There's no disadvantage to using a custom location for your Calibre library unless the location you specify is a network location you don't always have access to or you use Calibre's built-in Content Server feature.

In the next step of the Welcome Wizard, select Barnes & Noble from the list of manufacturers and then select Nook from the list of devices. (Don't worry if you have a NOOK HD+, NOOK HD, or NOOK Simple Touch because Calibre treats all of them as a generic Nook.) Calibre uses your choice here for the default conversion settings. In other words, because you are choosing a NOOK as your reading device, Calibre knows it needs to convert ebooks to EPUB format when it sideloads ebooks onto your NOOK.

In the final step of the Welcome Wizard, Calibre displays links for tutorial videos and the Calibre user's guide. The videos are an excellent way to learn all the features of Calibre, but if you just want information you need to manage your library and sideload ebooks onto your NOOK, you can skip them for now. (You can also access them at calibre-ebook.com/help.)

Adding Books to Your Calibre Library

When you first start using Calibre, your library is empty. To add books to your library, click the Add Books button on the toolbar. Select the books you want to add, and then click Open.

TIP: You can select multiple ebooks before you click Open; all the ebooks you select are added to your Calibre library.

Can I Add NOOK Books I've Purchased for My NOOK HD+, NOOK HD, or NOOK Simple Touch to My Calibre Library?

Absolutely! Although Calibre does not allow you to read books protected by DRM, you can manage protected books with Calibre. That includes managing the book's metadata and adding a cover graphic.

When adding ebooks protected with DRM, you need to make sure that they are in either eReader or EPUB format. However, unprotected ebooks can be in any format. When you sideload unprotected ebooks to your NOOK device, Calibre automatically converts them into the correct format.

NOTE: Your NOOK device cannot read eReader (PDB) formatted ebooks. Those books need to be converted to EPUB format, which you *cannot* do if they are secure eReader files.

Editing Metadata

As you add books to your library (see Figure 24.1), you might notice that some books have missing or incorrect metadata. For example, the book's title might not be formatted correctly or the listing in Calibre might be missing the author's name. You can edit the information Calibre uses for the book's listing by editing the book's metadata. You'll almost certainly want to be sure that your metadata is correct for all your ebooks because your NOOK device also uses metadata to display information about the ebooks.

FIGURE 24.1 The Calibre main window.

To edit metadata for an ebook, first select the ebook in Calibre, and then click Edit Metadata on the toolbar. Calibre displays the current metadata for the book you selected (see Figure 24.2). At this point, you can manually change the metadata or let Calibre retrieve metadata from either Google or ISBNdb.com.

To let Calibre automatically retrieve metadata for your ebook, click the Fetch Metadata from the Server button at the bottom of the Edit Meta Information dialog. Calibre uses the metadata shown in the dialog box to attempt a lookup on the book. If the metadata that already exists isn't sufficient, Calibre lets you know.

TIP: If Calibre cannot retrieve metadata for a particular book, enter the ISBN number (you can usually get it from BN.com or Amazon.com) for the book and try again. I've never experienced a problem when the ISBN number was entered first.

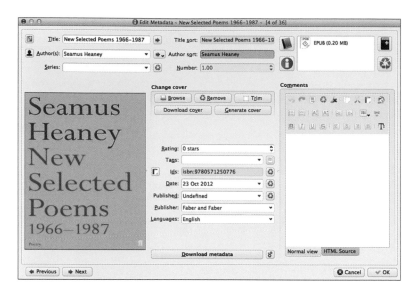

FIGURE 24.2   The Calibre Metadata Information screen.

By default, Calibre searches only Google for metadata. In most cases, Google has the metadata you need, but if it doesn't, you can also use ISBNdb.com as mentioned previously. To use ISBNdb.com, you need to sign up for a free account at ISBNdb.com/account. After you create your account, you must generate an access key that you can use in Calibre to authorize it to use ISBNdb.com. Here's how you do that:

1. Create an account at ISBNdb.com/account.

2. After you create your account, click Manage Keys at the top of the page.

3. Click Generate a New Key.

4. Enter a comment for your key. I entered "Calibre" so that I know that's what this key is for.

5. Leave the Daily Use Limit blank, which sets the limit to unlimited.

6. Click the Generate New Key button to generate your key (see Figure 24.3).

After you generate your key, copy it to your Clipboard. Switch over to Calibre and go to Preferences. Click Metadata Download, which opens the Metadata Download dialog. In Metadata Sources, click the check box for ISBNDB. Click Configure Source, and paste the key into the IsbnDB Key box. Click Save. From then on, Calibre will look up metadata in both Google and ISBNdb.com.

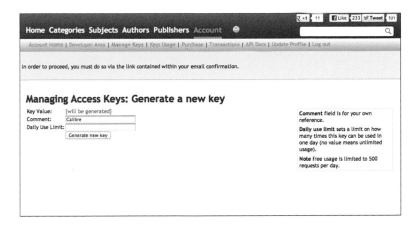

FIGURE 24.3   Generating a key is easy.

As you can see here, you have a wide variety of sources from which Calibre can obtain metadata. Click the ones you want it to use, and give it a cover priority. What that means is if a cover is found on Overdrive and Google, the higher priority (the lower the number) gets to provide the cover image. You can see a variety of options to the right. Depending on how you use the metadata, feel free to tweak the settings.

> NOTE: If it seems like too much work to create an ISBNdb.com account and generate a key, don't worry about it. Google almost always has complete metadata for most books. And you can add Overdrive or other sources.

> TIP: If you need to edit the title or author of an ebook, you can double-click the title or author name (and other metadata as well) in the Calibre library, type the new information, and press Enter.

If you want to update the metadata for a lot of titles, simply select them all, click the down arrow next to Edit Metadata, and click Download Metadata and Cover. You can choose to download only the metadata, only the covers, or both.

Adding Covers

Because books you sideload onto your NOOK are kept in My Documents, you can't browse them by cover. However, you can see the cover on the touchscreen while you're reading the book—assuming a cover image is available. Sideloaded books on your NOOK device, however, do show the cover when you view them in the Library.

NOTE: Recall that sideloaded books and content are ebooks and documents you have from sources other than B&N (for example, Fictionwise, Project Gutenberg, and so on).

Calibre can download covers for your ebooks automatically. You can even add covers to ebooks protected with DRM from the B&N NOOK Store or from another ebook store.

The easiest way to flip through cover images for your ebooks is to enable browsing by covers in Calibre. Click the Browse by Covers button (as shown in Figure 24.4) to enable this feature. You can then click either side of the current cover to flip to another cover or use the arrow keys on your keyboard to flip through your covers. To return to full library view, click the Browse by Covers button again.

FIGURE 24.4   The Browse by Covers button makes locating missing covers much quicker.

TIP: You can also browse ebooks by tags using the Browse by Tags button immediately to the right of the Browse by Covers button. Tags are part of the metadata for an ebook, so you can edit how an ebook is tagged by editing the metadata.

To add (or replace) the cover image for an ebook, select the ebook, and then click Edit Metadata. Click the Download Cover button to add a cover image.

You can add cover images to multiple books by selecting more than one book in the Calibre library. On Windows, you can press Ctrl+A to select all your books. If you want to select multiple books that are listed contiguously, click the first book, then hold the Shift key, and click the last book. If you want to select multiple books that are not contiguous, click the first book; then hold the Ctrl key as you select the other books.

After you select all the books to which you'd like to add covers, click the down arrow to the right of the Edit Meta Information button, and select Download Only Covers from the menu. Calibre automatically downloads covers for all the books you selected.

Sideloading Books with Calibre

Sideloading books onto your NOOK device with Calibre is fast and easy. After you connect your NOOK to your computer, Calibre detects it and displays an icon for it in the area directly under the toolbar. If you have a microSD card installed in your NOOK device, Calibre displays an icon for both your NOOK device and the microSD card.

> NOTE: When you connect your NOOK device to a Windows computer, Windows assigns drive letters to your NOOK device and to the microSD card if one is installed. Calibre assumes that the first drive letter assigned to your NOOK device is its main memory and the second drive letter is the microSD card. However, sometimes Windows assigns the first drive letter to the microSD card; when it does that, Calibre incorrectly identifies your NOOK device's main memory and the memory card.
>
> To resolve this problem, you need to explicitly assign drive letters to your NOOK device and its microSD card inside of Windows. For information on how to change drive letters in Windows XP, see www.online-tech-tips.com/computer-tips/how-to-change-the-drive-letter-in-windows-xp-for-an-external-usb-stick-or-hard-drive/. For Windows 7, see http://www.howtogeek.com/96298/assign-a-static-drive-letter-to-a-usb-drive-in-windows-7/.

> TIP: Sometimes Calibre, if it is already open when you plug in your NOOK device, won't recognize it as being installed. Close Calibre and restart it.

> NOTE: At this point in time, Calibre treats the NOOK device as the same device, so the image for your NOOK in Calibre is the NOOK. This is cosmetic only, and Calibre correctly interacts with your particular device.

To sideload one or more books onto your NOOK device, make sure your NOOK is connected to your computer. Select the books from your library, and click Send to Device on the toolbar. Calibre automatically converts any ebooks that are not already in a format compatible with your NOOK device and then transfers them to your NOOK. By default, Calibre transfers ebooks to your NOOK devices' main memory, but you can choose to transfer them to the microSD card if you want. Simply click the down arrow next to the Send to Device button, and select Send to Storage Card A from the menu (see Figure 24.5).

FIGURE 24.5   The Send to Device menu.

> TIP: You can also select Set Default Send to Device Action and select Send to Storage Card A. From then on, clicking the Send to Device button automatically sideloads any selected ebooks to your NOOK's microSD card.

Depending on what action is necessary, Calibre might take a while to sideload books. Calibre indicates that it's working and how many jobs it's currently processing using the Jobs indicator in the lower-right corner of the main window. If you click the Jobs indicator, a dialog appears where you can see details on what Calibre is doing.

If I Update Some Metadata Information for an ebook That's Already Sideloaded onto My NOOK Device and Sideload It onto My NOOK Device Again, Will It Overwrite the Existing Copy on My NOOK Device?

Yes. Both Calibre and your computer use the filename of an ebook to identify it as a unique ebook. If you change metadata information (such as the title, author, and so on) of an ebook that is already on your NOOK device, sideloading it onto your NOOK device will overwrite the existing copy. Essentially, you're just updating the metadata of the copy on your NOOK device.

There is one exception to this. If you sideload an ebook to your NOOK device's main memory and the same ebook is already on its microSD card, you will have a duplicate copy of the book and it will show up twice in your library.

> **Can I Read My ebooks Using Calibre?**
>
> You can read an ebook on your computer using Calibre as long as the ebook isn't protected with DRM. To read an ebook with Calibre, select the ebook, and click the View button on the toolbar. A new window appears for you to read the ebook.

Subscribing to News Content in Calibre

Calibre also has an excellent news subscription feature that makes it easy to subscribe to various news feeds that you can then sync to your NOOK device. To access this feature, click the Fetch News button, select a news feed, and set the subscription options that determine how often the feed is downloaded. Keep in mind that for feeds to download, Calibre must be running.

> TIP: I particularly like this feature (subscribing to news content in Calibre). I have print subscriptions to *The London Review of Books* and *The New York Review of Books*, which I paid for long before I got my NOOK. Although I could subscribe again to *The New York Review of Books* at BN.com, I would be paying for two subscriptions...so I use Calibre to fetch that news (using my account information from *The New York Review of Books* website). When my print subscription runs out, I will switch to the BN.com subscription...but for now, I pay for only one.

Calibre uses a collection of properties known as a "recipe" to subscribe to a particular news feed. If you don't see a news feed that you're interested in, you can find others and submit requests for new recipes by browsing to http://bugs.calibre-ebook.com/wiki/UserRecipes.

Converting ebooks in Calibre

Calibre can convert a wide variety of formats. Although your NOOK device can read Word and PDF documents, these are not treated as "real" ebooks by the NOOK device. What that means is that you cannot add notes or highlights, bookmark pages, and so on. So, although you can read those formats, you may want to convert them to the EPUB format so that they get the full ebook treatment.

Calibre's conversion options are rich, and I won't go into the details here. The standard default PDF to EPUB, HTML to EPUB, and such work quite well. To convert a document, follow these steps:

1. Add the document to your Calibre library if you haven't already. Do this just like adding a book: Click the Add Books button.

2. Select the book you want to convert.

3. Click the Convert Books button.

4. Click OK.

If you want more details about the vast number of options for conversion, go to calibre-ebook.com/user_manual/conversion.html.

> NOTE: PDFs are the most problematic documents to convert because of the way they are created. So, if the results are less than satisfactory, you might tweak some of the settings to see if you can get better results.

In this chapter, you've seen how powerful Calibre is for managing your ebook library. You've also seen how easily you can edit the metadata for your ebooks, add missing covers to your ebooks, and sideload ebooks onto your NOOK.

CHAPTER 25

Using My NOOK Library

All your B&N content is saved on the bn.com website in B&N's My NOOK Library. Using My NOOK Library, you can browse through your B&N content, lend and borrow books with LendMe, move items to and from your archive, see what your NOOK friends are up to, and delete items from your B&N library. You can even start reading your books. (**See** the section "Using NOOK for Web," in Chapter 23, "Reading Beyond Your NOOK: Desktop Apps.")

Accessing My NOOK Library

You can access My NOOK Library by browsing to http://mynook.barnesandnoble.com (see Figure 25.1). You can also get to this from the BN.com homepage by clicking My NOOK at the top of the screen. Log in if you have not already. From here, you can see recommendations, recent purchases, NOOK Friends activities, and links to your Library, Friends, Recommendations, and Manage My NOOK. You can now work your way through the top links. If you have a few other ways to access the same things (for example, to see your Library), you can click the Library link at the top or the Go to Library link right above titles.

Library

When you click Library, you see a variety of options and ways to interact with it (see Figure 25.2). The first option is Sort. Click this to sort by Most Recent, Title, or Author.

By default, all items in your B&N online library that have not been archived display in My NOOK Library. You can filter the view by clicking Books, Magazines, Newspapers, Apps, or Textbooks. You can also view any items that have been archived by clicking the Archived Items option.

Two views are available in My NOOK Library: Line view or Grid view. To switch between the two views, click one of the View buttons, as shown here, in the Layout category—the one that is a lighter gray is the one not in use.

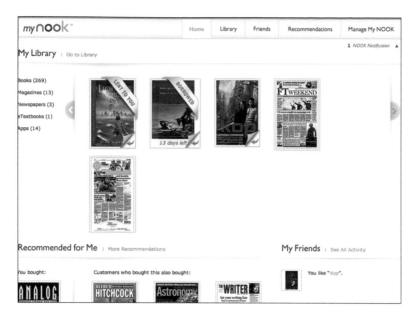

FIGURE 25.1 The My NOOK opening page.

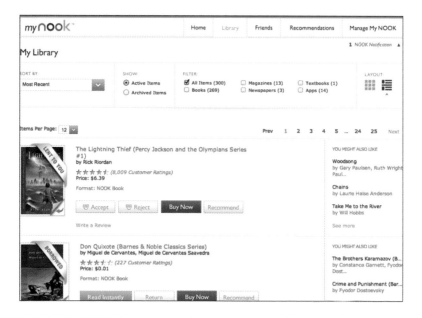

FIGURE 25.2 My NOOK Library page, where you can see all your purchases.

You can interact with individual books. You can download or recommend any books listed here that you've already purchased. You can also write a review, move to your archive, or delete permanently from your library. If the book is a sample or borrowed, you also have a Buy button. If it is a magazine or newspaper, you can manage your subscription.

> CAUTION: Be careful about deleting items. If you delete an item from your library, it will be removed from all your NOOK devices and apps where you access your B&N content. The only way to get it back is to buy it again. Archiving is the safe bet.

To archive an item, click the Move to Archive link. The item is moved to your archive on your NOOK device and apps as well. To move the item back to your library, click Archive under Show, find the item in the archive, and click Move to Active.

> TIP: Think of My NOOK Library as another way that you can view your NOOK Book library. When you interact with content via My NOOK Library, you also impact the content on your NOOK devices and apps.

Recommending and Reviewing Tools in My NOOK Library

You can Recommend or Write a Review of a book or magazine. If you click the Recommend button, you see the Share This Title dialog (see Figure 25.3). You can choose between emailing someone directly, posting to your Twitter, posting to your Facebook wall, or posting to a friend's Facebook wall. Select the option, enter the recipient if appropriate, enter a message, and click Recommend.

If you click the Write a Review link, you see the Rate and Review dialog (see Figure 25.4). No matter what, you are posting a review to BN.com, but you can also choose to copy that review to Facebook or Twitter. Click the number of stars you are giving to the book, type in a headline, write a review, and click Submit Review.

> NOTE: If you cannot post a review to Facebook or find Facebook friends to recommend that book to, you may need to link your accounts. Click a book cover, which opens a new page. Click the Link Accounts button on the left. Click the buttons for which you want to link accounts, and follow the instructions.

FIGURE 25.3   Recommend a title to a friend.

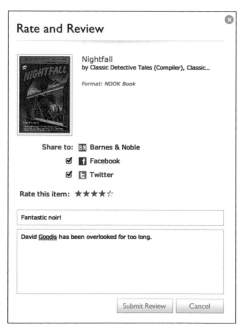

FIGURE 25.4   Write and share a review.

Managing Subscriptions in My NOOK Library

For a magazine or newspaper, you can click Manage Subscription, which opens a page like that in Figure 25.5. If you click the Cancel Your Subscription link, you are asked to confirm that you do want to cancel it. Click Confirm to do so, and your subscription is canceled.

FIGURE 25.5   The Manage Subscription page.

Downloading Content from My NOOK Library

You can download NOOK Books and subscription content from My NOOK Library for reading on your computer or for local archival purposes. You can download items to your computer and then sideload them onto your NOOK device later. However, if you do this, the item does not show up in My B&N Library on your NOOK. Instead, it shows up in My Documents just like all other sideloaded content.

When you download ebooks to your computer, you can then add them to your Calibre library. (**See** Chapter 24, "Managing Your ebooks with Calibre.") This is a convenient way to ensure that you have a backup of your B&N content in case you accidentally delete an item.

Can I Send an Item to My NOOK Device from My NOOK Library?

You cannot manually send an item to your NOOK device from My NOOK Library. However, because My NOOK Library is actually just another way to view your B&N online library, you should always see the same content on your NOOK devices and apps.

Friends

When you click Friends, you open the portal to interacting with your NOOK Friends from My NOOK Library (see Figure 25.6). This page is divided into three sections: actions you can take (listed under the My Friends heading), a list of yours and your friends' activities, and ways to add friends.

FIGURE 25.6   My NOOK Library Friends page.

You have four options available under the My Friends section:

▶ **Friends' Activities**: The default view on this page and the one shown in Figure 25.6.

▶ **About Me**: Gives you some information about yourself. The primary purpose of this page is to show or hide books in your library that are LendMe eligible. If you want to hide a book so that a friend cannot request to borrow it, click the Hide option. If want to hide *all* LendMe books from your friends, turn off the check mark for I Authorize My Friends to See My Lendable Books.

▶ **NOOK Friends**: Here you can remove friends (click Delete), see suggested friends, or invite others. To follow up on the suggestions from B&N, click the Invite button. The invitation is sent immediately. If you want to email a friend, click the Email Invite button, enter the address and message, and click Invite. Also, if you have been sent a friend request, you can review it here and accept or decline.

▶ **LendMe**: From here (see Figure 25.7), you can lend, borrow, and deal with pending LendMe requests. If you want to borrow a book, click Borrow. (If multiple friends have the book, you can click Borrow from the specific friend you want to borrow from.) The request is sent immediately.

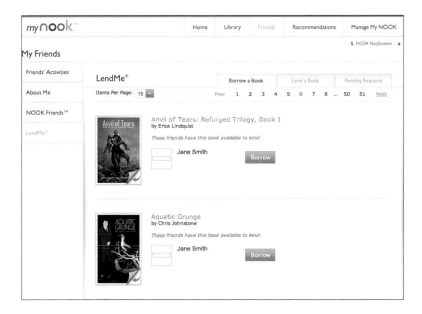

FIGURE 25.7 The LendMe page on My NOOK Library.

Click the LendMe tab to actively loan a friend a book. Click the LendMe button and enter the email address, or pick the Facebook friend. Enter a message and click Lend. The request is sent.

If you have received a lend offer, click Pending Requests to accept or decline that offer. In addition, you see a NOOK Notification beneath the

Manage My NOOK link at the top. Click that and you see a screen similar to Figure 25.8, where you can accept (click Borrow) or decline (click Ignore) the offer.

FIGURE 25.8   Accept or decline a LendMe offer.

Recommendations

When you click Recommendations, you arrive at the Recommendations page (see Figure 25.9). This page is actually a way to see book, magazine, and newspaper recommendations based on your previous purchases, bookseller picks, trending books, and so on. Click the cover to go to that book's page for more information.

Manage My NOOK

When you click Manage My NOOK, you arrive at the page with all your NOOKs. Hover your mouse over the NOOK, and you can see a few options (see Figure 25.10). Click Manage Payment Options to change your credit card information or add gift cards.

FIGURE 25.9 My NOOK Recommendations page.

FIGURE 25.10 Managing your NOOKs.

CHAPTER 26

Using PubIt to Sell Your ebooks

PubIt is a B&N feature that enables you to submit your ebook for sale through the B&N website. PubIt books are NOOK Books. When people visit BN.com and browse or search for ebooks, yours will be available. If they buy it, it downloads, can be lent, and can use the social features like any other NOOK Book.

Setting Up PubIt

Setting up and using PubIt is easy:

1. Go to http://pubit.barnesandnoble.com/pubit_app/bn?t=pi_reg_home.

2. Enter in your BN.com username and password and click Sign In, or create one from here. The Account Setup screen appears.

3. For PubIt, B&N needs to set up a PubIt account, although it uses your BN.com information. Update any information here.

4. Because you are publishing your work, provide a name and website if you want. Note: If you leave this blank, your first and last name will be used as the publisher. Click Continue. The Terms and Conditions page appears.

Important Information About PubIt Terms and Conditions

Normally, you might just blindly click I Agree or Accept when you see the kind of legalese included in the PubIt Terms and Conditions, but it is important that you understand something about PubIt before you agree to this.

B&N can update the pricing and payment terms whenever it wants. At the time of this writing, you, the publisher, can set a price for your content anywhere from $.99 to $199.99. For books priced $2.99 to $9.99, the publisher receives a 65% royalty. For books priced from $.99 to $2.98 or from $10.00 to $199.99, the publisher receives 40%.

B&N also requires that the publisher comply with the Content Policy. So, if B&N deems your content offensive, harmful, legally obscene, and so on, it can choose not to sell your content. It then provides some specific examples but certainly does not cover all areas.

You cannot include the following in the Product Data:

▶ Hyperlinks of any kind, including email addresses.

▶ Request for action (for example, "If you like this book, please write me a review.").

▶ Advertisements or promotional material (including author events, seminars, and so forth).

▶ Contact information for the author or publisher.

B&N will make your product available in the Read In and LendMe programs. In addition, 5% of the book's content will be provided as a sample for people to download to their NOOK devices apps to try before they buy.

A lot of other information is in this agreement (covering such things as withdrawing a book from the PubIt program, book rejection, reformatting, and so on), so I highly recommend reading through all the legalese before agreeing. This is your content, so treat this document as what it is: a contract.

5. If you agree with these terms, click I agree and Continue. The Payment Information screen appears.

6. Enter Bank Account, Tax Information, and Credit Card Information, and click Submit. A page appears indicating that your account is being set up.

Putting Content into PubIt

Now that your account is set up, load up your first title:

1. Click Add a Title (see Figure 26.1) and enter the required fields (see Figure 26.2).

2. To upload your ebook, click Browse, navigate to it, and click it. Click Upload & Preview. If the file you chose is not an EPUB file, B&N converts it to an EPUB file. Either way, you then see a virtual Nook with your text in it. Flip through pages to make sure you are satisfied with the appearance. If you need to tweak it, do so on the source file and then re-upload it.

3. Upload a cover in JPEG format between 750 and 2,000 pixels in length. (As a side note, because it's the first thing most potential buyers see, the cover image is hugely important.)

4. Enter the metadata info. Accurate and thorough metadata about the content, genre, and so on is important when visitors to BN.com search for a title. If your book is a spy eco-thriller taking place on the remote island of Tonga, you want to give potential buyers the best chance to find it.

FIGURE 26.1   The My Titles screen on PubIt.

FIGURE 26.2   Setting up a new title to sell.

5. Click the I Confirm box, and then click Put on Sale. A window appears indicating a 24–72 hour timeframe for it to be done (see Figure 26.3).

If you later want to adjust any of the information, from My Titles, click Actions, Edit. You can then modify the price, title, metadata, cover, and upload newer versions of the content.

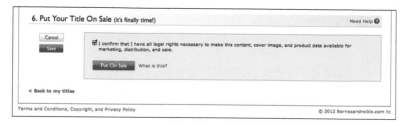

FIGURE 26.3   Soon your ebook will be for sale!

NOTE: The first time you upload a document, it can take 48–72 hours for the item to be on sale. Subsequent updates tend to update much faster, usually within 4–8 hours.

If I Update My Book with a New File, Does It Automatically Get Sent to Customers Who Purchased My ebook?

If you update your ebook after it has gone on sale with a new version of the content, customers who have purchased the original version do *not* automatically receive the new version. However, if they delete the local copy on the device, when they redownload it, they receive the latest version available.

With the other tabs in the PubIt interface, you can watch your sales (including any royalties coming your way), adjust your account information, and get support.

TIP: If your child has a kids' book idea, check out B&N Tikatok books at http://www.barnesandnoble.com/u/kids-activities-publish-a-childrens-book/ 379002382. Here, kids can create their own books that can be made into hardcover, softcover, or PDF.

CHAPTER 27

Reading Beyond Your NOOK: NOOK App for Windows 8

In April 2012, Microsoft and B&N inked a deal. Many speculated about what that deal meant. On November 13th, the first concrete evidence appeared in a Windows 8 NOOK App. This chapter walks you through using this app. Given that it was just released, I'm sure we'll see continued enhancements to it over time.

> NOTE: For the purposes of this chapter, I use the touch gestures associated with Windows 8 tablets, but you can use a mouse to interact with all the options as well.

The Basics

To obtain the app from the Windows Store, from the Charms bar, search for NOOK in the Store. Tap NOOK from the results to get to the NOOK App screen (see Figure 27.1). Tap Install. You'll see a notice that your NOOK App is installed, adding a tile to the Start screen.

Like any tile on the Start screen, swipe down on the tile to see various options (see Figure 27.2). This app features the standard tile options: pinning/unpinning, uninstalling, making smaller or larger, and turning off the live feature.

Tap the tile to launch the NOOK App. You are asked to enter your NOOK account or sign up for one. Enter your information and tap Sign In. If you don't have an account, tap Don't Have an Account? Sign Up and enter the requested information.

You see a Terms, License, and Privacy Policy screen. Tap Agree to move on. The screen loads and syncs your library with all your other devices and apps, so you can jump from your NOOK HD where you were reading the spine-tingling horror novel and pick up where you left off in the NOOK App on your Windows 8 tablet.

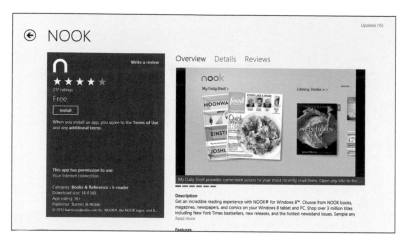

FIGURE 27.1   The NOOK App in the Store.

FIGURE 27.2   The NOOK App tile options.

Your screen now changes to the Home screen, which prominently displays My Daily Shelf (see Figure 27.3).

My Daily Shelf features the five most recent downloads and read items. Swipe left to see more options:

▶ **Just for You**: A set of recommendations from B&N based on your past purchases. You can tap Just for You to see more recommendations. You can also tap one of the covers (either on the Home screen or in the larger list) to open up the NOOK Store with an opportunity to purchase the item (or get a sample). **See** "Shopping from the NOOK App" later in this chapter for more details about shopping.

▶ **Library: Books**: Shows your NOOK Books. Tap a cover to either download it (if it has not been downloaded yet) or start reading. You can also tap the word Books to be taken to your full library of NOOK Books. **See** "Reading Books, PagePerfect Books, and Newspapers in the NOOK App" later for more details about reading your NOOK Books.

FIGURE 27.3   The NOOK App Home screen.

NOTE: Missing books? At this time, not every NOOK Book (for example, Read to Me Kids books) is supported on the NOOK App for Windows 8. If you are purchasing from BN.com, make sure you check what devices are supported before purchasing.

▶ **Library: Magazines**: Shows your NOOK magazines, if you have any. Tap a cover to either download it (if it has not been downloaded yet) or start reading. You can also tap the word Magazines to be taken to your full library of NOOK magazines. **See** "Reading Magazines and Comics in the NOOK App" later for more details about reading your NOOK magazines.

NOTE: Missing magazines? At this time, not every NOOK magazine is supported on the NOOK App for Windows 8. If you are purchasing from BN.com, make sure you check what devices are supported before purchasing.

▶ **Library: News**: Shows your NOOK newspapers, if you have any. Tap a cover to either download it (if it has not been downloaded yet) or start reading. You can also tap the word News to be taken to your full library of NOOK newspapers. **See** "Reading Books, PagePerfect Books, and Newspapers in the NOOK App" later for more details about reading your NOOK newspapers.

> NOTE: Missing newspapers? At this time, not every NOOK newspaper is supported on the NOOK App for Windows 8. If you are purchasing from BN.com, make sure you check what devices are supported before purchasing.

▶ **Library: Comics:** Shows your NOOK comics, if you have any. Tap a cover to either download it (if it has not been downloaded yet) or start reading. You can also tap the word Comics to be taken to your full library of NOOK comics. **See** "Reading Magazines and Comics in the NOOK App" later for more details about reading your NOOK comics.

▶ **Shop**: You can continue to scroll right to see many options here. **See** "Shopping from the NOOK App" later in this chapter for more details about shopping.

From the Charms bar's Settings selection, you have a few options. About gives you some details regarding which version of the app you have installed as well as provides a link to NOOK Support. If you tap Account, you can see who this NOOK App is currently registered to, as well as see existing gift card balances and add to it, change the default credit card used for the account, and sign out. Tapping Rate and Review takes you to the Windows Store where you can give a rating and write a review of the Nook App for Windows 8 that will be posted to reviews for the app.

Browsing Your NOOK Library

Browsing your library is easy. After you tap Books, Magazines, and so on, just swipe left or right with your finger to scroll.

To read an ebook, you first need to download it to your device. You can easily tell whether a book has been downloaded. If a Download button appears, you have not downloaded it to your device. Just tap the button to do so. After the ebook has been downloaded to your device, tap the cover to open the book.

If you swipe down on a cover, an Options bar appears (see Figure 27.4). Here you can download a book if it is not yet downloaded, view details, pin to the Start screen, archive the book, or sync that book. Also, if that cover is a sample, you see an option

titled Full Version Available, which, after you tap it, opens a screen for you to purchase the full version.

TIP: Want to archive a bunch of books quickly? Swipe down on the cover of
the first one. The Options bar appears. Then swipe down on additional covers.
Tap Archive when you have selected all the books you want to archive.

FIGURE 27.4   The Options bar for a NOOK Book.

Tap View Details to see the Details screen similar to Figure 27.5.

FIGURE 27.5   The Details Screen for a NOOK Book.

This screen differs a bit depending on the type of content. For books, you have a Read option with a short description. To the right, any customer reviews that have been written are available. (Tap Reviews to see the full complement of reviews and the full review.) Additionally, you see what other customers have purchased who purchased this item and what else the author has written; tap the cover to open the store. For magazines and newspapers, you also see a View Issues button, which you can tap to be taken back to the appropriate library displaying the full complement of issues you own.

For magazines, the library functions nearly identically. However, your magazines are grouped together by title, with the newest issue in the top left—if you have more than one (see Figure 27.6).

FIGURE 27.6   Your magazines.

Your newspapers are set up like your magazines, whereas your comics are set up like your NOOK Books.

From any of the libraries, if you swipe from the top edge down or the bottom edge up, you see additional options (see Figure 27.7).

If you tap Home, you go back to the Home screen. If you tap Shop, you are taken to the NOOK Store. You are in the Library, so the button in the Library screen does not offer much functionality, but if you were reading a book or magazine, you could tap Library to be taken back to the Library. In the top right, you see what you are currently reading. Tap the cover to open that book.

FIGURE 27.7 Additional options.

At the bottom, you see some Filter and Sort options, along with a Sync button. If you tap Filter, you see the following choices:

- ▶ **All of Library**: Tap this to see your entire library, regardless of type. Your magazines appear at the end of the books, followed by newspapers and then comics.

- ▶ **Books**: Tap this to view just your books.

- ▶ **Magazines**: Tap this to view just your magazines.

- ▶ **News**: Tap this to view just your newspapers.

- ▶ **Comics**: Tap this to view just your comics.

- ▶ **Archived**: Tap this to see a list of archived books, magazines, and so on. You can swipe down on a cover and tap Unarchive to remove it from this list.

- ▶ **Unsupported**: Tap this to see a list of your content that is not supported at this time for reading on the NOOK App for Windows 8.

The Sort options allow you to sort the list of titles by Most Recent, Title, or Author. Most Recent is selected by default. Tap if you want to change to a different sorting method.

Tap the Sync button if you want to force sync your library with B&N and your other devices.

TIP: Want to search your library easily? From the Charms bar, tap Search and begin typing in your search criteria. A list of results appears. Tap the result you want to open in the NOOK App.

Reading Books, PagePerfect Books, and Newspapers in the NOOK App

To read an ebook in the NOOK App, just tap the cover image to open it in reading mode. When there, to move to the next page, swipe your finger from right to left. To move to the previous page, swipe your finger from left to right. The reading screen, however, offers more options than just reading (see Figure 27.8), which you can access by swiping down from the top of the screen or up from the bottom of the screen.

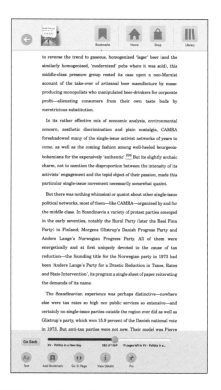

FIGURE 27.8   The NOOK App reading interface.

Newspapers, however, offer a tweak on the swiping through pages paradigm (though you can still do that). Figure 27.9 shows a typical section page of a newspaper.

FIGURE 27.9 *USA Today*'s news section page.

The front page (and section pages) offer links to the articles. In Figure 27.9, "In Brief" is the article headline followed by a bit of teaser text. You can tap the article's headline to jump right to that article. When reading an article, you typically have links at the top of the page that transport you quickly between articles and back to the section page.

If you do not see surrounding options bars in the reading screen, just tap the page, and they appear. Before discussing some of these options, take a quick tour:

▶ **Cover**: Tapping the downward arrow next to it opens the Table of Contents (see Figure 27.10). You can scroll and tap the appropriate link to go quickly to that spot in the ebook.

▶ **Bookmarks**: Tapping this opens a list of bookmarks in this book. Tap a bookmark to jump to that location. Tap Clear All to remove all bookmarks from this ebook. Tap Remove All to confirm.

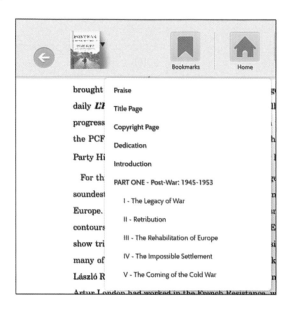

FIGURE 27.10   The NOOK App's Contents screen.

▶ **Home**: Tapping this returns you to the Home screen.

▶ **Shop**: Tapping this takes you to the NOOK Store.

▶ **Library**: Tapping this returns you to your NOOK library.

▶ **Scroll Bar**: Press and hold the button and drag to move quickly through the book. You an also tap a spot on the scroll bar to jump farther along.

▶ **Go Back**: This icon appears when you have jumped to a different page using the Table of Contents, a bookmark, or the Go To Page option. Tap it to go back to where you just came from.

▶ **Text**: Tapping this allows you to adjust the specific font, theme, margins, line spacing, font size, justification, rotation, and defaults.

▶ **Add Bookmark**: Tapping this adds a bookmark to the current location in the ebook. A blue bookmark with the NOOK logo appears in the top right.

▶ **Go To Page**: Tapping this opens a small box into which you can type a page number to be taken directly to that page.

▶ **View Details**: Tapping this brings up a page with details related to the book.

▶ **Pin or Unpin**: Tapping this opens the Pin screen, which allows you to pin this book directly to the Start screen. If this book is already pinned to the Start screen, tap Unpin and then Unpin from Start to remove it from the Start screen.

NOTE: At the time of writing, the NOOK App for Windows 8 does not support searching inside your NOOK Books, newspapers, or other content.

Adjusting Text Options

After tapping Text Options, you see a screen similar to Figure 27.11. The general purpose of this screen is to provide settings related to the reading experience in the NOOK App. To close the screen, tap anywhere outside of the Text Options screen.

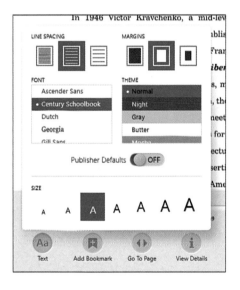

FIGURE 27.11   The NOOK App's Text Options screen.

The top-left set of icons determines line spacing. Think of this like single space, double space, and so on. The current setting is colored blue. Tap whichever you prefer. The screen adjusts.

Margins determine how close to the edge of the screen the text goes. The more "dark" space in the center, the more text appears on the screen. The currently selected Margin setting is colored blue.

Depending on what the publisher of an ebook allows, you can adjust the font. You can scroll through the available list. (A dot appears to the left of the currently selected one, which is also colored blue.) You have options between serif and sans serif fonts. Serif is a technical term that refers to the "hanging structure" on a letter. In Figure 27.11, looking at the word "Georgia," notice the little hanging things off the top of the G? That's a serif. Sans (French for "without") serif fonts lack these structures. In general, most people find reading serif fonts easier on the eyes. But go with whatever you want.

> NOTE: Of the available font options, Century Schoolbook, Georgia, and Dutch are serif fonts despite the fact that Dutch and Century Schoolbook in the Text options box itself do not appear to be serif. Ascender Sans, Gill Sans, and Trebuchet are sans serif fonts.

The Theme options provide a set of backgrounds and font colors. The default is normal, which is a white page with black text. The currently selected option has a dot to the left of the name and is colored blue. Select the theme you want, and the screen changes.

If you'd like, you can set Publisher Defaults to Yes, which sets the font, size, spacing, and so on, to what the Publisher feels is optimal. You can change it to Off at any time you want.

Clicking the A icon adjusts the font size. The current font size is in blue. As you tap different sizes, the Reading screen adjusts.

> NOTE: At the time of writing, the NOOK App for Windows 8 does not support adding notes or highlights, nor does it support viewing notes and highlights you have added in other NOOK Books.

Reading PagePerfect Books

PagePerfect books function the same as regular ebooks, except for two things:

- ▶ **No Text**: You cannot adjust font and margin settings in PagePerfect books, so the Text option is not available.

- ▶ **Zoom**: When reading, you can pinch and zoom in or out to get closer into the text. You can also double-tap the screen to zoom in quickly and double-tap again to zoom back out.

Reading Magazines and Comics in the NOOK App

Although you cannot read enhanced magazines (for example, *Time*), many magazines are available without video, and so on. Magazines offer thumbnails that you can scroll through. To see that, just tap the screen to get the reading options (see Figure 27.12).

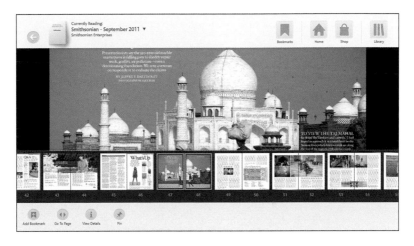

FIGURE 27.12   Reading a magazine.

> NOTE: Some magazines function more like newspapers when reading—for example, *Analog Science Fiction and Fact*.

You can scroll through the thumbnails to see what is covered on those pages. Just tap the thumbnail you want to go to that page. Tap the downward arrow next to the cover to see a vertical scrolling list of the magazine's contents. Tap Bookmarks to see the bookmarks you've added to this magazine and tap to jump to it.

When reading an article, you can pinch and zoom in or out to get closer into the text. You can also double-tap the screen to zoom in quickly and double-tap again to zoom back out.

Shopping from the NOOK App

You can shop for new books, magazines, and newspapers directly within the NOOK App. You can get to the NOOK Store in one of two ways:

▶ **From the Home Screen**, scroll right until you see the Shop section.

▶ **From the Options bar**, tap Shop.

Either way, you land at the NOOK Store (see Figure 27.13). This screen is divided up into several parts.

FIGURE 27.13   The NOOK Store.

You can tap Books, which takes you right into a list of current bestsellers. You can scroll right to see even more options. The basic gist of all of these is a series of lists: Most Popular Magazines, Favorite Comics, National Book Aware Nominees, and so on. You can tap each category to drill further down and see what content is available for purchase.

Additionally, you have NOOK Channels, which are lists of related titles. Channels are descriptive and—I have found—useful ways of categorizing titles. Instead of just a big collection of history books, you have History by Plot, Notorious American History, and History Buff. The Channels descriptions are themselves evocative of the types of content you will find. Additionally, Channels allow for titles from multiple genres to appear (Science-Fiction Science-Fact is a good example).

Farther to the right, you have large categories: Books, Magazines, Newspapers, Kids, and Comics. Again, you can drill down further to get to specific listings. Once there, you can tap the downward arrow to see more categories (see Figure 27.14). These are further refinements. Tap to your heart's content.

If you want to search the NOOK Store for a specific title, from the Charms bar, enter the criteria in the Search box and tap Search.

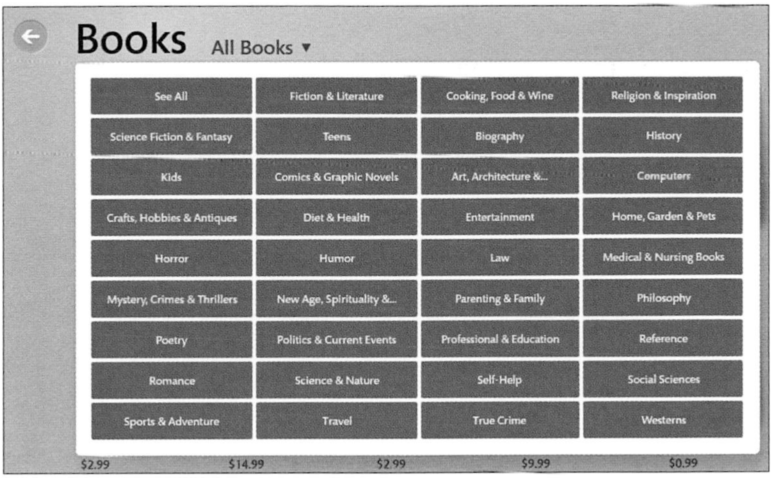

FIGURE 27.14   Refining categories in books.

Once you get to a book you like, tap the cover and you are taken to a Details screen (see Figure 27.15).

FIGURE 27.15   Book Details screen.

Reviews gives you an idea of what others have to say about the book. Customers Also Bought shows books that others have purchased who also purchased the one you are looking at. More by This Author shows additional titles that that author has written.

If you want to sample the content before purchasing, tap Free Sample, and a sample downloads to your app and other devices. If you want to buy the book, tap the Buy button and then tap Confirm. The Free Sample and Buy buttons are replaced by the single Read button.

> NOTE: Samples never expire. You can keep a sample for as long as you want.

Magazines and newspapers offer Free Trials instead of Free Samples (see Figure 27.16).

FIGURE 27.16   Magazine Details screen.

If you tap Free Trial, you get the current issue free, which is downloaded to your app and devices. After 14 days, you will be charged an ongoing rate for the subscription. If you want to cancel your subscription, you'll need to cancel your subscription at BN.com (**see** the section "Managing Subscriptions in My NOOK Library" in Chapter 25, "Using My NOOK Library," for more information about managing your subscriptions). If you want to buy the current issue, tap Current Issue and then tap Confirm. This adds that issue to your library. You will not automatically receive the next issue. For that, you must subscribe. If you have never subscribed to the newspaper or magazine, you can tap Free Trial and then tap Confirm to begin your trial.

When you subscribe to a newspaper or magazine, you receive a 14-day free trial. If you cancel your subscription within that 14-day period, you will not be charged. If you cancel after the 14-day trial period, you will be refunded a prorated amount based on when you cancel.

You can use a trial subscription only once for any particular item. For example, if you subscribe to *The Wall Street Journal* and cancel your subscription within the 14-day trial period, you will be charged beginning immediately if you were to subscribe to *The Wall Street Journal* again because you have already taken advantage of a trial subscription.

NOTE: Subscriptions can be canceled only using My NOOK Library at BN.com. You cannot cancel a subscription using your NOOK App.

What About LendMe?

At the time of writing, you can read LendMe titles that others loan you, but you need to accept the request on a NOOK device or at BN.com. When you do so, the book downloads to your NOOK App for Windows 8.

Unfortunately, you cannot offer to lend books to any of your friends from the app itself. You can from a NOOK device or BN.com, and when you do so, you will not be able to read the book until the lending period expires—just like a normal LendMe book.

Understanding ebook Formats

An Overview of ebook Formats

You can use the following types of ebooks on your NOOK:

- ▶ EPUB (including Adobe Digital Editions)
- ▶ PDF

> NOTE: That's right. If you purchase secure eReader (PDB) files from Fictionwise or eReader.com, your NOOK device cannot read those files.

You can use the following types of ebooks on your NOOK:

- ▶ EPUB (including Adobe Digital Editions)
- ▶ Non-DRM eReader from third parties

Can I Read Word Documents or TXT Files on My NOOK Tablet or NOOK?

If you want to read Word documents or TXT files on your NOOK Tablet and treat them as ebooks versus Word documents, you need to first convert them into EPUB files.

Calibre can convert TXT files to the EPUB format for your NOOK Tablet. If you want to read a Word document, you should save the file as a PDF file. (Recent versions of Word provide this functionality.) If you cannot save the Word document as a PDF, first save it as an HTML file, and then use Calibre to convert it for your NOOK Tablet.

For more information on using Calibre to convert ebooks, **see** Chapter 24, "Managing Your ebooks with Calibre."

EPUB Format

EPUB (electronic publication) is an open-source format for ebooks. That means the format isn't owned by any single entity, making it an ideal format for electronic books. EPUB ebooks have a file extension of .epub, but EPUB files are actually Zip files (a compressed collection of files) that contain content files for the book along with other supporting files that specify the formatting.

> NOTE: The EPUB format was created to replace the Open eBook format, a format that was widely used in the first ebook readers.

EPUB ebooks are actually just HTML files—just like the files used for web pages. The same technologies used in displaying web pages are used to display EPUB ebooks. If you rename an EPUB book and give it a .zip file extension, you can open the file to see all the files contained in the EPUB archive.

EPUB ebooks can be protected with *digital rights management (DRM)*, which is designed to prevent unauthorized users from accessing digital content such as ebooks. When you purchase a book on your NOOK or from bn.com, that content is tied to your bn.com account using DRM. B&N uses its own DRM mechanism for books purchased from B&N, but your NOOK also supports Adobe Digital Editions DRM.

Using Adobe Digital Editions

Adobe Digital Editions (ADE) is software that manages ebooks that use ADE DRM. Your NOOK is compatible with ADE DRM and can be configured as an authorized device in the ADE software.

> NOTE: You can download ADE software free from adobe.com/products/ digitaleditions/.

To authorize your NOOK for ADE DRM, connect your NOOK to your computer while ADE is running. When you do, you see a dialog box informing you that your NOOK was detected and needs to be authorized (see Figure A.1). Click the Authorize Device button to authorize your NOOK.

FIGURE A.1   Authorize your NOOK to use ADE ebooks.

> NOTE: Sometimes I have to connect the NOOK Tablet or NOOK first before starting ADE.

After your NOOK is authorized, ADE displays an icon for your NOOK in the bookshelf on the left side of the main window. If you click that icon, you see all the content on your NOOK that is compatible with ADE. Any content in EPUB or PDF format is available for reading directly in ADE.

> NOTE: ADE does not yet distinguish between the different NOOKs. It simply refers to it as NOOK.

> TIP: I have a few ADE books I have purchased that I could not read on my iPhone or iPad because apps such as Stanza, eReader, and others did not support ADE books. However, the Bluefire eReader app does support ADE, so check it out.

Sideloading Adobe Digital Editions

To sideload ADE content to your NOOK, connect your NOOK to your computer, and launch ADE if it's not already running. Drag the ebook from your ADE library to the NOOK icon in the bookshelf.

ADE supports both protected PDF files and protected EPUB files.

TIP: One of the most popular ebook stores for ADE books is ebooks.com.

When ADE books are copied to your NOOK, ADE creates a folder called Digital Editions, and the books are copied to this folder. Unlike protected books from eReader.com and Fictionwise, ADE ebooks don't require you to enter any information to open them. As long as your NOOK is an authorized device, you can open ADE EPUB books.

TIP: When you sidcload content onto your NOOK, you find the items in My Documents. You need to tap Check for New Content before the new item is visible in My Documents.

NOTE: ADE does not yet distinguish between the NOOK. It simply refers to it as NOOK.

You don't need to use ADE to sideload ADE EPUB books onto your NOOK. I prefer using Calibre to manage all my ebooks and use it to sideload ADE books. **See Chapter 24 for more information about Calibre.**

Sources for ebooks Other than B&N

EPUB Sources

You can buy EPUB books or download free EPUB books that you can read on your NOOK from numerous places. Here are just a few:

- ▶ Gutenberg.org
- ▶ Fictionwise (www.fictionwise.com)
- ▶ Feedbooks.com
- ▶ eBooks.com
- ▶ Google Play (play.google.com/store/books)
- ▶ Smashwords (www.smashwords.com)
- ▶ BooksOnBoard (www.booksonboard.com)
- ▶ Kobo Books (www.kobobooks.com)
- ▶ Diesel eBook Store (www.diesel-ebooks.com)
- ▶ Powells.com
- ▶ Weightless Books (weightlessbooks.com)
- ▶ Baen (www.baen.com)

Some of these sites offer ebooks in several formats, so ensure you select carefully and get the EPUB or PDF version.

Perhaps one of the greatest benefits to having an ebook reader that supports the EPUB format is that you can read ebooks from many public libraries. Check with your local library to see if it offers the capability of checking out EPUB ebooks. If it doesn't, you might still get a library card from a nearby library. Check out the Overdrive website at www.overdrive.com. You can enter your ZIP code and it will

give you a list of libraries in your area that support Overdrive for checking out
EPUB books.

Use Calibre to Search for ebooks

In 2011, Calibre came out with a release that added an ebook search function. One of
the great things about Calibre's features is that you can control which locations to
look at and get DRM status. Calibre does not let you purchase a book through them,
but it can give you a quick look at what's available.

Open Calibre and click Get Books. The Get Books dialog opens (see Figure B.1).

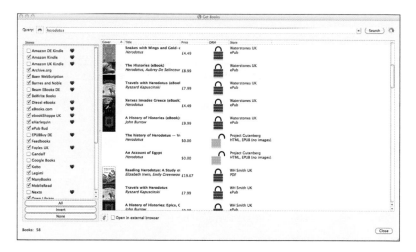

FIGURE B.1   Use Calibre to search for ebooks.

You can adjust which stores to search by clicking the appropriate check boxes in the
Store list. In the Query box, type your search criteria. Click Search.

If you double-click a title in the search results, Calibre opens that web page.
Alternatively, you can click Open in External Browser, and when you double-click a
title, your default browser opens to that web page. As usual, Calibre offers extensive
settings options, so feel free to explore.

Libraries and ebooks

Many libraries offer selections of ebooks that you can read on your NOOK. A popular
ebook lending service for libraries is Overdrive. If you are curious if your library

offers ebook lending services, go to http://www.overdrive.com/ and enter your ZIP code. A list of libraries appears. Select the link to your library to see what they have available.

To check out library ebooks, you first need to have a valid library card from that particular lending library. The specifics can be found at that library. Using the library's website, select the title you want. Most offerings from libraries are either PDF or EPUB, both of which you can read on your NOOK.

Download the file as instructed by the library. Most of the time, you need to open the file using Adobe Digital Editions (**see** the "Using Adobe Digital Editions" section in Appendix A, "Understanding ebook Formats," for information about using that software). You can then sideload the book to your NOOK.

> NOTE: Libraries have their own policies, guidelines, and requirements, so be sure to check all the available information on the library's website to understand the options related to ebook lending. You can also contact the library directly and speak to a librarian to get answers.

Can I Read This Here?

With all the devices available for reading NOOK Books, the following should help you distinguish which formats can be read on each device.

	NOOK HD/HD+	NOOK Simple Touch	NOOK for PC/ Mac App	NOOK for iOS[1]	NOOK for Android[2]	NOOK for Kids for iPad	NOOK Study	NOOK Tablet	NOOK Color
NOOK Books	Yes	Yes	Yes	Yes	Yes	Yes	Yes	Yes	Yes
NOOK Books for Kids with Read to Me	Yes	No	No	No	No	Yes	No	Yes	Yes
NOOK Books for Kids with Read and Play	Yes	No	No	No	No	No	No	Yes	Yes
NOOK Books for Kids with Read and Record	Yes	No	No	No	No	No	No	Yes	Yes
eTextbooks	No	No	No	No	No	No	Yes	No	No
Newspapers	Yes	Yes	Yes	Yes	Yes	No	Yes	Yes	Yes
Magazines	Yes	Yes[3]	No	Yes[3]	Yes[3]	No	No	Yes	Yes
Enhanced NOOK Books	Yes	No	No	No	No	No	No	Yes	Yes
Supports LendMe	Yes	Yes	Yes	Yes	Yes	No	Yes	Yes	Yes
PagePerfect	Yes	No	No	Yes	No	No	No	Yes	Yes[4]
Comics	Yes	No	No	No	Yes	No	No	Yes	Yes[4]
NOOK Video	Yes	No	No	No	No	No	No	No	No

[1] iPhone, iPad Mini, iPad, and iPod Touch.
[2] Android phones and tablets.
[3] Most magazines are readable—check the magazine's product page at BN.com to verify.
[4] You must update your NOOK Color to 1.4 before reading PagePerfect books.

Index

G–H

I–J

K–L

M

O–P

Q–R

U–V

W–Z

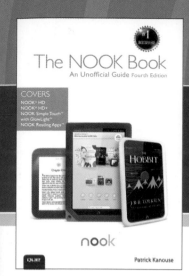

Your purchase of *The NOOK® Book* includes access to a free online edition for 45 days through the **Safari Books Online** subscription service. Nearly every Que book is available online through **Safari Books Online**, along with thousands of books and videos from publishers such as Addison-Wesley Professional, Cisco Press, Exam Cram, IBM Press, O'Reilly Media, Prentice Hall, Sams, and VMware Press.

Safari Books Online is a digital library providing searchable, on-demand access to thousands of technology, digital media, and professional development books and videos from leading publishers. With one monthly or yearly subscription price, you get unlimited access to learning tools and information on topics including mobile app and software development, tips and tricks on using your favorite gadgets, networking, project management, graphic design, and much more.

Activate your FREE Online Edition at
informit.com/safarifree

STEP 1: Enter the coupon code: NOWYQZG.

STEP 2: New Safari users, complete the brief registration form. Safari subscribers, just log in.

If you have difficulty registering on Safari or accessing the online edition, please e-mail customer-service@safaribooksonline.com